BRYCE CANYON

MOUNT RAINIER

CRATER LAKE

GRAND CANYON

LASSEN VOLCANIC

MOUNT McKINLEY

OLYMPIC

KINGS

YOSEMITE

SEQUOIA

National Parks of the West

A Sunset Book

Supervising Editor: Paul C. Johnson, Editor of *Sunset Books*

Travel Editor of *Sunset* Magazine: Martin Litton

Technical Consultant: Dorr Yeager, former Regional Chief of Interpretation,
National Park Service

Book Design Consultants: Adrian Wilson, Richard S. Coyne

Graphics Coordination and Layout: Judith Whipple

Maps: James M. Cutter, Doris Marsh

Illustrations: Earl Thollander, E. D. Bills

NATIONAL PARKS OF THE WEST

By the Editors of Sunset Books and Sunset Magazine

Lane Magazine & Book Company · Menlo Park, California

Foreword

THIS BOOK IS A PICTORIAL INTERPRETATION of the national parks in the West, the score of scenic preserves whose very names are household synonyms for spectacular beauty—Yosemite, Yellowstone, Grand Canyon, Zion, Mount McKinley, Olympic—parks that encompass within their 10 million acres most of the nation's finest mountain and desert scenery.

As its title indicates, this is a book about *national parks*, which are defined as areas of outstanding scenic beauty that have been set aside by Congress to be preserved in their natural state for the benefit and enjoyment of the people. Although some *national monuments* partially meet this definition, and all of them are operated by the National Park Service, we have treated them only briefly in the appendix (pages 310-313) and have confined our coverage to areas officially designated as national parks.

As the second half of the title specifies, this book is limited to national parks in the *West*—an elastic word that could be stretched to take in almost any territory. We have restricted our coverage to the eleven states west of the Rockies plus Hawaii and Alaska, and within these have grouped the parks into five geographic regions: the Northwest, California, the Southwest, Rocky Mountains, and Offshore. Even with this Western limitation, the book encompasses two-thirds of the national parks in the United States.

Some of the material in this book has previously appeared in *Sunset* Magazine, but most of it is new, specifically created for this book. Our pictorial interpretation of the parks is offered with the wish that it may partly accomplish what John Muir hoped his own book on the national parks would do when it was published in 1898. Like Muir, we have tried "to show forth the beauty, grandeur, and all-embracing usefulness of our wild mountain forest reservations and parks, with a view to inciting people to come and enjoy them, and get them into their hearts, that so at length their preservation and right use might be made sure of."

Contributors and Consultants

PHOTOGRAPHERS AND PICTURE SOURCES

R. W. Abolin
Ansel Adams
Barry Anderson
William Aplin
Ray Atkeson
Bancroft Library
Clyde Childress
Glenn C. Christiansen
Frances Coleberd
Kenneth Cooperrider
Robert Cox
Cornelia Fogle
Jon H. Gardey
Fred Harvey
Haynes Foundation
J. M. Heslop
Philip Hyde
Lloyd G. Ingles
Forrest Jackson
Bill Jones
Ruth Kirk
Kolb Studios
Martin Litton
Modesto Bee
Peyton Moncure
David Muench

Josef Muench
National Park Service
Leigh N. Ortenburger
Charles J. Ott
William A. Pawek
Richard G. Prasil
John Robinson
Hal Roth
Save-the-Redwoods League
The Sierra Club
Bob and Ira Spring
Clyde Sunderland
Paul V. Thomas
Union Pacific Railroad
University of California
William L. Van Allen
Darwin Van Campen
Joseph Van Wormer
Elton Welke
Western Ways
Robert Wenkam
Joseph Williamson
Steven C. Wilson
Ginny Hill Wood
Cedric Wright
Yellowstone Park Co.

CONSULTANTS

Henry Berrey
Howard L. Cogswell
George Downes
Gunnar Fagerlund
Emanuel Fritz
James Godbolt
Ed Johns
Leigh Ortenburger
Robert Wenkam
Gil Winger

CONTRIBUTORS

Eldon Dye
Roger Flanagan
Cynthia Hecht
Bob Iacopi
Eugenie B. Johnson
Chad Michel
Neil Sundermeyer
Harolyn Thompson
Dorr Yeager

NATIONAL PARK SERVICE CONSULTANTS

WE WISH TO ACKNOWLEDGE with appreciation the excellent cooperation that we received from the National Park Service, from Washington down to the individual parks, in the supplying and checking of technical information for this book. We would like to thank specifically the following superintendents and ranger naturalists who worked with us—absolving them of any responsibility for errors of fact or interpretation that may have crept into the book:

PARK SUPERINTENDENTS

JOHN M. BROADBENT, Carlsbad Caverns National Park, New Mexico
EDWARD T. DAVIES, Lassen Volcanic National Park, California
JOHN M. DAVIS, Sequoia-Kings Canyon National Parks, California
OSCAR T. DICK, Mount McKinley National Park, Alaska
RUSSELL E. DICKENSON, Zion National Park, Utah
FRED C. FAGERGREN, Grand Teton National Park, Wyoming
BENNETT T. GALE, Olympic National Park, Washington
NEAL G. GUSE, Haleakala National Park, Hawaii
LOUIS W. HALLOCK, Bryce Canyon National Park, Utah
CHARLES E. HUMBERGER, Petrified Forest National Park, Arizona
FRED T. JOHNSTON, Hawaiian Volcanoes National Park, Hawaii
GRANVILLE B. LILES, Rocky Mountain National Park, Colorado
JOHN S. McLAUGHLIN, Yellowstone National Park, Wyoming
KEITH P. NEILSON, Glacier National Park, Montana
RICHARD A. NELSON, Crater Lake National Park, Oregon
JOHN C. PRESTON, Yosemite National Park, California
JOHN A. RUTTER, Mount Rainier National Park, Washington
HOWARD B. STRICKLIN, Grand Canyon National Park, Arizona
CHESTER A. THOMAS, Mesa Verde National Park, Colorado

CHIEF PARK NATURALISTS

MERRILL D. BEAL, Grand Canyon National Park, Arizona
RICHARD M. BROWN, Crater Lake National Park, Oregon
DWIGHT L. HAMILTON, Hawaiian Volcanoes National Park, Hawaii
DOUGLASS HUBBARD, Yosemite National Park, California
CARL E. JEPSON, Zion National Park, Utah
LOUIS G. KIRK, Olympic National Park, Washington
JOHN J. PALMER, Glacier National Park, Montana
RICHARD W. RUSSELL, Bryce Canyon National Park, Utah
PHILIP VAN CLEAVE, Carlsbad Caverns National Park, New Mexico

Contents

The first national park in the world was established in the West to preserve the natural wonders, protect wildlife, and provide a "pleasuring-ground" for the benefit of the people.

The Northwestern Parks

Largest mountain in the United States, cloud-hidden and glacier-mantled, object of veneration to the natives; at its base, a veritable zoo of wildlife ranges over the tundra.

Three parks in one—an untamed seacoast, beachcombers' delight; moss-festooned rain forests as lush as the Amazon basin; and a highland of glacial ice and wildflower parks.

Home of "The Mountain," a beacon to the State of Washington and a challenge to mountain climbers for more than a century; a glacier factory garlanded with wildflowers.

A saucer of indescribably blue water enclosed within the walls of an ancient volcano that collapsed within the memory of man; peaceful and serene, best when encircled with snow.

The California Parks

Steam and hot gasses still rise from the boilerworks of this slumbering volcano that blew its top a half century ago; signs of catastrophe now softened with forests and lakes.

The cliffs, domes, and waterfalls have earned renown for Yosemite Valley; but it occupies only 7 out of 1,200 square miles of the park, and there is much more to see.

Home of the Big Trees, the giant redwoods that are among the oldest and largest of living things; gateway to the shining world of the High Sierra.

A hiker's paradise, open to the traveler who carries his world on his back or a pack animal; remote, astringent, and wide-open; a granite wilderness of tarns, spires and vistas.

The Southwestern Parks

Awesome and humbling, the gigantic cleft in the earth sears the memory with its immensity; down in the canyon, the story of the earth itself, a vast lesson in geologic history.

Rocky Mountain Parks

Offshore Parks

THE NATIONAL PARK IDEA

"THOUSANDS OF TIRED, NERVE-SHAKEN, OVER-CIVILIZED people are beginning to find out that going to the mountains is going home; that wildness is a necessity; and that mountain parks and reservations are useful not only as fountains of timber and irrigating rivers, but as fountains of life." So wrote John Muir, naturalist, conservationist, and pioneer spokesman for the national parks.

When Muir expressed these sentiments, the year was 1898. There were only four national parks in existence—three of them in California—and they could be reached only by an endless stage ride over backbreaking roads. The fact that thousands were making this arduous trip is an indication of the depth of the need that was felt even then to "go home to the mountains."

What Muir sensed as a significant truth then is even more cogent today, as 15 million visitors converge each year on the Western national parks, seeking spiritual and physical renewal and the reassurance of contact, however brief and communal, with nature.

Westerners are fortunate to have within their domain the lion's share of the nation's spectacular scenery, and most of it is contained within the boundaries of the national parks lying west of the Continental Divide. Here, held in trust for the country as a whole are a dozen scenic superlatives—the deepest canyons, highest waterfalls, tallest peaks, and biggest trees in the nation. Here the traveler can stand witness to the awesome forces of earthbuilding: the power of running water or grinding ice to shape the surface of the earth; the restlessness pent up within the planet, revealed in fire-fountains of lava or spouting columns of steam. He can observe the grand cycle of life, seen in the wash of spring wildflowers, the frolicking bear cubs, or the golden fires of October aspen. In a few weeks' travel, a vacationer can see perpetual snow and active glaciers,

WITHIN THE BOUNDARIES OF THE WESTERN NATIONAL *parks are a dozen superlative waterfalls, such as the wild and beautiful Lower Falls of the Grand Canyon of the Yellowstone, described as the "embodiment of momentum" by one of the first chroniclers to see it.*

ANSEL ADAMS

"To the traveler, the parks offer the soul-stretching experience of being alone in a world of wide-open space, of grand vistas of forest and mountain and great storms rumbling across the land."

petrified forests and mountains of glass; he can follow a trail through a wild-flower park, watch armies of elk on the move, or walk through a dead city that was a vital community 1,500 years before Plymouth Rock. Within the parks, motorists can drive over the spine of a continent, and hikers can safely roam for weeks in a primeval wilderness, unchanged from the days of the cavemen.

To devotees of the national parks, it is often things subtler than geysers, fumaroles, and the riven earth that bring them back vacation after vacation. To the camper, it is the camaraderie of the campfire or the trail; to the fisherman the park is a place where time stands still while he trolls a lake or casts into a rushing stream. To parents it is a place where the flash of wonder and delight glows on the faces of their children when they first feel a running stream against their shins, or see a fawn, a thieving jay or chipmunk, or Smokey in all his natural majesty. To some, it is a garden of trees and wildflowers, stones and lichens; an aviary; and a place to watch animals going about their daily chores. To all, the parks offer the soul-stretching experience of being alone in a world of wide-open space, of grand vistas of forest and mountain and great storms rumbling across the land. The experience is remembered for the tang of fresh mountain air, the blessing of pure silence, the benediction of alpenglow. In short, the parks offer a return to nature, and the renewal that comes from re-contact with a wild and primitive environment.

To make sure that all who want to enjoy the parks can do so, at whatever level of experience, is the dedicated mission of the National Park Service.

THE SEED OF THE NATIONAL PARK IDEA was planted more than a century ago in California, where commercial exploitation of Yosemite Valley and the sense-less cutting of giant sequoias had aroused great public concern. A handful of men banded together to put pressure on Congress to preserve the beautiful valley and a grove of the irreplaceable trees, both of which were on federal property. With little debate, a law was passed in 1864 and signed by President Lincoln, then in the heat of the Civil War, that granted Yosemite Valley and the Mariposa Grove of Big Trees to the state of California. This was the first time that any government anywhere had set aside public lands purely for the preservation of scenic values, and, as such, the law was a landmark in conservation.

The portion of Yosemite turned over to the state was only a 10-square-mile strip that included the famous valley and a square mile of trees 35 miles to the south. In size, it was far from the huge park of today. Furthermore, as a grant to a state, this was not a "national" park in today's meaning of the term, but a state park. The first true national park was created in Yellowstone eight years later, and it is from it that the National Park Service dates its official beginning.

The idea for a national park was first presented before an historic campfire in 1870 by a Montana attorney named Cornelius Hedges. He was a member of a famous exploring party known as the Washburn-Langford-Doane expedition

WILLIAM APLIN

To a child, a national park *may be remembered as the place where she first saw wild creatures going about their daily chores, or where, specifically, she fed half a sandwich to an ill-tempered marmot named Freddie.*

THE NATIONAL PARK IDEA   13

ONE HUNDRED AND TWENTY-SIX *men, women, and children, dressed in their Sunday best, pose on the stump of a freshly felled Big Tree in 1872. Obviously, to some people the cutting of a 3,000-year-old tree was no different from the felling of a pine or fir, the redwood was just bigger and gave the woodsman more opportunity to prove his prowess. But the cutting of these trees stirred the consciences of other citizens, and the sequoias were placed under national park protection—but not until 8,000 acres of them had been logged off.*

that surveyed the wonders of Yellowstone (see page 233) with the purpose of puncturing or confirming the incredible rumors then circulating about the thermal spectacles in the area.

After exploring the region for more than a month, on their last night before returning home, the party held a campfire meeting at the junction of two rivers in western Yellowstone. Under the laws of the day, all were entitled to stake claims on the land and its geysers. As the men were discussing how they would divide this wonderland among themselves, Hedges made a far-reaching proposal. Turning the conversation away from private gain, he eloquently proposed that they work for the preservation of the whole area under government protection. The men enthusiastically endorsed the idea (all but one hold-out), and after their return, several of them campaigned for a law to set aside the area. So effective was their presentation that Congress passed the necessary legislation only 17 months after the expedition's return, thus creating the first, and as far as anyone then knew the last, national park.

The law established a standard that was copied for later national parks, and it is still the cornerstone of the Park System. It was partly influenced by the earlier statute that established Yosemite as a state park, but since Yellowstone was not in a state—Wyoming was still a Territory—the federal government retained full control.

The Yellowstone Act specified that the park area was to be "reserved and withdrawn from settlement . . . and dedicated and set apart as a public park or pleasuring-ground for the benefit and enjoyment of the people." The act empowered the Secretary of the Interior to provide for the "preservation from injury or spoliation, of all timber, mineral deposits, natural curiosities, or wonders within said park, and their retention in their natural condition." The Secretary was also authorized to grant 10-year leases of land for the construction of visitor accommodations, and to spend all income from such leases on the management of the park and the construction of roads and bridle paths. He was also to provide against the "wanton destruction of fish and game . . . and their capture or destruction for the purposes of merchandise or profit."

Forward-looking as the law may have been for its day, it had a number of flaws. The notion that income from leases to concessioners would be sufficient to run the park and build all the needed roads and bridle paths proved unrealistic from the start, yet Congress did not appropriate a single penny for Yellowstone for five years, and for some time thereafter, it launched new parks with almost as niggardly restrictions.

The 10-year limitation on leases did not always attract the highest type of business men, because the lease period was too short for long-term capital investment. Leases were often handed out to political favorites or given to get-rich-quick operators who built shoddy accommodations ("room and path" was the order of the day), offered poor service, and failed when competition drove prices below costs. Only in the parks where one or two concessioners dominated, or where one held a monopoly, was service to the public of high quality. The railroads—Santa Fe, Great Northern, and later the Union Pacific—provided excellent accommodations and helped to promote and upgrade the parks where they operated. The 10-year limit was dropped eventually in all the parks and uniformly high-quality concessions evolved.

So pinched for funds were the first parks that the Secretary of the Interior had to make extra-legal arrangements with the Army to manage or patrol them and to build roads. The troops ran Yellowstone from 1886 to 1916 and patrolled Yosemite and Sequoia from 1890 to 1914. The cavalry had its hands full expelling trespassers, evicting squatters, and dispersing bands of sheep and cattle. In Yosemite, for instance, the troops drove 7,000 head of sheep out of the park in 1896, and when the cavalry was withdrawn to serve in the Spanish-American War, a tidal wave of animals entered illegally. Forces were finally mustered to evict them, and a total of 1,000 cattle, 300 horses, and 189,500 sheep were driven out of the park!

After the creation of Yellowstone, there was a lull of 18 years before any more parks were established. During these years, the national park idea was gaining recognition, and articulate spokesmen began to press for extension of the Yellowstone formula to other areas. Most eloquent of these was John Muir, a well educated Scotsman who had come to Yosemite in 1868, walking to the

Two great conservationists, *President Theodore Roosevelt and John Muir, stand on Glacier Point in Yosemite, where they camped together for 5 days in 1903. As a result of this meeting, Roosevelt returned to Washington determined to expand the federal protection of the nation's scenic, historic, and natural heritage. In the next few years, he brought protection to several million acres by proclaiming national monuments.*

Valley from Oakland, 200 miles away. He herded sheep (for which he developed a lifelong distaste), worked in a hotel, and explored the Sierra from one end to the other. In 1878 he began writing his remarkable descriptions of the California mountains for *Century Magazine.* His eyes took in everything. He revelled in nature—ascending the ice cone beneath Yosemite Falls at peril of life and limb, climbing a 100-foot pine in a windstorm to share in the wild phenomenon, calmly observing a forest fire close at hand, riding an avalanche, dodging boulders released by an earthquake. No activity of animal, bird, or insect escaped him, and no geologic evidence went unobserved and unanalyzed. His writings were read, his voice listened to by important and influential people, and in his 45 years of campaigning for national parks and the preservation of the wilderness, he helped immeasurably to advance the park idea. In this zealous work, he had the support of the militant Sierra Club (organized in 1892), of which he was president from 1892 to 1914.

Largely as the result of Muir's campaigning, three new parks were created in 1890. These were Yosemite (which formed a ring around the earlier park, still being operated by the state), Sequoia, and General Grant. They were established to preserve the Sierra forests from timbering and over-grazing by sheep, which Muir referred to as "hoofed locusts."

After the turn of the century, thanks to the prodding of President Theodore Roosevelt, Congress passed another far-reaching conservationist measure, the Antiquities Act of 1906. This law was designed to protect the ancient Indian ruins of the Southwest from the vandals who were destroying them. The looting was being conducted on a grand scale, with companies organized to remove pottery and artifacts from the ancient dwellings for sale to museums and private collectors. In searching for these treasures, the vandals blasted holes in the walls to let in light, burned roof beams for firewood, and destroyed some of the finest ruins that had stood unmolested—every bowl and olla left where the last occupants had put them—for the preceding 700 years. The new law made these acts illegal and gave the President the power to withdraw lands with historic relics and natural wonders from the public domain and proclaim them as "national monuments." President Roosevelt made prompt and generous use of the law by proclaiming 1.4 million acres of federal land as national monuments during his term of office.

The name "national monument" was and is a confusing term because of the diversity of objects preserved within them. At present, they include battlefields, forts, cliffs, canyons, sand dunes, caves, islands, missions, homesteads, birthplaces of famous men, deserts, cacti, and trees (see pages 310-313). Most of the monuments are smaller than national parks, encompass scenic or geologic items of less magnitude or significance, and are not provided with developed road and trail systems or accommodations.

NATIONAL PARK SERVICE

DENVER POST
★ THE BEST NEWSPAPER IN THE U. S. A. ★ Census, 1910 ... 213,38
U. S. Census, esti
DENVER, COLO., WEDNESDAY, JANUARY 20, 1915. mate, 1914 ... 245,52

GOOD BOY, ENOS!
I ALWAYS KNEW YOU WERE ALL RIGHT, ENOS!

COLORADO—"ENOS, I'M PROUD OF YOU!"

Many national parks owe their *existence to the tireless work of one man or a small handful of dedicated proponents. Rocky Mountain National Park was created largely because of the promotion of a famous naturalist, Enos A. Mills, "John Muir of the Rockies." The park was approved by Congress in 1915, and in recognition of this event and Mills' part in it, the Denver Post ran this front-page cartoon.*

18 THE NATIONAL PARK IDEA

The next national park? *Establishment of national parks is a continuing process and new areas are still being added to the system. If proponents of a new national park in Washington State have their way, tranquil Image Lake and Glacier Peak would become features of a new North Cascades National Park.*

19

At first, the monuments were distributed among the federal departments that held jurisdiction over the land they occupied, but they were later all transferred to the Department of the Interior. Many of the national monuments proclaimed by Roosevelt—Grand Canyon, Lassen, Mount McKinley, Petrified Forest, Mount Olympus—were later advanced to park status by Congress.

Probably the biggest boost in the development of the national park system came with the creation of the Park Service in 1916 and the appointment of an extraordinary man, Stephen Mather, to head it. Prior to this time, the parks had operated catch-as-catch-can within the huge, disjointed Department of the Interior. The nine parks then in existence were under the harried supervision of a part-time assistant. There was no central purchasing facility, each park operated independently under its own set of rules, each had different contractual relations with concessioners, and the main means for exchanging information was an annual conference of the superintendents.

Establishment of central control of the parks was inevitable, and it was legislated into existence in 1916, and turned over to Mather with an able assistant, Horace M. Albright. Mather, a handsome man with a magnetic personality and prodigious energy, was a tireless worker and a born promoter. Having made a fortune in borax, he was immune to political pressure, and he contributed personally to the parks from his own pocket.

During his term of service under three presidents, he added 12 parks to the system, established the ranger service and the interpretive program, standardized concession contracts, and fought off repeated forays against the parks by power, grazing, lumbering, and mining interests.

Mather pushed himself mercilessly, suffering three breakdowns during his tenure, and literally worked himself to death, dying while still in office in 1928. Although he was aided in his great work by many competent men in his department, in Congress, and outside the government, it is little wonder that there are peaks, mountain passes, and highways named after him in the parks, and that many parks display a memorial plaque with the tribute, "There will never come an end to the good that he has done."

Men of great competence have followed him in the Directorship—Horace Albright, Arno B. Cammerer, Newton B. Drury, and Conrad Wirth—all have contributed to maintaining the policies of Mather and those who preceded him.

Entrusted with the care of this great natural heritage, the National Park Service operates within a two-pronged policy. The Park Service is charged with the dual responsibility to (a) preserve for all time the wonders within its boundaries in a natural state and (b) to make them available for the enjoyment of all the people. To a certain extent, these two objectives are contradictory, and their successful administration is therefore a grand compromise.

Under its commitment to preserve the parks in their natural state, the Park Service is required to protect wildlife from trappers and hunters and to preserve the forests, streams, and lakes from despoliation. Thus, timber cutting is pro-

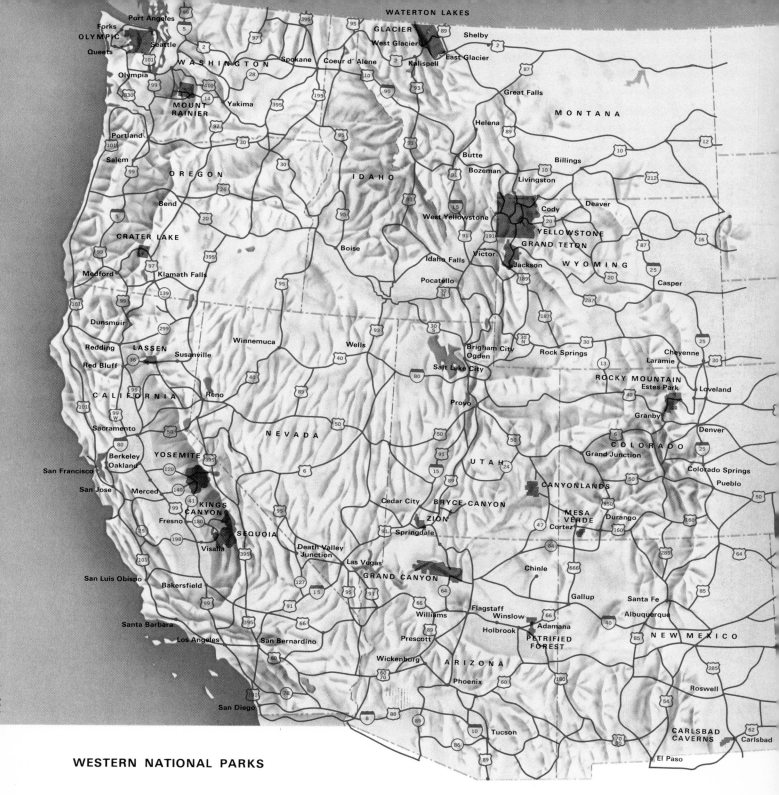

WESTERN NATIONAL PARKS

WITHIN THE ELEVEN STATES *west of the Continental Divide there*
are 18 national parks, set aside from the public domain by congressional
action over the last century. Maps of the individual parks are included in
each chapter. For information on access by air and for location of national
monuments, recreation areas, and historic sites, see the map on page 290.
Maps of Alaskan and Hawaiian parks are shown in their respective chapters.

hibited and trees are left to topple of old age or to be blown down in a wind-storm. Once fallen, they are left where they fell. Mining and extraction of petroleum are forbidden, and so is the grazing of sheep and cattle. Private cabins cannot be built within a national park, and the only structures permitted are those needed by government services and the concessioners.

To make the parks accessible to everyone, the Park System builds and maintains roads and trails and assures food, housing, and services by granting long-term concessions to corporations, usually only one or two to a park. Such concessions are closely supervised by the Service (and to a certain extent, by Congress) and are largely staffed by eager college students, who earn paid vacations by working for the summer as a "savage," "heaver," or "bubble queen."

To promote understanding of the natural wonders within their borders, the parks provide museums, visitor centers, booklets, and indestructible roadside labels for every prominent feature. Ranger naturalists, many of them "90-day wonders" (summer recruits from the teaching profession), give interpretive lectures and conduct nature walks, ranging from a gentle stroll around a lily pond to a stiff, full-day hike up a glacier and back.

In the public mind, national parks are frequently confused with national forests, and yet the two are basically different. Many of the activities that are prohibited in a national park are permissible in a national forest. Unlike the Park Service, the Forest Service permits controlled harvesting of timber, extraction of oil and minerals from the soil, hunting, grazing by sheep and cattle, and the building of private cabins and business structures. The Forest Service is dedicated to the regulated utilization of its natural resources for the benefit of the public; the Park Service to the preservation of its scenic resources for the enjoyment of all. (For further distinctions, see the chart on page 307.)

PRESERVATION OF THE NATURAL SCENE by the Park Service so that all the people may enjoy it often calls for skillful balancing of opposing needs.

Under its charter, the Park Service must welcome all who wish to come to the parks. With improved roads and the proliferation of the automobile, the parks have become more accessible to more people each year, and crowded conditions prevail in seasons of heavy tourist travel. Yellowstone clocks 1,000 cars an hour on its east-west highway, Yosemite checks in 45,000 visitors over a Fourth of July weekend, and in both parks the tourists head instinctively for the centers of popular interest, thereby compounding congestion. Although the Park Service tries to interest tourists in outlying areas and encourages off-season visits, these measures do not solve the problem. Crowding increases each year, threatening to submerge the parks, scenic wonders and all.

NEWEST NATIONAL PARK *in the system is Canyonlands (1964), located in an astonishing geologic jumble in eastern Utah. Development of accommodations and access routes are presently under way. For an idea of the height of the cliffs in this scene, compare them with the width of the road winding across the plateau.*

PHILIP HYDE

The park dilemma shows up in minor ways, as well. In Yellowstone, if the public were allowed to exercise its legal right to wander at will through the geyser basins, the fragile volcanic crust would be damaged and many tourists would be scalded and burned. To prevent this, the Park Service has built miles of wooden catwalk that conduct viewers safely among the spouting geysers but at the same time add an unsightly feature to the natural scene, in technical violation of the mandate to preserve scenic features in their natural state.

Or, take the "bear problem." Black bears are native to nearly all the Western parks, virtually a part of the scenery. The Park Service has an obligation to the bears to let them live out their allotted span and to the tourists to let them meet the beasts in their native haunts. Unfortunately, some of the bears become addicted to human food, thanks to the pampering by a minority of the touring public, and they become testy if deprived of it. Thus, scores of tourists are mauled each year by bears who suspect them of withholding treats, and countless campers' ice boxes, cars, and even tents are ripped open by bears rummaging for human food. The rangers exile offenders to the wilderness, but the wily animals find their way back for further depradations, a capital offense. The rangers have no choice but to destroy repeaters, yet each dispatched bear is a loss to the wholeness of the park.

All in all, it is remarkable that the Park Service and its concessioners cope as successfully as they do with the basic paradox that is built into the laws that govern them. A working compromise is the best that can be expected. Even at that, this compromise is remarkable and unique among the nations of the world. No other country has developed such a progressive way of making its scenic wonders available to its citizens.

What of the future? Tradition and legal precedent do not guarantee that the national parks can be kept to their designated mission without vigilant adherence to the policies that have governed them.

It is theoretically possible to create a new national park anywhere within the federal domain today, but in areas containing mineral deposits, harvestable timber, dam sites, or grazing land, opposition is almost inevitable. Our newest national park, Canyonlands, located in a mineral-rich area of Utah, was long a subject of controversy, and was much shrunk in size from earlier proposals. And it is not surprising that national park proposals in Washington's North Cascades and in California's coast-redwood belt are vigorously opposed, not only by timber industry spokesmen but by spokesmen for communities dependent on the timber industry.

The Park Service still has many problems to solve, notably the handling of the massive crowds heading towards the parks in the future, the controlling of wildlife in parks with more animals than can be handled, and the resisting of pressure to build dams and freeways on protected lands. Public understanding of the problems facing the parks can help to ease the burdens imposed on the park authorities in carrying out their dual mission to preserve the natural beauty of the land for the enjoyment of all.

National Parks of the West

MOUNT MᶜKINLEY
OLYMPIC
MOUNT RAINIER
CRATER LAKE
LASSEN VOLCANIC
YOSEMITE
SEQUOIA
KINGS CANYON
GRAND CANYON
BRYCE CANYON
ZION
PETRIFIED FOREST
MESA VERDE
CARLSBAD CAVERNS
ROCKY MOUNTAIN
GLACIER
YELLOWSTONE
GRAND TETON
HAWAII VOLCANOES
HALEAKALA

MOUNT McKINLEY

HOME OF THE INVISIBLE MOUNTAIN

PARK FACTS: *Discovered:* 1896. *Established:* February 26, 1917. *Size:* 3,030 sq. mi. *Altitude:* 1,400-20,320 feet. *Climate:* Cool, wet, and windy; temperatures —50° to 80°. *Season:* June 1 to September 15. *Visitors in 1964:* 19,175. *Access:* By highway, railroad, and private and nonscheduled aircraft.

MOUNT McKINLEY, THE HIGHEST MOUNTAIN IN NORTH AMERICA, lies only 250 miles south of the Arctic Circle. Guarding the Alaska Range with its neighbor Mount Foraker, this great peak rises to the sublime height of 20,320 feet. Small wonder the Indians of the region called it *Denali* (Home of the Sun).

Mount McKinley National Park is one of America's largest parks, and in its 3,030 square miles man has intruded but slightly. There is only one road and one area of major development.

Long before you reach the park, you can see the glacier-mantled mountain, stark and forboding, a giant among giants. The first glimpse is from a point 8 miles out on the park road to Wonder Lake, but the mountain does not appear in its full glory until the last 25 or 30 miles. The views are less obstructed, here, and although the summit is still 20 miles from the road at its nearest point, it appears so near that one is sure a 10-minute walk should bring him to the snowy slopes. Unfortunately, it is not visible from McKinley Park Hotel.

Probably the best view, and certainly the most photographed, is from near the end of the road, with Wonder Lake in the foreground. Mount McKinley is a stunning sight at midday, when the sunlight glistens on its snow and glaciers, but at sunrise or during the long subarctic twilight it is magnificent. Then delicate pastel shades enshroud it, changing with every shift of light, softening and transforming it from a great mass of granite, ice, and snow into a thing of ethereal beauty.

Weather is the enemy of visitors to this park. Summers are cool and windy, and you can count on rain half the time. You can be in the area for days and never see the mountain at all because of low-hanging clouds. Yet, even when

"THE BIG ONE," *highest peak on the North American continent, Mount McKinley rises 20,320 feet above sea level, dominates a great wilderness province 250 miles south of the Arctic Circle.*

27

the mountain is not visible, there is much else of interest. The park is a sanctuary for wildlife, and you can see many animals from the road, especially if you drive slowly, park frequently, and use field glasses.

The mighty Toklat grizzly is frequently seen. Moose are not uncommon and are usually seen browsing on willow shoots in the thickets. But the greatest wildlife show is provided by the barren-ground caribou, close relative of the domesticated reindeer. The annual migratory route of these animals crosses the park, and for a few days in late June and early July thousands can be seen moving leisurely over the slopes and along the river bottoms. There is no telling exactly when the migration will occur, and you can count yourself extremely fortunate if you are in the right place during the short time it is visible from the road.

Most of the park lies above timberline, but in this northern latitude this does not mean the altitude is high; it ranges, in fact, between 2,500 and 3,000 feet. Alpine tundra, not to be confused with arctic tundra, covers much of the park. It is of two types, wet and dry. Wet tundra is characterized by a luxuriant growth of grasses, mosses, lichens, and low shrubs. Small ponds frequently dot this dense mat, and hiking is difficult. Dry tundra, on the other hand, is typical of higher, well-drained soils, but it too is composed of dwarf plant forms, prostrate and matted, although usually not as dense as the ground cover at lower levels.

The park road varies in elevation from 1,600 feet at the entrance to about 4,000 feet near Eielson Visitor Center. At present it cannot be called a highway, since the surface is gravel, although a few sections have been oiled. The road is hilly and winding, with frequent sharp curves and rough sections. Ordinarily it is open from June 1 to September 10. Seven campgrounds with fireplaces and water are conveniently spaced along the road.

Considering its isolation, Mount McKinley National Park is surprisingly accessible. During the summer the Alaska Railroad takes passengers daily almost to the door of the hotel. The Denali Highway, open from about June 1 to September 15, serves the park and connects with the Richardson Highway at Paxson, 160 miles from the entrance.

The park was established in 1917 primarily to protect wildlife from extinction by an army of hunters that was expected to arrive when the Alaska Railroad was completed to the area. Conservation groups, such as the Boone and Crockett Club of New York and the Campfire Club of America, worked under the leadership of the "Father of McKinley Park," Charles Sheldon, to persuade Congress to establish the park, which it did six years before the rails reached it.

Another reason for creating the park was to establish a reserve around the largest mountain on the continent. The "Big One," known to explorers and prospectors for a century, was officially named in 1897 for President McKinley by a prospector named W. A. Dickey, who bestowed the name in a fit of exasperation. After spending several weary days listening to a pair of fellow prospectors advance arguments in favor of free silver, he chose in retaliation to name the peak for the leading advocate of the gold standard.

TYPICAL OF THE LAKES *that abound in the wilderness around Mount McKinley is Deneki on the outer edge of the park, just off the Denali Highway. It is a favorite haunt of moose and waterfowl.*

JON GARDEY

MOUNT MCKINLEY   29

THREE GLACIERS FLOW TOGETHER *to form a single massive ice sheet in the southwestern corner of the park. The dark ribbons are deposits of rock and soil (medial moraines) pushed aside by the advancing ice. The scalloped ice (ogives) is thought to be some sort of an annual ring. The extreme range of elevation within the park—from 1,400 to 20,320 feet—provides both the altitude to form, and the slope to move, glacial ice.*

Sudden storms and treacherous ice *make the ascent of Mt. McKinley a risky venture. Only a few dozen climbers have reached the summit since it was first conquered in 1910; some have died in making the attempt. Parties ranging from poorly equipped amateurs to elaborately outfitted expeditions have climbed it to study weather and cosmic rays, field-test cold-weather food and gear for the army, retrieve bodies from a crashed military transport plane, or, simply, to conquer the continent's highest mountain.*

MOUNT MCKINLEY NATIONAL PARK

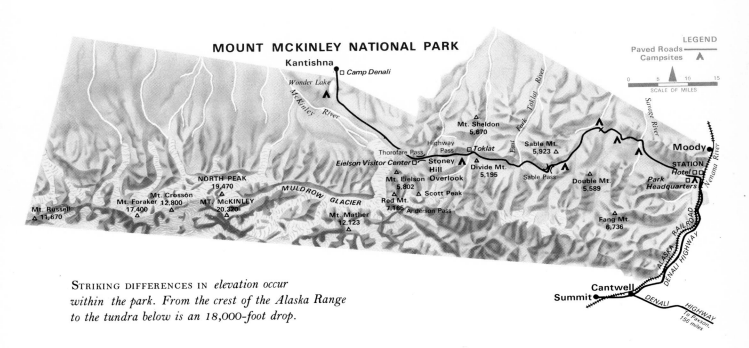

LEGEND
Paved Roads
Campsites ▲

0   5   10   15
SCALE OF MILES

Kantishna
□ Camp Denali
Wonder Lake
McKinley River

Mt. Sheldon
5,670

East Fork Toklat River

Sable Mt.
5,923

Savage River

Highway Pass
Thorofare Pass   □ Toklat
Eielson Visitor Center □   Stoney Hill ▲   Divide Mt.
Overlook   5,195
Sable Pass   ▲

Moody
STATION
Hotel □□
□□

NORTH PEAK
19,470
△
MULDROW GLACIER
Mt. Crosson 12,800
△
Mt. Foraker 17,400
△
MT. McKINLEY
20,320
△
Mt. Eielson
5,802
△
△ Scott Peak
Red Mt.
7,165   Anderson Pass

Double Mt.
5,589
△

Park Headquarters

Nenana River

Mt. Russell
11,670
△

Mt. Mather
12,123
△

Fang Mt.
6,736
△

Striking differences in *elevation occur within the park. From the crest of the Alaska Range to the tundra below is an 18,000-foot drop.*

ALASKA RAILROAD
DENALI HIGHWAY
Cantwell
Summit ●
DENALI HIGHWAY
To Paxson,
156 miles

MOUNT McKINLEY   31

ONE OF THE MOST INCREDIBLE SIGHTS *in the park is the annual migration of the caribou in great herds, sometimes numbering as many as 5,000 animals. The herds travel slowly on a broad front, leaving behind scores of parallel trails only a few feet apart. They follow general route patterns within a region 200 to 300 miles in diameter, traveling several hundred miles in their annual circuit. They winter north of the park and return to it in spring for two or three months before swinging north again. Caribou feed on lichen, and their wide-ranging migration keeps it from being over-grazed.*

CHARLES J. OTT

EXCELLENT SWIMMERS, *moose spend a great deal of time wading and swimming in ponds in search of aquatic plants, their principal source of summer food, and escaping the torment of the insects that plague them. Moose can graze as easily under water as in a meadow. The great antlers are grown annually and only by the males.*

RED FOX PUP (LEFT), *grooming himself in his burrow opening, stays close to shelter to escape the talons of swooping golden eagles, his natural enemy. Foxes live off mice, squirrels, rabbits, and ptarmigan (RIGHT), a plump bird that changes to white in winter.*

UNIQUE AMONG MCKINLEY NATIVES *are the Dall sheep that roam in bands over the higher slopes. At home on slippery scree, they are relatively safe on steep slopes from attack by less-sure-footed wolves.*

COMMON THROUGHOUT THE PARK, *grizzlies are best viewed at a respectful distance. The big, hump-shouldered beasts appear in a range of coloring, from blonde to cinnamon brown. The species was once common from Mexico to Alaska, but has been exterminated over much of its original range and may only be seen in the United States in McKinley and Yellowstone parks.*

SUNLIGHT GLINTS ON THE MILKY WATER of *Teklanika River, flowing down its braided path to lower ground. The milky water is a slurry of mineral particles, ranging from "rock flour" to pebbles and small stones, ground off the mountainsides by glaciers. The rock dust in suspension gives the water its milky cast. The travelling pebbles collect here and there to form little dams and levees that force the water to seek new channels, thus creating the braided pattern of flow. Needless to say, the river is impossible for fishing and is risky to ford, because its opacity conceals potholes.*

Caribou bull in his autumn uniform *is a picture of wild grace and power. Caribou are members of the deer family that have adapted to Artic conditions. Both sexes grow antlers, but the male sheds his first and is for a time at the mercy of his barbed mate. Prehistoric cave drawings indicate that caribou have been hunted by man since the Stone Age.*

OLYMPIC

THREE GREAT PARKS IN ONE

PARK FACTS: *Discovered:* 1774. *Established:* June 29, 1938. *Size:* 1,400 sq. mi. *Altitude:* Sea level to 7,965 feet. *Climate:* Summers cool and sunny, but rain likely; winters wettest in the conterminous United States. *Season:* All year, but some main roads closed by snow. *Visitors, 1964:* 1,343,600.

OF ALL THE NATIONAL PARKS, THE MOST DIVERSIFIED in character and climate is Olympic. Here you will find seacoast and mountain peak, rain forest and glacier, and an unbelievably abrupt change of weather patterns. The western side of the park has the wettest winter climate in the United States, with nearly *12 feet* of precipitation annually. The eastern side is the driest part of the Pacific Coast outside of Southern California.

Located on the Olympic Peninsula in the extreme northwest corner of Washington, the park contains one of the last virgin wilderness areas between Mexico and Canada. Through it wind hundreds of miles of hiking and horseback trails. Along the trails, as welcome retreats in case of sudden storm or the arrival of darkness, are many simple overnight shelters.

The Olympic Mountains are centered on the peninsula between the Pacific Ocean to the west and Hood Canal to the east. The land rises gently from the water and suddenly steepens, culminating in the heights of Mount Olympus. In comparison with the altitudes of inland mountains, the summit of Olympus— 7,965 feet—and those of other peaks above 7,000 feet do not sound impressive. But this range rises from sea level, and it is massive. Jagged peaks shade the deep canyons, more than 60 glaciers lie in the cirques, and shaggy forests climb from the sea up to timberline.

The rain forests are the strangest portions of the park, and to many the most fascinating. Their vegetation is as luxuriant as that of the Amazon jungles. Great ferns spring from beds of thick moss. Dense thickets of vine lend mystery, and gigantic trees trail heavy draperies of moss that filter the sunlight to an eerie yellow-green. There are three such forests—in the valleys of the rivers

THE SIGHT AND SOUND OF RUNNING WATER *is everywhere in this forested land. Fed by glaciers, streams run all year, reach a crescendo in summer when sun speeds melting of the ice. Rustic bridge across Soleduck Falls, in northern part of park, connects trails on each side of river.*

39

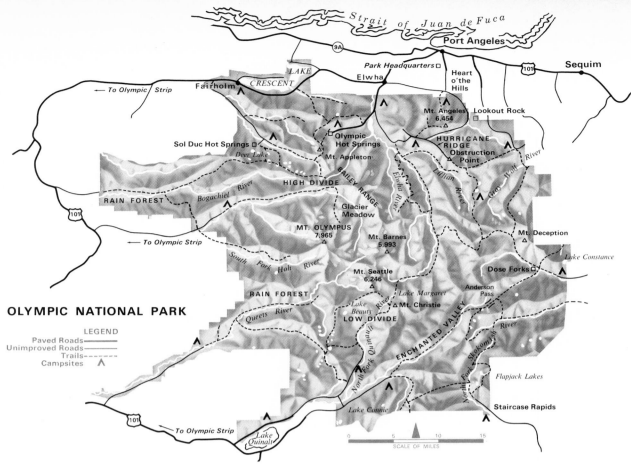

OLYMPIC NATIONAL PARK

LEGEND
Paved Roads ——————
Unimproved Roads ——————
Trails ------------------
Campsites Λ

Strait of Juan de Fuca

Port Angeles

9A

Park Headquarters □ Heart o'the Hills

Sequim

101

← To Olympic Strip

Fairholm

LAKE CRESCENT

Elwha

Mt. Angeles 6,454 △ Lookout Rock

Sol Duc Hot Springs □

□ Olympic Hot Springs

HURRICANE RIDGE
Obstruction Point

Deer Lake

Λ

Mt. Appleton △

Bogachiel River

HIGH DIVIDE

BAILEY RANGE

Elwha River

Lillian River

Gray Wolf River

RAIN FOREST

101

Glacier Meadow

MT. OLYMPUS 7,965 △

Mt. Barnes 5,993 △

Mt. Deception △

← To Olympic Strip

South Fork Hoh River

Mt. Seattle 6,246 △

Lake Margaret △ Mt. Christie

Lake Constance

Dose Forks □ Λ

Anderson Pass

RAIN FOREST

Lake Beauty

LOW DIVIDE

Queets River

Quinault River

ENCHANTED VALLEY

North Fork Skokomish River

Λ

Flapjack Lakes

101

← To Olympic Strip

Lake Quinalt

Lake Connie

Λ

Staircase Rapids

0   5   10   15
SCALE OF MILES

OLYMPIC NATIONAL PARK IS DIVIDED *into two parts: a thin coastal strip (map on page 42) and an inland block. Roads connect the two sections, but the park boundaries do not surround both. Most of the main body of the park is up-and-down country, a confusing mass of mountains and canyons.*

BARRY ANDERSON

FISHERMEN TROLL *for rainbow and cutthroat trout on Lake Crescent, largest body of water in park, which fills a deep east-west glacial trough close to the northern boundary. Easily accessible, lake is a popular resort center.*

Hoh, Queets, and Quinault—and in them are found the world's largest specimens of Sitka spruce, Douglas fir, and Western hemlock.

Six thousand Olympic elk dwell in the park. Blacktail deer live here, and so do black bears and a host of smaller animals.

Like a few other national parks, Olympic is a land of water, and it boasts not only lakes and rivers but the ocean as well. To preserve the rugged beauty of unmodified coastline with jagged cliffs, islands, and coves, the park takes in 50 miles of shoreline, perhaps the most primitive remaining in this country.

Along with hiking, mountain climbing attracts many to Olympic. Many of the lesser peaks can be conquered in safety by the inexperienced, but the more difficult demand skill. Once attained, the heights offer views that are all-embracing —peaks on every side, snow and ice, flower-strewn meadows, and the heavy coniferous forest. Beyond are the waters of the Pacific, Strait of Juan de Fuca, and Puget Sound, and the cities and towns of northwest Washington.

No trip to this peninsula would be complete without a visit to the Indian fishing village of La Push, at the mouth of Quillayute River on the ocean strip. Here fishermen still use dugout canoes and dip nets to take silversmelt in spring.

OLYMPIC HAS HAD A LONG AND EMBATTLED HISTORY. Over a span of 40 argumentative years, it has been set up in turn as a forest preserve (1897-1909), a national monument (1909-33), and, finally, a national park (1938). It has been shifted back and forth between the Department of Interior (1897-1905, 1933 to date) and the Department of Agriculture (1905-1933), and it has ranged in size from an initial 615,000 acres, down to a low in 1915 of 300,000 acres, and back up to its present size, 896,000 acres. Its boundaries have been adjusted a half dozen times.

Principal reason for this checkered history has been strong local opposition to the park built on the conviction that it would withdraw thousands of acres of harvestable timber needed to sustain the state's giant lumbering industry. First moves to set aside the area were introduced in the 1890's, and though repeated attempts were made in later years, including a bill in 1905 to establish it as Elk National Park, the park was not created until 1938. The protracted battling surged in and out of congressional committee hearings, reached into the President's Cabinet, and even drew President Franklin Roosevelt to Port Angeles in an attempt to compromise the disputed issues. In time, proponents of the park were able to win their point that creation of the national park would bring long-run benefits to the state, as well as the nation, that would greatly outweigh the short-run benefits to be derived from logging off the trees, and the park was finally legislated into existence.

The name chosen for the park harks back to an English sea captain, John Mears, who sighted the high mountains from the coast in 1774 and named the highest peak Mount Olympus, believing it deserved the dignity of association with the Greek home of the gods. For 24 years, Olympic was known as Mount Olympus National Monument, and the park was very nearly named Mount Olympus National Park when it was established.

OLYMPIC OCEAN STRIP

WITH THE HARD, WET SAND UNDER FOOT, the beachwalker finds the Olympic Strip a fascinating realm of spray and mist, where every twisting mile reveals subtle changes in the scenery and surprises along the trail.

The wide trail picks its way through barricades of driftwood, tossed on the beach by the waves in massive piles of jackstraws. Wedged among the rocks or bobbing in the surf are occasional glass floats, broken loose from fishing nets off Japan and carried across the Pacific by the current on a year-long voyage. Here and there are battered timbers and twisted ironwork, mementos of the countless ships that have been smashed to bits against the cliffs.

In season, the running of the smelt brings out fishermen en masse; and during the clamming months, throngs of diggers, equipped with shovels and buckets, probe feverishly for razor clams that retreat deep into the sand to elude the clutching hand. An abundance of marine life thrives in the tide-pools, where it may be viewed under the guidance of ranger naturalists, who conduct walks through this chill and slippery realm.

RUTH KIRK

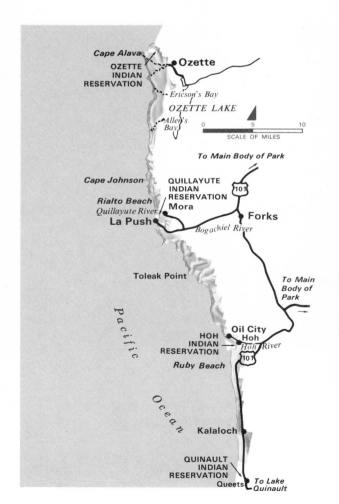

MUSSELS CROWD TOGETHER *in an intertidal environment that is so favorable that the creatures living in it multiply and compete for food and living space.*

THE COASTAL STRIP *of Olympic National Park is separated from the main body of the park that lies a few miles inland.*

CAMPERS IGNORE A LOWERING SKY *as they pitch camp on a natural jetty near Point Toleak. Damp weather does not deter those who are drawn to this dramatic coastline, a place of primeval and unspoiled grandeur.*

INQUISITIVE HARBOR SEALS *are often
seen from the beach. Squashy pawprints in
the wet sand reveal the presence of black
bear, who emerge at dusk to fish in the
surf or feed on carrion. Other permanent
residents of the strip include elk and deer,
who frequently come down to the beach,
and raccoons that catch crabs in tidepools.*

THERE IS NO WAY TO GO ASTRAY *on nature's wide trail between sea and wooded hills. The 50-mile strip of sand is itself the path—the forests that press to the waterline are too dense to penetrate. Hikers carry tide tables so they can pass the sections that are covered by high tide.*

STEVEN C. WILSON

A LONE DUGOUT CANOE, *propelled by an outboard motor, drones into the estuary of Goodman Creek bay. Indians living along the strip still use these venerable craft for offshore transportation and for fishing. Carved from a single cedar log, dugouts have been known to last 50 years or more.*

DUGOUTS AND DINGHIES *share berthing space at the dock at La Push, only seaport in the strip and center of Quillayute Indian Reservation. Boats used by Indians for deep-sea fishing for salmon. The few cedar dugouts being made today are rough-shaped with chainsaws, finished by hand.*

COMMON MURRE, *bobbing in a tidepool is one of several species of birds that nest in the nearby wildlife refuges.*

RAIN FOREST

THE LUMINOUS WORLD OF THE RAIN FOREST is filled with a soft green light reflected and refracted by the mosses and the translucent maple leaves. To a well-traveled Westerner, there are no strange or unknown organisms. Everything that grows in the rain forest, except the Sitka spruce, grows in other places. The differences are not so much in species as in habit. Water-loving things, be they microbes, mushrooms, or Douglas firs, are literally in their element. Their growth and functioning in the life community are stepped up here.

With all its exuberance, the whole forest is unexpectedly fragile. The trees are shallow-rooted, as they can be where food and water are plentiful and where the forest cover is so uniform and continuous that the wind cannot get a "bite."

Within the rain forest, trees grow large and undergrowth is abundant. Olympic has the world's record specimens of Douglas fir, Western red cedar, Western hemlock, and Sitka spruce. The undergrowth, though luxuriant, is seldom impenetrable. It is yielding and pleasant to the touch, with winding aisles that invite strolling. The foliage is kept in check partly by the browsing of the park's most famous wild creature, the Roosevelt elk, who spend 9 months of the year here before migrating to high ground for the summer.

ROOSEVELT ELK ROAM THE RAIN FOREST *in winter, move to the high country in summer. Also known as Olympic elk, these animals were one of the principal reasons for creation of the park, which was nearly named in their honor.*

FILLED WITH SOFT GREEN LIGHT, *the Olympic rain forest invites the visitor to stroll down its moss-festooned paths between luxuriant growths of maidenhair, swordfern, and deer and licorice ferns.*

CAUSES OF WASHINGTON RAIN FOREST

1. HEAVY RAINFALL. *Caused by steep rise of mountains forcing storm clouds to ascend and release moisture.*

2. CONCENTRATED MOISTURE. *Rain plus runoff from mountain sides plus slow river flow concentrates moisture in the valley.*

3. SEA-LEVEL TEMPERATURES. *Long, almost level floor of valley extends moderate, sea-level temperatures deep inland.*

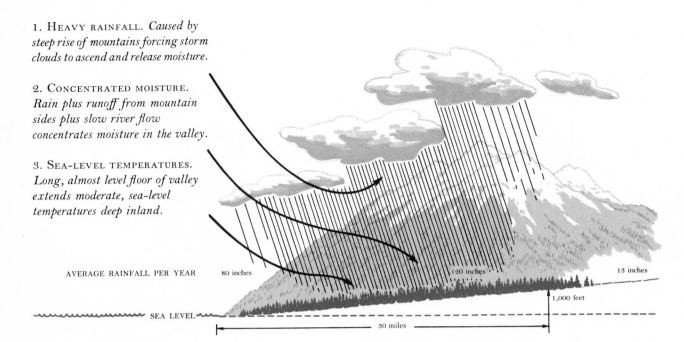

AVERAGE RAINFALL PER YEAR 80 inches 120 inches 13 inches

1,000 feet

SEA LEVEL

30 miles

ROADS PENETRATE *just the fringes of the park, and the only way to enjoy most of its primitive grandeur is to hike or ride horseback. A network of trails follows the stream courses through the forests. Simple trailside shelters, spaced a few miles apart, offer protection from drizzle, overnight accommodation, and eliminate need for carrying tents in the backpack. Girl scouts make camp at a typical leanto.*

CATHEDRAL-LIKE FORESTS *of immense Douglas-fir trees with Western hemlock and Western redcedar fill river valleys.*

50 OLYMPIC

LIFE CYCLE OF A RAIN FOREST: *After a tree topples, forest starts to return it to soil; bacteria and fungi slowly break down its fibres; mosses cover it, give surface in which tree seeds germinate, sprout; seedling takes root; in time, a new tree grows.* RIGHT: *Key to typical plant community (ABOVE).*

KEY TO PLANTS IN TYPICAL RAIN FOREST COMMUNITY

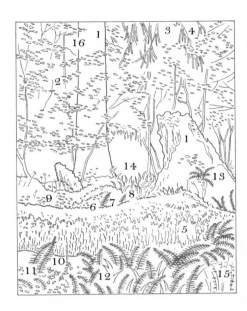

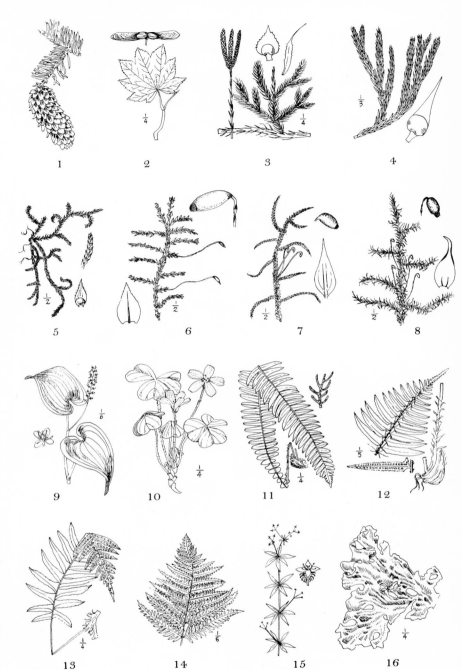

1. SITKA SPRUCE *identifies the rain forest. Its life begins on rotting logs and stumps.*

2. VINE MAPLE (Acer circinatum) *gives the deep forest a cheerful luminescence.*

3. RUNNING PINE (Lycopodium clavatum). *Common clubmoss found on trees, logs, stumps, rail fences, and the ground.*

4. FIR CLUBMOSS (Lycopodium selago).

5. SELAGINELLA (S. oregana) *forms the graceful curtains on the maple boughs.*

6. MOSS (Eurhynchium oreganum) *is one of the true mosses of the Olympic forests.*

7 AND 8. MOSSES (Rhytidiadelphus loreus *and* Rhytidiadelphus triquetrus) *typical of the rain forest, range across the continent to Evangeline's "forest primeval."*

9. BEADRUBY (Maianthemum dilatatum). *Glossy leaves highlight carpets of moss.*

10. WOOD SORREL (Oxalis oregana). *The commonest leafy plant of the forest floor.*

11. DEER FERN (Lomaria spicant). *Look for erect, thin fertile leaves in center.*

12. WESTERN SWORDFERN (Polystichum munitum). *Each leaflet has own stalk.*

13. LICORICE FERN (Polypodium vulgare) *grows on logs, stumps, rocks, mossy trees.*

14. LADY FERN (Athyrium filix-fœmina) *looks something like bracken minus stalk.*

15. FRAGRANT BEDSTRAW (Galium triflorum).

16. LICHEN (Lobaria oregana) *is colony of interdependent fungi and algae.*

HIKERS' HIGHLANDS

THE HEART OF THE PARK IS A DEDICATED MOUNTAIN WILDERNESS. Without question, it is not for everyone. Yet, even with all the aloofness of haughty Olympus itself, no other wilderness is more inviting, more unlocked, or more approachable.

This highland domain is all up-and-down country, its peaks and ridges separated by the valleys of rivers sliced so deep into the yielding rock that some have reached their ultimate level. Irregular and complex as they are, the Olympics contain two principal "ranges": a "wet" range that roughly parallels the western boundary of the park and traps the bulk of the moisture-laden air from the Pacific Ocean, and a "dry" range that marks the eastern edge with a series of peaks separated by short, steep, river canyons. Mount Olympus, monarch of the wet range, is not easy to see from afar. Unlike its distant neighbor, Mount Rainier, which rises high above the countryside, Olympus is a puzzling cluster of crags that are barely clear of the ice cap and nearly lost in a jumble of peaks.

Few roads penetrate to this mountain fastness, and access is largely by trail—600 miles of it. Hikers familiar with conditions in the Sierra or Rockies find the Olympics easy going because of the lower altitudes, the fresh, cool weather, plentiful water, and soft, spongy trails.

BOB AND IRA SPRING

THIS IS A HIKER'S PARK *that offers its best rewards to the strong-legged and self-sufficient. Trails cover a variety of terrain, from wet to dry, moss-covered to ice-encrusted. Only hikers skilled in snow and ice climbing, or those trained in the basic techniques, are permitted to ascend into the glacial highlands. The roped party above is on icy leg of trail to Mount Olympus.*

BREATHTAKING VISTAS OPEN WITH *every bend in the trail that climbs to the summit of Mount Olympus. The up-and-down nature of the terrain produces long views of deep canyons and towering mountain ridges.*

OLYMPIC 55

HIGH ABOVE A CLOUD-FILLED CANYON, *deer graze on the meadows of
"panorama country" in the northeast corner of the park. Hurricane Ridge
is noted for its magnificent outlooks over the Strait of Juan de Fuca
and the snowcapped peaks around Mount Olympus, as well as the view
of the towering peaks to the east. Highest alpine area in the park
that can be reached by automobile, Hurricane Ridge is approached by a
hair-raising road that corkscrews up from sea level to 5,000 feet in 18 miles.*

WILDFLOWERS BURST INTO BLOOM *while snow is still on the
ground at Hurricane Ridge. Fields of alpine lilies cover
the high meadowlands. The snow-covered Bailey Range
looms on the horizon.*

DARWIN VAN CAMPEN

MOUNT RAINIER

SNOW-CAPPED BEACON TO A STATE

PARK FACTS: *Discovered:* 1792 by Vancouver expedition, mountain named for British Admiral Rainier; area explored 1833. *Established:* March 2, 1899. *Size:* 378 sq. mi. *Altitude:* 1,914 to 14,410 feet. *Climate:* Mt. Rainier perennially snow and cloud capped. *Season:* All year. *Visitors, 1964:* 1,439,922.

ON A CLEAR DAY, THE SNOW-MANTLED CREST OF MOUNT RAINIER dominates the skyline of northwest Washington, even in cities and towns on Puget Sound more than 50 miles away. At a distance its great height and some trick of the atmosphere make it seem much closer. Those who live within sight of its gleaming peak seem to draw a sense of security and well-being from its presence; they are cheered when the clouds roll away and they can tell one another, "You can see the mountain today." The Indians felt its guardianship so strongly they called it The Mountain That Was God.

It is easy to imagine the impact the mountain had on Captain George Vancouver of the British Navy, when he cruised the Pacific Coast in 1792. He was probably the first white man to see it, and he promptly gave it its present name, in honor of his friend Admiral Peter Rainier. Later it became an unmistakable landmark for pioneers bound for the Oregon Country, who knew when they saw it that they were nearing the end of their journey.

The mountain was born of fire. It is one of several great volcanoes of the Cascade Range, and it inspired John Muir to write: "Of all the fire mountains which, like beacons, once blazed along the Pacific Coast, Mount Rainier is the noblest."

Despite the steam caves and warm mineral springs that prove the volcanic furnaces are not completely extinguished, more than one-tenth of Mount Rainier National Park's 378-square-mile area is ice. There are a dozen major glaciers, and 26 that are important enough to have names; and they are among the most accessible in the United States. Some can be reached by a short walk from the road, and several others can be viewed from close-up vantage points.

THIS IS MOUNT RAINIER *as it reveals itself to mountain explorers based at Klapatche Lake on the western slope of Rainier. Add to this scene the tang of crisp, clean mountain air and the whisper of wind in the trees and you begin to share the secrets of "The Mountain."*

BOB AND IRA SPRING

BOB AND IRA SPRING

"A PERFECT FLOWER ELYSIUM," *is the way John Muir described the wildflower parks that encircle Mount Rainier. A bright wreath of ever-changing color carpets slopes between glaciers and forest. Floral display comes in two intense seasons: first in early July, as snow recedes; second, the next month.*

PAUL V. THOMAS

Canadian dogwood   *Phlox*   *Buttercup*   *Avalanche lily*

Until recently, for as long as men have been studying them, the glaciers have been gradually receding. Now they are advancing again—very slowly, of course, and perhaps only temporarily.

Below the ice fields is an unspoiled preserve of alpine meadows and dense forests, home of countless birds and animals—tiny as the chickadee, large as the black bear, rare as the mountain goat. Wildflowers brighten the lower slopes in late spring and move upward in an unfolding tapestry as the snow melts.

Rainier rations its beauty and grandeur, as if to make sure it will be appreciated. Much of the time it retires behind a heavy cloud cover; on other days it tantalizes its admirers by hiding behind a thin curtain of vapor. Then, when the mood is right, the veil suddenly is lifted, and there is the matchless crown of ice and snow shining in the sunlight.

Weather is uncertain at Mount Rainier, but a good share of warm, clear days can usually be expected between early July and mid-September, and sometimes into October, when the wooded slopes renew their annual display of autumn color. In the course of the year the park receives heavy rain and snowfall, for the Cascades are a major barrier to moisture-laden winds from the Pacific. Precipitation averages about 100 inches a year at Paradise, where as much as 80 feet of snow has fallen in a single winter to leave a snowpack of 30 feet.

Hiking is popular here, and the choice of trails ranges from short nature walks to a hike along the Wonderland Trail, which completely encircles the mountain and samples the whole variety of terrain the park has to offer. Typical of the shorter walks is the Trail of the Shadows, a special delight in spring when the rivulets are full and the air is fragrant with the odor of evergreens, damp earth, and growing things.

For those who enjoy mountain climbing, Rainier is a worthy challenge. It requires a strenuous ascent over lava, glaciers, and ice fields, though without the danger of the vertical faces to be scaled elsewhere in the West. Some 800 climbers—all carefully screened first by park authorities for fitness, ability, experience, and equipment—reach the summit each year.

The park is open year round, although the Carbon River, White River, and Stevens Canyon entrances are closed from the first heavy snowfall (usually around November 1) until about the last half of June. Mount Rainier is a favorite of campers, and one of the campgrounds—Sunshine Point, near Nisqually Entrance—is available for use through the winter. On winter weekends and holidays the skiers come to Paradise.

In several ways Mount Rainier is one of the least remote of the national parks of the West. Its peak is visible over a vast area. It is one of the nearest to large centers of population. And, in a sense, it can be seen from the highway by the passerby, for the roads along the southern and eastern edges provide spectacular views of its snow-clad monarch.

But few who glimpse its beauty as they pass are satisfied until they return for a longer visit.

Up to 80 feet of snow *in one winter has been recorded in the Paradise area, a major winter recreation center. Snow lingers here until mid-May, and as it melts, the white fields are replaced by bright carpets of wildflowers. Located near an active glacier, Paradise offers base for glacier exploring.*

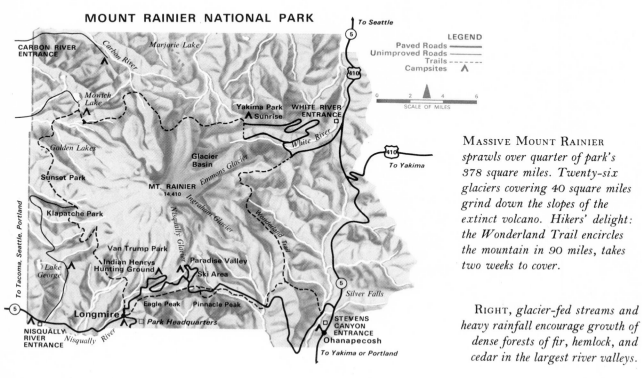

MOUNT RAINIER NATIONAL PARK

Massive Mount Rainier *sprawls over quarter of park's 378 square miles. Twenty-six glaciers covering 40 square miles grind down the slopes of the extinct volcano. Hikers' delight: the Wonderland Trail encircles the mountain in 90 miles, takes two weeks to cover.*

Right, *glacier-fed streams and heavy rainfall encourage growth of dense forests of fir, hemlock, and cedar in the largest river valleys.*

ANSEL ADAMS

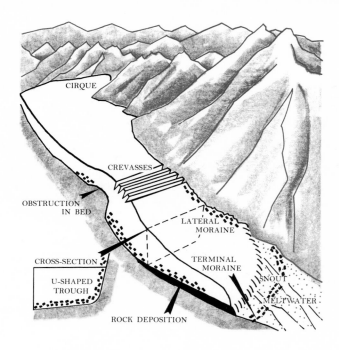

HOW DOES A GLACIER WORK?

GLACIERS ARE FORMED *where snowfall is so heavy that the winter's accumulation cannot be carried off by evaporation in spring. The snow piles deeper and deeper, becomes denser and denser, and finally turns to a near-solid, ice. Tremendous weight of the built-up mass causes it to slide downhill at a slow pace. Where the river of ice reaches lower and warmer elevations, it melts and changes to a running stream or river, depending on its size. At the point where its progress is arrested, it forms a bulging tongue called a "snout."*

The flowing ice carries rock debris with it, some dislodged from the mountainsides, some from the bed of the valley that it occupies. This residue gives the lower end of a glacier a dirty, messy look quite unlike the pristine white of its upper reaches. In time, the rocky mass is deposited either at the sides or at the snout in massive accumulations known as moraines. The gouging processes of a glacier are most active where it starts, thus causing the formation of bowl-like cavities known as cirques.

Where glacial ice flows around sharp bends or over obstructions in its bed, the brittle mass cracks open to form deep crevasses, as in the photograph (RIGHT) of the Winthrop Glacier on the north side of Mount Rainier.

A PURPLE GLOW *infuses the ceiling and walls of ice grottos inside glaciers.*
Sunlight passing through the compressed ice changes to the blue-purple side of the spectrum. Snow
climbers catch their breath in a grotto at the 10,000-foot level on Cowlitz Glacier.

ICE-CLIMBING TOOLS

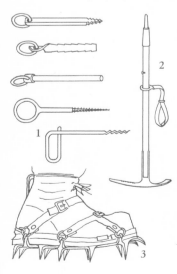

SPECIAL GEAR *is similar to that used by rock climbers (see page 262).*
1. ICE PITONS *and ice screws for securing climbing ropes.*
2. ICE AXE, *versatile tool for cutting steps in ice, securing rope, and serving as a brake or rudder for downhill slides.*
3. CRAMPONS, *claw-like soles to be strapped to hiking boots.*

SINCE 1833, *ascent to the 14,410-foot summit of Mount Rainier has challenged mountain climbers. Nearly 800 leather-lunged hikers a year now secure climbing permits and make the two-day climb to the crest.* RIGHT: *Climbers picking their way past seracs on the Ingraham Glacier at 11,000 feet use some of same techniques as rock climbers*

BOB AND IRA SPRING

CRATER LAKE

BLUE SAUCER ON A VOLCANO SITE

Park facts: Discovered: June 12, 1853. *Established:* May 22, 1902. *Size:* 250 sq. mi. *Altitude:* 4,405-8,926 feet. *Climate:* Snow covers park nearly 8 months of year, but main roads kept open all year. Summer weather is very unpredictable, with warm days and chilly nights. *Visitors in 1964:* 494,057.

THE KLAMATH INDIANS TELL US that long ago, before there was a Crater Lake, the volcanic mountain called Mazama served as the passageway between the domain below the earth and the world topside. When Lao, chief of the world below, visited the surface, he could be seen as a dark form towering above the white snows. When Sahale Tyee, chief of the world above, appeared on earth, he rested atop Mount Shasta, south of Mazama.

The day came when these two deities quarreled, and the anger of Lao shook the ground, sent thunder and burning ashes into the sky, and spilled lava down the mountainside.

The medicine men interpreted Lao's violence as a curse directed at least in part toward the tribe for wickedness and error. To make atonement, they climbed to the top of Mount Mazama and threw themselves into the crater.

The chief of the world above was so impressed by this sacrifice that he renewed his war with Lao and finally drove him underground. As the chief of the world below retreated and disappeared, the mountaintop fell in upon him and his door to the surface was sealed. Never again did Lao frighten the Indians; the crater of his mountain filled with pure waters and became a scene of peace and quiet.

The Indian legends have helped geologists reconstruct the violent eruptions that climaxed with the collapse of Mount Mazama's cone. The timetable is necessarily inexact, but all evidence indicates that the bowl containing Crater Lake was created within the last 10,000 years.

Before its collapse, Mazama was a 12,000-foot volcano that stood out with the mountains now called Baker, Rainier, Adams, Hood, and Shasta as giants of the Cascade Range. The peak had built up from repeated flows of molten lava

THE INTENSE BLUES of Crater Lake must be seen to be believed. Ranging from indigo to turquoise, depending on water depth, the color is thought to be caused by scattering of sunlight in water of great depth and clarity. Blue is reflected, other rays absorbed.

DAVID MUENCH

and the debris of explosive eruptions. Glaciers filled the valleys of its sculptured slopes, and thick forests covered the foothills.

The climactic eruptions recounted in legend must have been horrendous by any standards. Earthquakes were followed by enormous clouds of gases and steam that blocked out the sun for weeks. Embers and ashes fell over a vast area, covering the land with gray powder and igniting the forests. The glaciers melted and new rivers washed down the steep slopes.

And then came the greatest explosion of all. A dense cloud of dust, expanding gases, and red-hot lava fragments burst from the crater and spilled down the slopes, traveling at great speed. The avalanche crushed every form of life for 35 miles around.

Long fissures opened beneath the volcano. The violence underground continued for days, with additional eruptions and expulsions, until Mazama's peak became a heavy shell over an empty pocket. Shaken by the violence and deprived of support, the top of the volcano fell in with a roar that must literally have staggered the Indian witnesses.

When the skies finally cleared, the mountain peak was gone, and the foreshortened slopes of Mazama rose to a huge bowl more than 5 miles across and 4,000 feet deep.

The caldera (Spanish and Portuguese for caldron) began to fill with rain and melting snow. The first pools were turned to steam by the boiling mud and hot rocks in the bottom of the basin, but as the mountain cooled the caldera filled with water. Eventually the water level reached a point higher than that of today, then receded to its present depth of about 2,000 feet.

There are many calderas in the world, but none is quite as spectacular as that of Crater Lake. The broken lines of the old volcano contrast with the quiet surface of the deep, blue water. Visitors who drive around the lake are impressed with the immensity of the mountain and the tremendous forces that caused its downfall. Geologists find Mazama one of the best places on earth to study volcanism.

Most of the park's roadways and points of interest are related to the caldera and its surrounding slopes. The major exception is the Pinnacles. These needle-like rock formations are remnants of the avalanches of volcanic pumice that preceded Mount Mazama's collapse. The pumice spread out in sheets and cooled rapidly on top, but the hot rocks beneath continued to send gases to the surface through vents. These hot emissions hardened the pumice around the vents to form "pipes." When the rest of the pumice eroded away during succeeding centuries, the pipes remained as thin pinnacles.

The Indians long believed that only punishment could come to men who looked upon a lake that was sacred to the spirits. "Do not look upon this place," the legend warned, "for it will mean death or lasting sorrow." Fortunately, the ominous warning no longer applies. The thousands who stand in awe each year on the brink of Crater Lake come away not in sorrow but with a new and exultant realization of nature's power and beauty.

HOW CRATER LAKE WAS FORMED

1. ERUPTIONS *of lava from crater built up Mt. Mazama over period of time.*

2. VOLCANO *spent itself in series of violent eruptions that emptied underlying lava chamber.*

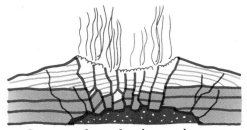

3. CAVE-IN *of top of peak, caused by withdrawal of underground support, created caldera.*

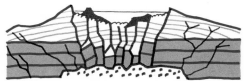

4. WATER *filled caldera to form lake. Wizard Island formed 6,000 years later by new eruption.*

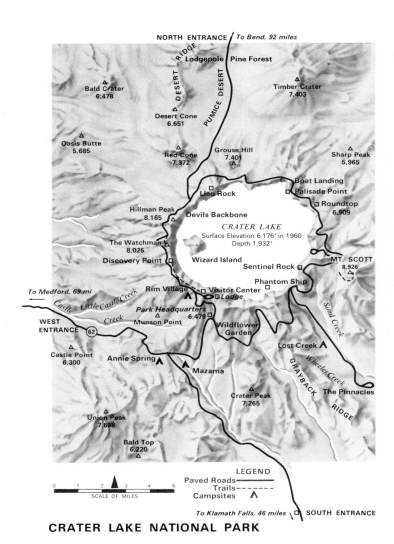

CRATER LAKE NATIONAL PARK

CORE OF THE *250-square-mile national park, Crater Lake's 22 square miles of water is contained within a 20-mile circle of cliffs. Pumice flow spewed out of crater of now-dead Mount Mazama filled all valleys now within park boundaries and raced 20-30 miles to east and west. Lighter pumice, blasted into the air, was wind-borne for 80 miles, covered 5,000 square miles.*

THE MISSING PEAK, *old Mount Mazama, can best be sensed from the air where the full immensity of the cavity is visible. Before its collapse, the top of the peak probably stood on a level with the airplane from which this photograph was taken. Few other calderas in the world equal Crater Lake's in size or beauty. Although the lake is supplied only by snow, rain, and spring water, it maintains a constant level year in and year out, rarely fluctuating more than 3 feet.*

CRATER LAKE X-RAY

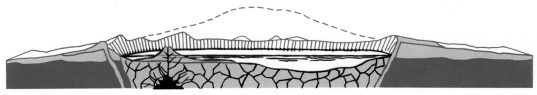

SECOND DEEPEST LAKE *in the Western Hemisphere, Crater Lake plummets to a depth of 1,932 feet at its extreme point. Around the rim, volcanic cliffs slope sharply down to the water. Extinct volcano Wizard Island rises 1,900 feet from floor of caldera, 760 feet above the water.*

GLOWING PROJECTILES *rising above the rim of the caldera and the roar of explosions within*
accompanied the birth of the volcanic cone, Wizard Island, a thousand years ago.
The cataclysm terrified the Indians, who feared that the eruption
signaled a repetition of the catastrophes that their ancestors had suffered when Mount Mazama
collapsed. The island was formed by an outpouring of lava from the crater, which is
clearly visible from the rim and can be reached by a trail from the
boat landing. Growth rings indicate the age of the oldest trees on the island as 900 years,
thus establishing the approximate date of the eruption.

WINTER CASTS *a magic spell over Crater Lake when heavy snow rims the indigo water and cloaks the firs and hemlocks with a quilt of dazzling white. Lying on the crest of the Cascade Range above 6,500 feet, the park annually receives more than 50 feet of snow, which covers much of it for nearly 8 months, starting as early as September and lasting almost to July. Access is kept open through the thick of winter, and visitors drive between towering snowbanks and enter buildings through tunnels from the cleared parking areas. The big rambling lodge (RIGHT) is shuttered and closed for the winter, but a coffee shop is kept open to thaw the sightseers and skiers.*

EVERYWHERE YOU LOOK *are the black-grey-and-white Clark nutcrackers, crow-sized birds as common here as the jay. Harsh-voiced, sociable, and thievish, these birds thrive on tourist's scraps. Ravens, eagles, and falcons may sometimes be seen flying over the lake. California gulls often light on the water, and ducks and geese stop here on their migration route.*

CRATER LAKE 75

THE PHANTOM SHIP, *rising dramatically above surface of the lake,*
is formed of two kinds of volcanic rock: brown-black sails are of molten rock,
pale green hull of volcanic ash. Sails are part of a volcanic dike.

HOW THE PINNACLES WERE FORMED

GLOWING AVALANCHES *once filled the deep valleys surrounding the ancient peak with a white-hot blanket of pumice. The super-heated substance took years to cool, and while it was still hot, it released steam and gases through vents and tubes. The hot gases cooked the walls of these passageways into hard-baked chimneys, and these ancient vents now stand alone —as at the Pinnacles (*RIGHT*)—the softer surrounding material having long since been carried away by erosion.*

DARWIN VAN CAMPEN

LASSEN VOLCANIC

THE SMOKE CLOUD ROSE FIVE MILES

PARK FACTS: *Discovered:* Probably in early 1800's. *Established:* August 9, 1916. *Size:* 160 sq. mi. *Altitude:* 5,680-10,457 feet. *Climate:* Warm, pleasant summers; snow in winter. Snow recreation area kept open in winter in southern section of the park; other areas closed. *Visitors in 1964:* 407,700.

WHEN THE FIRST WHITE SETTLERS CAME to northeastern California, they assumed that volcanic Lassen Peak was extinct. The earth around it was pockmarked with bubbling sinks, but the mountain itself appeared cold and lifeless.

But on May 30, 1914, they changed their minds. Without warning, a great column of steam and gases spouted from the top of the peak, throwing out small pieces of lava and debris on the upper slopes. The eruption was brief, but it opened a new vent in the old crater and signaled the beginning of renewed activity that lasted more than two years.

Lassen erupted more than 150 times during the next year, spouting dust and steam high in the air and flinging cinders and small boulders around its base. But no lava appeared, and spectators were more curious than concerned.

During the winter of 1914-15, snowfall was unusually heavy. It piled deep on the upper slopes of Lassen, and all that fell within the new crater immediately melted and drained down into the earth. Some scientists believe that this build-up of water below the surface was partly responsible for what happened in the spring.

On the evening of May 19, molten lava bubbled up to the crater rim. On the southwest edge, it trickled over and flowed a thousand feet down the side before cooling into a solid sheet. On the northeast side, a much more dramatic performance was developing. Lava spilled over the rim, steam roared out of a hole in the mountainside near the top, and chunks of lava fell on the slopes. The heat melted the deep drifts of snow, and this water combined with the debris of earlier eruptions to create a devastating mudflow. The deluge of mud surged down the mountain, growing in volume and violence, and funneled into the

QUIESCENT LASSEN PEAK *looms above the scene of its devastating eruptions of 1914-15. The skeletal tree is one of the few remaining of the thousands that were flattened in a few seconds by a violent blast of steam from the side of the mountain in 1915.*

79

valleys of Hat and Lost Creeks. It peeled the bark off trees up to 18 feet and submerged the meadows with as much as 6 feet of debris.

Despite this cataclysm, Lassen Peak was not yet spent. Three days later a spectacular column of smoke mounted 5 miles into the air and a blast of steam shot out of the mountainside. This time the force of the steam jet was horizontal. Trees in its path were knocked down like matchsticks, and the earth was scrubbed bare.

With that release of pressure, Lassen seemed all but appeased. The volcano shuddered a few more times—there were eight minor eruptions in June, six in July—but by 1917 all visible activity had subsided.

There are still many signs of these volcanic eruptions—which are the most recent in the United States except for Hawaii and Alaska—but nature is gradually covering the wounds. The devastated area is clearly defined, although a few trees are taking root in the rocky crust. You can hike to the top of Lassen Peak and look into the crater, but the crucible has long since cooled and the mountain once again wears a cap of perpetual snow.

Well below the surface, however, the volcanic pot is still boiling. At those places where the crust is broken or cracked (there are six within the park), gases and steam hiss up through fumaroles and keep the mud bubbling like porridge on a hot stove. Sulfurous vapors taint the air.

Although the 1915 eruption poured forth molten lava, Lassen is actually a plug volcano, made of stiff lumps of lava pushed upward by subterranean forces but too thick to flow like liquid. Not old, it was probably formed no more than a few thousand years ago.

There are other significant examples of volcanism in Lassen Volcanic National Park. South of Lassen Peak are traces of another giant that once existed here— Mount Tehama, a huge cone 15 miles in diameter and 11,000 feet high. It eventually collapsed, and the fractured remnants include Brokeoff Mountain, Mount Diller, Pilot Pinnacle, Mount Conard, and Diamond Point.

Chaos Crags are the remains of three plug volcanoes, much like Lassen but without craters. Prospect Peak, Mount Harkness, Red Mountain, and Raker Peak are shield volcanoes similar to those of Hawaii—volcanoes that have been built up from layers of molten lava that flowed out and then cooled into "shields."

What about the future of Lassen Peak? Will it awaken again, or has it settled into a deep and lasting sleep? Many geologists believe the volcano is well on its way to extinction. The thermal activity underground continues, but only a few wisps of steam are ever seen atop the mountain. Another series of eruptions would come as a great surprise.

Of course, that's what they were saying back in 1913.

SMOKE COLUMN *from the 1915 eruption climbed 5 miles into the sky and was visible for 50 miles; 5-ton rock bombs were catapulted into the air. Touring party watches pyrotechnic display from a discreet distance.*

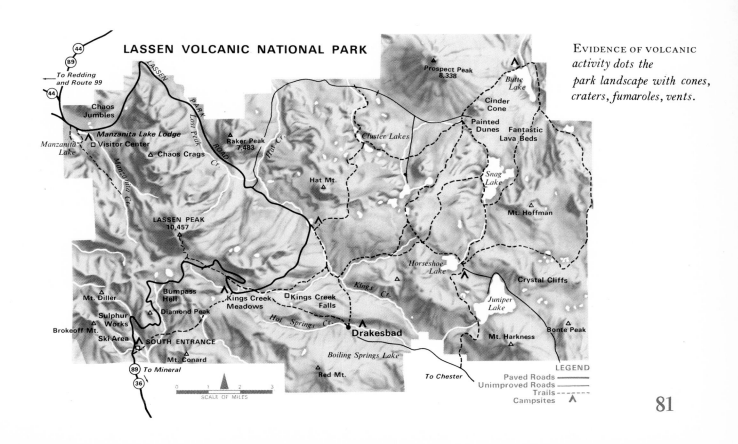

LASSEN VOLCANIC NATIONAL PARK

EVIDENCE OF VOLCANIC *activity dots the park landscape with cones, craters, fumaroles, vents.*

44
89
To Redding and Route 99
44

LASSEN
PARK
Lost Peak Cr.
ROAD
Chaos Jumbles
Manzanita Lake Lodge
Manzanita Lake
Visitor Center
Chaos Crags
Manzanita Cr.
Raker Peak 7,483
Hat Cr.
Hat Mt.

Prospect Peak 8,338
Butte Lake
Cinder Cone
Painted Dunes
Fantastic Lava Beds
Cluster Lakes
Snag Lake
Mt. Hoffman

LASSEN PEAK 10,457

Mt. Diller
Bumpass Hell
Diamond Peak
Kings Creek Meadows
Kings Creek Falls
Kings Cr.
Horseshoe Lake
Crystal Cliffs
Juniper Lake
Sulphur Works
Brokeoff Mt.
Ski Area
SOUTH ENTRANCE
Mt. Conard
Hot Springs Cr.
Drakesbad
Mt. Harkness
Bonte Peak

89 To Mineral
36
Red Mt.
Boiling Springs Lake
To Chester

0 1 2 3
SCALE OF MILES

LEGEND
Paved Roads ————
Unimproved Roads ————
Trails ------
Campsites ∧

81

A VOLCANO BLOWS ITS TOP

FROM MANZANITA LAKE *the eruption, only 4 airline miles away, was a spectacular sight. Over the centuries, occasional eruptions of lava, forced to the surface by pressure of magma below, built up peak with layer upon layer of volcanic rock.*

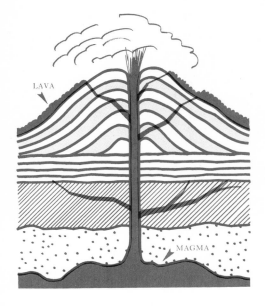

TRANQUIL MANZANITA LAKE *reflects a very different scene from the one it mirrored a half century ago. The mineral-rich soil and plentiful water encourage luxuriant growth of conifers and shrubby plants. Birds nest in the willow and alder thickets, orchids bloom in the bogs, and deer and bear seek the water at dusk.*

IN THE CRISP AIR OF WINTER, steam rising from fumaroles carries the white world into another dimension. Areas such as Bumpass Hell can only be reached by ski after heavy snows close the main highway.

BOILING MUD POTS fling blobs of red mud into the air, forming a rim around the vent. Color comes from iron oxide in the soil. The mud is dangerously hot— about 200° Fahrenheit.

FORREST JACKSON

Bᴜᴍᴘᴀss Hᴇʟʟ ɪs ɴᴀᴍᴇᴅ *for a pioneer who suffered the misfortune of plunging a leg into the steaming mud while showing the area to a visiting newspaperman. The rising steam and hissing vents give evidence of the thermal tumult that is close to the surface here.*

CINDER CONE rises symmetrically, 700 feet above the surrounding countryside. A true volcano (it erupted in 1851), it was formed of lava so charged with gases that it was thrown out with explosive violence. When it reached the air, the lava cooled and dropped in an even fall of cinders.

THE STEAMING WATER of Boiling Springs Lake is so transparent that the varicolored bottom is clearly visible. The water boils and bubbles (125°), and the land around it roars and hisses with jets of escaping steam. Near Drakesbad.

Snowplant   *Penstemon*   *Indian paintbrush*   *Leopard lily*   *Lupine*

THE MOONSCAPE TERRAIN *of Chaos Jumbles was created about 300 years
ago by steam explosions along base of the crags that caused great rockslides
of pink lava chunks to roll down the mountainside and cover 2 square miles.*

FALL COMES EARLY *to Lake Manzanita and touches the alders and cottonwoods
with orange and gold after the first snows fall. Thus ends a short
but luxuriant display of wildflowers that thrive in the park. Spring reveals
Indian paintbrush, bleeding heart, monkey flowers, tiger lilies,
and a host of other blooms, many of which persist throughout summer. The
showy red snowplant is abundant, and in the higher mountain meadows,
mountainheath, lupine, and penstemon put on their finest display in
mid-August. Orange wallflower, bog Kalmis, senecio, balsam root,
marsh marigold, monkshood, shooting stars, the dainty white rein orchid, and
blue, false forget-me-not carpet the meadows or brighten
the forest trails from early June to late September.*

YOSEMITE

ICE, THE GREAT SCULPTOR

PARK FACTS: *Discovered:* 1849. *Established:* State park, 1864; national park, 1890. *Size:* Approx. 1,200 sq. mi. *Altitude:* 2,000 to 13,114 feet. *Climate:* Dry, mild summers; relatively warm winters with heavy snow pack. *Season:* Valley, all year; high country summer only. *Visitors, 1964:* 1,547,000.

"AS I LOOKED AT THE GRANDEUR OF THE SCENE a peculiar exalted sensation seemed to fill my whole being, and I found my eyes in tears with emotion." So wrote one of the discoverers of Yosemite Valley in 1851, recording an experience that has moved thousands of visitors who have since followed the trail into the Incomparable Valley.

Although it represents less than one-half of one percent of the total area of the park, the Valley contains more than its share of scenic beauty, and, historically, it accounts for the very existence of Yosemite as a national park.

The valley was known to the Indians for centuries, but because of its remoteness and inaccessibility it was not discovered by white men until the 1850's, when the Gold Rush attracted thousands of inquisitive miners to the nearby foothills and made its disclosure inevitable. It was a pair of miners, tracking a wounded bear in 1849, who were the first Americans to see the Valley. They were followed two years later by a punitive expedition, known as the Mariposa Battalion, that entered the Valley in pursuit of marauding Indians. Convinced that they had made an important discovery, they named the Valley, calling it "Yosemite" for the Indians they had driven out. The name was from an Indian word "Uzumati," meaning grizzly bear.

Word of the discovery was slow in spreading, but by 1855 the first tourist parties had followed Indian trails into the Valley to look at the reported wonders. One enterprising young miner by the name of James Hutchings was so impressed by what he saw that he launched into the business of attracting and serving tourists. He started a journal, *Hutchings California Illustrated* that featured Yosemite, published a series of guidebooks to the area, and built a hotel in the

A THREE-QUARTER MOON *rises over the shoulder of snow-dusted Half Dome, evoking the magic that enchants the visitor to Yosemite. First white man to see the great monolith named it "Rock of Ages," but the name did not stick. The rock rises 4,800 feet above the Valley floor.*

ANSEL ADAMS

Valley. Soon afterward, other hotels were opened, toll routes built, and the Valley began to welcome tourists of a sufficiently durable cast to survive the long and arduous trip by stage and saddle horse.

While commercial development was in progress, agitation for protection of the natural beauty of the park was also under way. John Muir and others published articles extolling the glories of the Valley, congressional interest in the area was aroused, and in 1864 President Lincoln issued the historic proclamation that ceded the Valley and the Mariposa Grove of Big Trees to California, "to be held for public use, resort, and recreation, unalienable for all time."

The Valley and the Mariposa Grove, 35 miles apart, were administered as a state park for 42 years before being returned to the federal government in 1906. In the meantime, a national park was established in 1890 that surrounded the original grant, and Yosemite was thus administered as two separate parks for 16 years. Administration of the national park was largely entrusted to units of the United States Cavalry until 1916.

Within the 1,200 square miles of the park today, there is of course a great deal more to see than the wonders compressed within the Valley. Glaciers, giant sequoias, alpine meadows, 13,000-foot Sierra peaks, emerald lakes, and sparkling streams are scattered in profusion throughout the vast domain. Those who know the park well know it as a rich and varied playground that is capable of sustaining years of rewarding exploration.

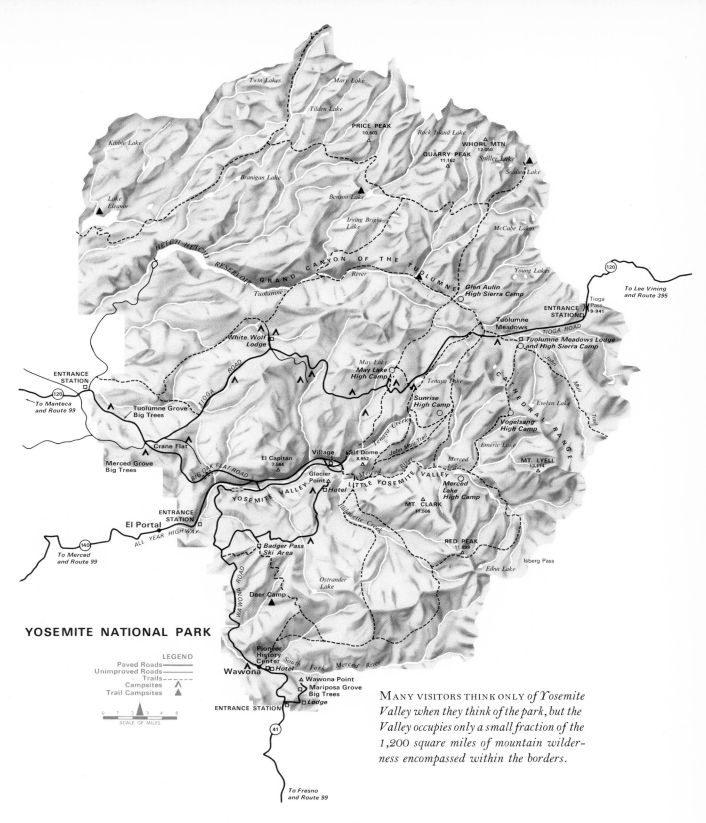

YOSEMITE NATIONAL PARK

Twin Lakes
Mary Lake
Tilden Lake

PRICE PEAK
10.603

Rock Island Lake
WHORL MTN.
12.050

Kibbie Lake

QUARRY PEAK
11.162
Spiller Lake
Saddie Lake

Branigan Lake

Benson Lake

Lake
Eleanor

Irving Bright
Lake

McCabe Lakes

HETCH HETCHY RESERVOIR
GRAND CANYON OF THE TUOLUMNE
River
Tuolumne
Young Lakes

Glen Aulin
High Sierra Camp

To Lee Vining
and Route 395

ENTRANCE
STATION
Tioga
Pass
9.941

TIOGA ROAD
Tuolumne
Meadows

Tuolumne Meadows Lodge
and High Sierra Camp

White Wolf
Lodge

May Lake
May Lake
High Camp

Tenaya Lake

CATHEDRAL RANGE

Evelyn Lake

John

Muir

Trail

ENTRANCE
STATION

120

To Manteca
and Route 99

Tuolumne Grove
Big Trees

TIOGA ROAD

Sunrise
High Camp

Tenaya Creek

Vogelsang
High Camp

Crane Flat

BIG OAK FLAT ROAD

El Capitan
7.564

Village

Half Dome
8.852

John Muir Trail

Emeric Lake

MT. LYELL
13.114

Merced Grove
Big Trees

Glacier
Point

Hotel

YOSEMITE VALLEY

Merced

LITTLE YOSEMITE VALLEY

River

Merced
Lake

Merced
Lake
High Camp

ENTRANCE
STATION

El Portal

ALL YEAR HIGHWAY

Illilouette Creek

MT. CLARK
11.506

140

To Merced
and Route 99

Badger Pass
Ski Area

RED PEAK
11.699

Isberg Pass

WAWONA ROAD

Ostrander
Lake

Edna Lake

Deer Camp

Pioneer
History
Center

Hotel

South Fork Merced River

Wawona

Wawona Point
Mariposa Grove
Big Trees

Lodge

ENTRANCE STATION

41

To Fresno
and Route 99

LEGEND

Paved Roads————
Unimproved Roads————
Trails------
Campsites ⋀
Trail Campsites ▲

0 1 2 3 4 5
SCALE OF MILES

MANY VISITORS THINK ONLY of Yosemite
Valley when they think of the park, but the
Valley occupies only a small fraction of the
1,200 square miles of mountain wilderness encompassed within the borders.

PRESIDENT THEODORE ROOSEVELT and a distinguished party guided by John
Muir pause before passing through the Wawona Tree in the Mariposa Grove.
Roosevelt's 1903 visit to the park encouraged him to press for protective
legislation to save more Big Trees and other valuable natural wonders.

YOSEMITE 93

THE VALLEY

FOR WELL OVER A CENTURY, the fabled grandeur of Yosemite Valley has drawn enchanted travelers to the park. The majesty of the granite cliffs rising above the forested floor, the beauty of the tumbling waterfalls, and the tranquility of the Merced River have combined to mesmerize generations of Americans.

The Valley is a profound gorge, cut by a river and gouged by glaciers, that is 7 miles long, a mile wide, and 3,000 feet deep. Its walls are actually mountain-sized rocks, separated from each other by side canyons. So deep did the glaciers and the river cut into the granite, that they left behind the tributary streams, which cascade from hanging valleys around the rim of the canyon in waterfalls of extraordinary height.

As the central tourist attraction of the park, it is here that most of the recreational opportunities and accommodations are found. All roads into the park end at Yosemite Village. Despite the efforts of the Park Service to shunt visitors to other sections of the park, hordes of tourists pour into the compact canyon on long summer weekends. The congestion partly cancels the value of coming to the park—but it is understandable. Once seen and felt, the Valley becomes a part of the beholder, and it is with reluctance that he settles for anything less.

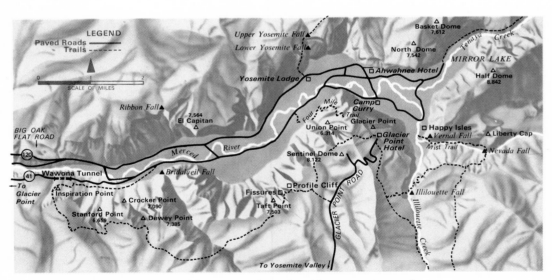

WITHIN A GLACIAL VALLEY *7 miles long and 1 mile wide are concentrated most of the spectacular domes, cliffs, and waterfalls in the park. Here, too, are the major resorts and campgrounds, located along the Merced River.*

LARGER THAN THE ROCK OF GIBRALTAR, *El Capitan stands sentinel at the lower end of the valley. Said to be the largest single block of granite in the world, its sheer cliff attracts rock climbers—to the discomfort of park authorities, who disapprove of the paralysis that this feat creates in Valley traffic when visitors gather to watch.*

NATIONAL PARK SERVICE

THE FALLS OF YOSEMITE *are world-renowned for their height and beauty. Bridalveil Fall* (ABOVE) *runs a solid torrent in spring, exploding in clouds of mist where it strikes the rocks at its base, 620 feet below; in low-water months it turns into a thin, gossamer veil—whence its name. Yosemite Falls* (RIGHT), *one of the highest in the world (2,425 ft.), tumbles over the north wall in spring with a vigor that shakes the ground, then wanes to a trickle by September.*

THE FULL FORCE OF THE MERCED RIVER *pours over Vernal Fall (317 ft.) and races down the canyon in foaming violence. The head of the fall, a popular hike, is reached by the Mist Trail, a slippery, spray-drenched climb. When the sunlight is right, a rainbow forms in the mist.*

LOOKING LIKE AN ANCIENT GLACIER, *a blanket of clouds fills the Valley from wall to wall on a wintry day.*

HOW YOSEMITE VALLEY WAS FORMED

 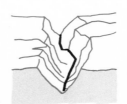  

1. BROAD VALLEY STAGE   2. V-SHAPED CANYON STAGE   3. GLACIAL STAGE   4. POST-GLACIAL STAGE

GLACIERS FORMED YOSEMITE VALLEY *during the Ice Age. 1. First, the land now occupied by the Sierra was covered with low ridges, rolling hills, and broad valleys. The ancestral Merced River flowed gently. 2. A gradual upheaval tilted the Sierra block, causing the sluggish Merced to rush seaward, carving a 2,000-foot, V-shaped canyon. 3. A change in climate caused ice to accumulate in the high country. In time, glaciers gouged the valley to U-shape and rounded the peaks to domes. 4. The glaciers advanced and receded three times, then melted and left a lake dammed behind the terminal moraine. Eventually, the lake dried up, leaving the level floor of today's meadows.*

LAST WISPS OF A NOVEMBER STORM *drift away to the northeast after having dumped a heavy quilt of snow on the Valley area. Winter holds a mild grip on the Valley, for at 4,000 feet it receives only a few feet of snow, which melts quickly. But the surrounding mountains receive and retain a heavier fall that seals the passes until spring. The snowpack in the high country draws the winter sportsman and in spring creates the burgeoning flow of water over the Valley's dozen waterfalls.*

AUTUMN FLASHES BRIGHTLY *in Yosemite Valley, helping to relieve the somber cast of the conifer forest. Within the Valley is a concentration of broadleafed trees that brings forth a more varied display of fall color than in the Yosemite forest in general. At higher altitudes, off the Tioga Road and the highway to Glacier Point, are groves of aspen that turn to shimmering gold in autumn. The glowing colors are caused by pigments left behind in the skeletonized leaves after the tree has transferred all nutritive elements from them to other parts where they can be drawn upon through the winter.*

RIPPLELESS MIRROR LAKE *reflects without flaw the rugged profile of Mount Watkins, named for a pioneer photographer whose stereoscopic views of Yosemite (1861) helped to introduce its grandeurs to the nation. A changeable lake, it freezes in winter and dries up in late summer after the end of the run-off. Easter sunrise services are held in this serene setting, sometimes with late snow on the ground, when both congregation and participants sit bundled, scarfed, and mittened against the cold.*

"LET THE FIRE FALL!" *bellows a stentorian voice at Camp Curry in the Valley, and in a moment the faint response drifts down from the summit 3,200 feet overhead: "The fire falls!" Then down into the night cascades a shower of embers, falling halfway down the cliff. This famous spectacle has been enthralling visitors since 1872 and has been a favorite subject for generations of postcard writers, as evidenced in the 1920 sample on the left. (For a look at the other end of this performance, see page 108.)*

CAMP CURRY'S FIRE FALL.

CLYDE CHILDRESS

"DEER AND BEAR ARE WILD AND DANGEROUS *animals!" warns the park brochure and every bulletin board within the boundaries. Yet some tourists find them fascinating and get as close to them as they dare—sometimes to the animal's annoyance, as when photographers surround a puzzled deer; and sometimes to the animal's delight, as when a bear discovers camper's food cached in an open car.*

GLENN C. CHRISTIANSEN

CAMPING DELUXE IN CONCRETE-SLAB TENT-HOUSES *along the Merced River is one of the several ways that the traveler finds shelter within the park, where accommodations range from luxury hotel to open campgrounds redolent with cedar smoke from the punky campfires. Though crowded during the summer, the camps and resorts offer an idyllic grace period just before and after the season, when the park is uncrowded and the visitor can enjoy the spectacular surroundings in relative peace and quiet.*

YOSEMITE 103

104   YOSEMITE

"THE GRAND WINTER STORMS," *wrote John Muir*, "*seldom set in before the end of November. The fertile clouds, descending, glide about and hover in brooding silence, as if thoughtfully examining the forests and streams with reference to the work before them; then small flakes or single crystals appear, glinting and swirling in zigzags and spirals; and soon the thronging feathery masses fill the sky and make darkness like night.*"

SOUTH OF THE VALLEY

IN THE RICHLY DIVERSIFIED AREA south of the Valley, most of the main attractions are located right on the highway.

Climbing out of the Valley, the road pauses at a turnout for a last sweeping view of the canyon, then winds upward through conifer forests. It passes Badger Pass, a crowded ski center in winter and a quiet wildflower park in summer, and ends at the tip of Glacier Point, a breathtaking overlook. Here, pressed against the guard rails, the traveler can look down 3,200 feet to the floor of the Valley or up the great gorges whence came the glaciers that carved it.

Continuing south, the highway passes through bucolic Wawona, one of the earliest settlements in the park and location of a hotel that has been serving the touring public since 1875. Nearby is the park's prime historical exhibit: a frontier village recreated from pioneer buildings gathered from all over the park. Finally, the road sidetracks to the cathedral-like groves of Big Trees, containing some of the finest and largest specimens in the state.

NEARLY BURIED UNDER A MAT OF SNOW, *Badger Pass Ski Hut is the center of a carefully planned ski area that accommodates up to 4,000 skiers on a weekend without detracting from the scenic values of the park.*

CROSS-COUNTRY SKIERS EXPLORE *the crystalline purity of snow-covered Glacier Point with its sweeping vistas mantled in white. The skiers follow orange trail stakes from Badger Pass.*

FRESH, UNSCORED SNOW *records the exuberance of a party of skiers on their way to the point.*

FRANCES COLEBERD

FORREST JACKSON

"One of the most photographed trees in the world," is the tenacious Jeffrey pine on the top of Sentinel Dome, a mile from Glacier Point. The lightning-scarred and stunted tree draws its sustenance from cracks in the granite. In a forest, the Jeffrey is often mistaken for yellow pine and normally grows straight and tall, ranging from 60 to 170 feet in height.

No place for the giddy, the tip of Glacier Point is an exhilarating stop for tourists. It is here that a half-cord of fir bark is lit in the late afternoon and pushed off the cliff a few hours later to produce the firefall. Here, too, the traveler clings to the reassuring rail while he looks down at the Valley, 3,250 very vertical feet below.

YOSEMITE CREEK DROPS *down
from a hanging valley to join
the Merced River, which in
geologic ages past once ran on
the same level. Best view of the
full sweep of Yosemite Falls is
from Sentinel Dome or Glacier
Point. The Upper Fall drops
1,430 feet, probably the longest
fall of its kind in the world.*

110   YOSEMITE

FROM GLACIER POINT, *a breathtaking sweep of Yosemite high country, diffused with what John Muir called "good-night alpenglow," spreads to the horizon under a mountain sunset. Two great glacial canyons sweep around Half Dome and enter the Valley: to the left, Tenaya Canyon; to the right, the Little Yosemite, through which the Merced River flows, down Nevada and Vernal falls.*

STOPPING PLACE FOR PRESIDENTS *and a favorite of vacationing families since the 1880's, peaceful Wawona in the south end of the park exudes an old-fashioned tranquility. Though fully modernized, the gingerbread buildings look the same today as they did when this photograph was taken in the 1930's or when they were built (left to right, 1889 and 1917).*

A FIELDSTONE JAIL, LOG CABINS, *and early clapboard buildings from all over the park were carefully taken apart, transported, and reassembled at the Pioneer History Center at Wawona. Nearby stands the only covered bridge in a national park. It served the park's first highway from 1857 to 1931.*

112   YOSEMITE

A THOUSAND YEARS OLDER THAN CHRISTIANITY, *these giant trees humble the viewer with their enormous size, venerable age, and stately proportions. Protection of the Mariposa Grove from the saw and the axe had much to do with the creation of Yosemite as a park in 1864.*

YOSEMITE 113

NORTH COUNTRY

NORTH OF YOSEMITE VALLEY, a 700-square-mile province of forest, rivers, and mountains spreads to the boundaries of the park. This is a land of solitude, of fresh and unspoiled country, inviting and accessible alike to hiker, camper, and motorist. Traversed by a single east-west highway, which crosses the highest pass (9,941 ft.) of any road in the state, the area is spotted with campgrounds and laced with trails that radiate from beautiful Tuolumne Meadows.

It was from the north that the first tourist routes penetrated to the Valley after it became known to the public in the 1850's. The first travelers entered the Valley on horseback, spending 12 saddle-sore hours on the rough trail. For 22 years the only access was by foot or on a horse, then toll wagon roads were opened in 1874 and 1883. Most notorious of these was the famous Tioga Road, a hair-raising mining road that was not completely modernized for 78 years. The old roads form the basis of the present intensively-used highways.

STAGE PASSENGERS RODE ENVELOPED *in a cloud of dust on the Big Oak Flat Road, one of two toll roads that entered the Valley from the northwest in 1874. The narrow road zigzagged down the north wall of the canyon by a series of switchbacks. Passengers endured 20 hours of jouncing in the ride from the railhead. The toll road operated for 35 years and was put out of business when a railroad reached El Portal near the park's west boundary.*

THE LAKE BACKED UP BEHIND HETCH HETCHY DAM *fills a beautiful glacial canyon similar to Yosemite Valley. It was created after a bitter 10-year battle between conservationists and the city of San Francisco. Wrote John Muir, "Dam Hetch Hetchy! As well dam for water-tanks the people's cathedrals and churches, for no holier temple has been consecrated by the heart of man." The contest begun in 1903 was ended by congressional approval of the dam in 1913 and its construction in 1923. It is accessible by automobile from the Big Oak Flat Road.*

SKIMMING ALONG THE EDGE *of the north rim of Yosemite Valley, the Tioga Road reveals to the motorist the shining land of the High Sierra that once belonged only to the hiker and backpacker. Great vistas sweep into view at frequent intervals. Here is a look down Tenaya Canyon, with the familiar cap of Half Dome at the right, Cloud's Rest at the left.*

ORIGINALLY BUILT IN 1883 *as a wagon road to service a mine, the Tioga Road was not completely modernized for 78 years, and driving it was until recently a nerve-racking adventure. For 60 twisting miles, it snaked between trees and boulders, roller-coasted up and down hills, and skirted precipices. Until its realignment in 1961, many miles were still in the same condition as the vintage scene at the left.*

STRANDED BOULDERS AND GLACIAL POLISH *near the highway are close-at-hand evidence of the power of the ice sheet that carved the canyons out of solid granite and rounded the peaks to domes. The boulders were left behind by the melting glaciers.*

DAVID MUENCH

YOSEMITE 117

MODESTO BEE, FORREST JACKSON

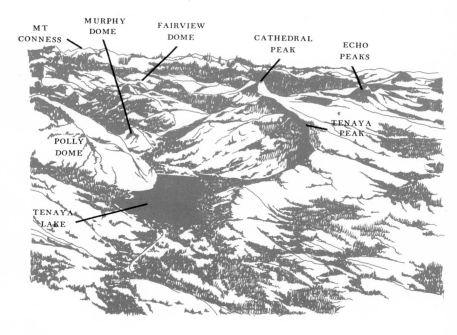

MT
CONNESS MURPHY
DOME FAIRVIEW
DOME CATHEDRAL
PEAK ECHO
PEAKS

POLLY
DOME TENAYA
PEAK

TENAYA
LAKE

THE NORTH COUNTRY SEEN FROM THE AIR *takes on dramatic qualities when coated with early snow. In November, when this photograph was taken, the first storms are often relatively light. The highway is covered and Tenaya Lake gleams like a bright emerald set in the cottony landscape. Within a few weeks, the snow will pile deeper, the lake will freeze to a sheet of paraffin, and the road will be lost to sight until the end of May.*

PHILIP HYDE   GATEWAY TO THE NORTH COUNTRY, *Tuolumne Meadows (8,700 ft.) is regarded as one of the most beautiful subalpine meadows in the Sierra. Sparkling air, a feeling of spaciousness, and the quiet absence of crowds endears the area to its devotees. Trails to High Sierra destinations fan out from the meadow, which is itself one stop in a loop of five High Camps, one of the most popular week-long hikes in the park.*

THE HAUNTING SONG OF MULE BELLS
*sounds clearly in the still mountain
air as a pack train leaves for a
fishing rendezvous in the high country.*

WATCHDOGS OF THE HIGH TRAILS,
*marmots are often seen above timberline.
Their shrill whistles inform their relatives
up the trail that nonmarmots are
approaching. These self-important little
animals are cousins of the prairie dog,
but found only at higher elevations.*

SEQUOIA and KINGS CANYON

BIGGEST TREES, DEEPEST CANYONS

PARK FACTS: *Discovered:* Sequoia, 1890. *Established:* Sequoia, Sept. 25, 1890; Kings, March 4, 1940. *Size:* Sequoia, 604 sq. mi.; Kings, 710 sq. mi. *Altitude:* Sequoia, 1,700-14,495 ft.; Kings, 4,600-14,242 ft. *Climate:* Summers hot; winters snowy. *Visitors, 1964:* Sequoia: 654,140; Kings, 831,623.

THE TWIN PARKS, SEQUOIA AND KINGS CANYON, located next to each other on the ridgepole of California, are administered as one and share many features in common.

Within the boundaries of each are several thousand acres of sequoias, the largest trees on earth. Each park encompasses a hikers' domain of spectacular peaks and canyons, threaded with an intricate trail system. The two parks are accessible to the same highway on the west, and they share the opposite ends of one of the most spectacular roads in the park system, the Generals Highway, that runs along the shoulder of a mountain ridge and reveals sweeping views of high mountains and deep valleys.

SEQUOIA, THE SECOND OLDEST NATIONAL PARK, was established in 1890 as a sanctuary of 252 square miles to protect the largest remaining sequoia groves from the logging destruction that had befallen their larger and more accessible neighbors.

The trees were considered a species of the genus (also containing *Sequoia sempervirens*, the coast redwood) which had been named for Sequoyah, inventor of the Cherokee alphabet. The giant sequoia (common name), Big Tree (poetic and unmistakable), Wellingtonia (British), Sierra redwood (Forest Service) are one and the same: *Sequoia gigantea*, which some authorities are now giving a new, unmusical name, *Sequoiadendron giganteum*.

The largest tree (by volume) in the world, the sequoia is a relic of a pre-glacial genus that was once distributed over much of the world. During the Ice Age, glaciers swept away all but the few stands in the Sierra that had been

"SEE ONE BIG TREE *and you want to see another and then another," so say the visitors to the Big Tree groves. To many, it is not the size or the age of the sequoias that is the most appealing, but their mystic beauty. Few other trees possess such powers of enchantment.*

DAVID MUENCH

123

SEQUOIA NATIONAL PARK *is named for the great redwood trees which in turn were named for a Cherokee Indian, Sequoyah (ca. 1760-1843), who invented an alphabet of 86 characters for his tribe and taught his fellows to read and write. His deeds so impressed the Austrian botanist who named the redwoods that he registered the trees under the name* sequoia. *In Cherokee language, the name had an odd meaning: as nearly as it can be translated it meant "neither this nor that" and it was appropriately applied to the oppossum.*

growing on land higher than the obliterating ice. These residues of a once-encompassing forest now constitute the groves that are mostly within the protection of the two national parks and adjoining national forests.

Extensive as the present-day groves appear to be, nothing that can be seen today begins to match the vast sequoia forest that was still intact just a century ago. Between 1862 and 1900, logging operations wiped out the finest forest in the world, containing at least two trees—and possibly four or more—that must have been bigger than the world's largest tree, the General Sherman in Sequoia's Giant Grove. Ironically, two of these giants were not cut for their wood, but simply so that sections of their trunks could be exhibited at two world's fairs.

At an early date, public-spirited citizens and conservationists became alarmed by the rapidity with which lumbering activities were destroying the Big Trees. One of the last straws was the building of a sawmill about 9 miles from the Giant Forest, as part of an ill-fated co-operative colony. Determined action resulted in creation of the national park that placed the trees under permanent protection. President Harrison signed the bill creating Sequoia National Park on September 25, 1890. Established at 252 square miles, the park was enlarged 36 years later to its present 604.

For 22 years after the park was established, it was administered by the Army. Congress did not appropriate sufficient funds to support a resident administration, and the development of facilities and trails was entrusted to cavalry units that served in the park during the summer months. The troops withdrew each fall and left the area open for 9 months of poaching, trespassing, and illegal grazing. In time, adequate sums were appropriated, and the park administration was taken over by civilian administrators in 1914. Under the direction of a sequence of able and dedicated superintendents and enlightened concessioners, the park has been developed with integrity and naturalness.

THE DISTINCTION OF BEING BOTH one of the oldest and one of the newest national parks belongs to Kings Canyon. When the park was established in 1940, it absorbed tiny General Grant National Park, the 50-year-old sanctuary that had been established almost as an afterthought 3 weeks after Sequoia was created in 1890, and had been administered by Sequoia ever since. It is now known as the General Grant Grove.

The Kings Canyon area had been proposed for park status long before the move was approved by Congress. John Muir campaigned for it in 1891 and the idea was reopened in 1926 at the time Sequoia was more than doubled in size.

The park bears the name of the river, named by a Spanish explorer in 1805 for the Three Wise Men—*El Rio de los Santos Reyes*, The River of the Holy Kings.

AN ENTERPRISING FORM OF THE VANDALISM *that ravaged the sequoia groves in the late 1800's was this project that involved stripping bark from a tree and reassembling it at the Chicago Worlds Fair in 1893, where many fairgoers thought it a fake. Its stump is now known as the Chicago Stump.*

SEQUOIA and KINGS CANYON   125

THE BIG TREES

WITHIN THE REDWOOD GROVES of Sequoia and Kings Canyon National Parks stand several thousand giant sequoias, the largest trees in the world.

Hundreds of these giants far outstrip the largest specimens of any other species. Many sequoia stumps show more than 3,000 annual growth rings, and it is a safe guess that some of the trees now standing were alive in the Bronze Age, 3,500 to 4,000 years ago. Largest of them all is Sequoia's General Sherman, conceded to be the biggest of the world's measured trees. Second place is usually assigned to the General Grant Tree in Kings Canyon, although one set of computations places the Lincoln and President trees in second and third place ahead of General Grant.

The great trees owe their long lifespan partly to a natural vigor that makes them outgrow all other species in a forest complex and partly to their thick, disease and fire-resistant bark that permits them to survive forest fires and the ravages of insect blight. Although the sequoias in the parks are among the last of their species, they are reproducing themselves adequately to continue in existence until the next Ice Age—providing Man leaves them in peace.

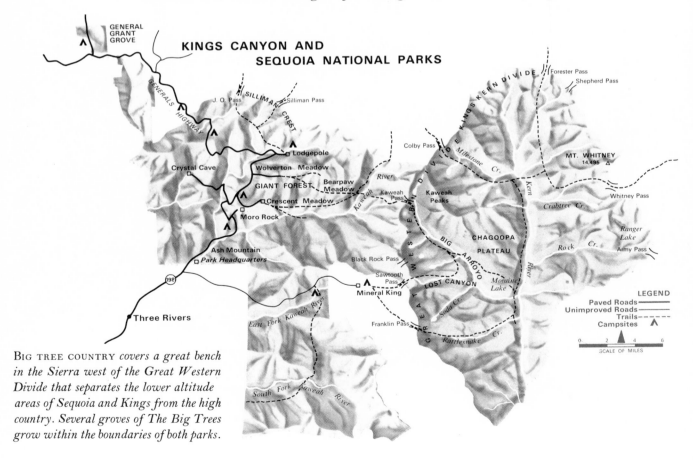

BIG TREE COUNTRY *covers a great bench in the Sierra west of the Great Western Divide that separates the lower altitude areas of Sequoia and Kings from the high country. Several groves of The Big Trees grow within the boundaries of both parks.*

126   SEQUOIA and KINGS CANYON

MORO ROCK LOOMS ABOVE *the trees near Giant Forest Village, can be seen*
for miles from the grade leading up from Ash Mountain. A giddy foot path,
safeguarded with handrails and rest stops, leads up the bare spine of the
rock to its summit 300 feet above the parking area. From the crest (6,719 ft.),
a 360-degree panorama takes in the Central Valley 6,000 feet below
to the west and the Great Western Divide 7,000 feet above to the east.

SEQUOIA and KINGS CANYON   127

Two small boys peering *out of the shell of a burned-out Big Tree are dwarfed by the massive proportions of the hulk. Where the trees are massed in a grove, they seem in scale and proportion, and their enormous size is hard to grasp. But a downed or burned-out giant conveys the great size with more immediacy. A walk down the length of a fallen trunk, a clamber through a tangle of upturned roots, or a saunter through a hollow trunk—such experiences bring home the pygmy size of man relative to these giants.*

A snug and comfortable home *fashioned out of a fallen tree by the first white settler in the park, Hale Tharp, is preserved as an historical exhibit. Tharp was led to the area by friendly Indians in 1858. He carved his name and the date of the visit on the tree—the inscription was still visible under a protective glass plate at the time this photograph was taken several years ago. Tharp returned to the area a few years later and made the tree his permanent summer home. He grazed cattle in the park for several years.*

COAST   SIERRA

THE TWO REDWOODS

Two kinds of redwoods *grow in California, one along the coast, the other in the Sierra. Though not of the same genus, the two are often compared. The Big Tree is not so tall as the Coast redwood, but is more massive, has thicker bark and heavier, more angular limbs; its cones are larger, needles scalier.* RIGHT: *General Grant Tree, second-largest in world and the "Nation's Christmas Tree."*

(For comparative dimensions, see page 306.)

SNOW-STARVED CALIFORNIANS *ascend to Wolverton and Lodgepole to ski, toboggan, or try their blades on the ice rink. The main road is kept open all winter, passes through cathedral aisles of white-robed trees, in a world of flawless white where no sound is heard but the crunching of spotless snow under the tires.*

THE THRILL OF HER FIRST SLED *ride lights the face of the little girl, defying gravity on a slick slope. For many children raised in temperate California, the pre-bunny slopes at Sequoia offer the first exciting experience with snow.*

FROM THE SUMMIT OF MORO ROCK *a grand winter's scene spreads into view. Snow covers the Great Western Divide to the east, sealing off the barricade to the High Sierra until spring. Framing the view, the pendulous branches of a sugar pine seem to offer benediction. These magnificent trees, with their 18-inch cones, are striking individuals in forests in the 4,500-9,000 foot range. Fire or axe wounds in the wood of a living tree cause it to exude a white, sweet, chewable but cathartic gum that was used by Indians and early settlers.*

SEQUOIA and KINGS CANYON **131**

HIGH COUNTRY

FOR NINE MONTHS OF THE YEAR, the high country in Sequoia and Kings Canyon National Parks belongs to the native wildlife; during the other three, this roadless domain is a playground for a varied lot of devotees, some hiking alone, some in small groups, and some in organized parties as large as small armies.

The main traffic arterial is the John Muir Trail, which begins in Yosemite Valley and runs south for 225 high-elevation miles to Whitney Portal, about half of its route lying within the boundaries of Kings Canyon and Sequoia parks. This remarkable pathway, which took 40-odd years to complete, was first conceived by the Sierra Club in 1892. Its route was surveyed over several years, construction was begun in 1915, and it was finally finished in 1938. The trail was named in honor of John Muir, who died just before construction was started.

A network of supplementary trails within the two parks gives access to the full variety of High Sierra terrain: cool, silent forests of fir and pine; knife-edged passes; snowbanks; hundreds of lakes; marshy alpine meadows sprinkled with wildflowers; and talus slopes where marmots sun themselves.

MARTIN LITTON

EARLY MORNING RISERS *stuff their backpacks with lunches and fishing gear at Bearpaw Meadow camp, located on a breathtaking perch on the shoulder of a deep canyon.*

Most of the true High Sierra *lies within Kings Canyon and Sequoia national parks. The eastern edge of this high domain runs along the spine of the Sierra block and drops down steeply to the Owens Valley outside the parks' boundary. Several major rivers rise within the drainage basins in the two parks. Main barricade to the west is the 12,000-foot Great Western Divide that isolates this roadless land. A net of trails provides access to almost every corner of the two parks. Main artery is the north-south John Muir Trail; next in importance, the High Sierra Trail from Giant Forest to Mount Whitney.*

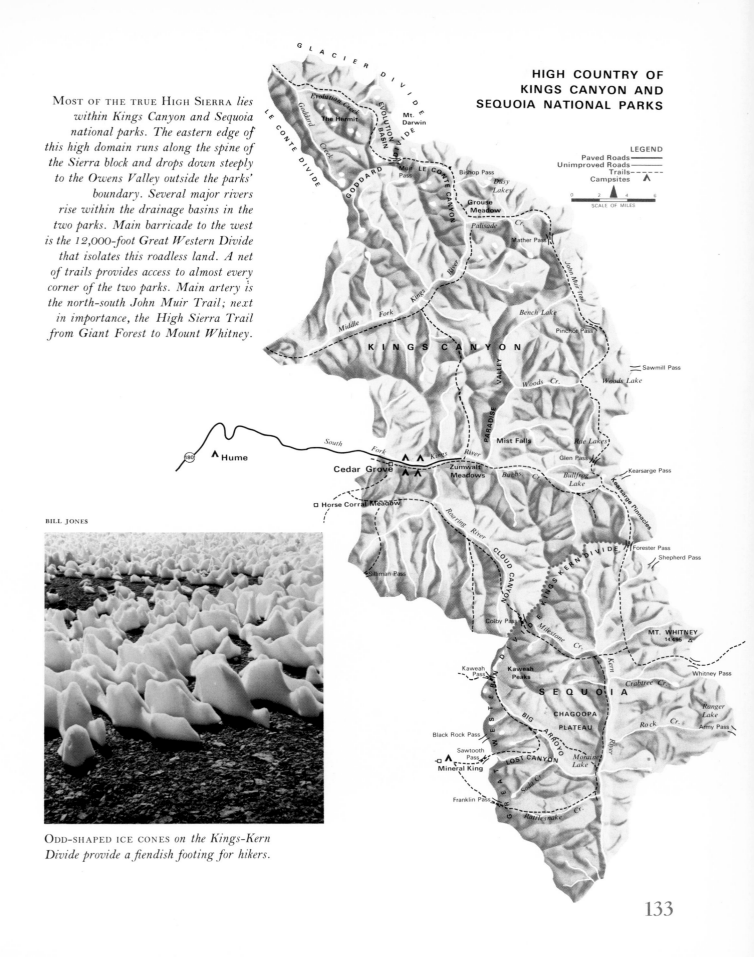

HIGH COUNTRY OF KINGS CANYON AND SEQUOIA NATIONAL PARKS

LEGEND
Paved Roads ———
Unimproved Roads ———
Trails - - - - -
Campsites ∧

0   2   4   6
SCALE OF MILES

GLACIER DIVIDE

Evolution Creek

The Hermit

Mt. Darwin

LE CONTE DIVIDE

Goddard Creek

EVOLUTION BASIN

EVOLUTION DIVIDE

Muir Pass

GODDARD DIVIDE

LE CONTE CANYON

Bishop Pass

Dusy Lakes

Grouse Meadow

Palisade Cr.

Mather Pass

Bench Lake

Pinchot Pass

John Muir Trail

Middle Fork Kings River

KINGS CANYON

PARADISE VALLEY

Sawmill Pass

Woods Cr.

Woods Lake

Mist Falls

Rae Lakes

Glen Pass

Kearsarge Pass

South Fork Kings River

∧ ∧

180 ∧ Hume

Cedar Grove ∧ ∧

Zumwalt Meadows

Bubbs Cr.

Bullfrog Lake

Kearsarge Pinnacles

□ Horse Corral Meadow

Roaring River

CLOUD CANYON

KINGS-KERN DIVIDE

Forester Pass

Shepherd Pass

Silliman Pass

Colby Pass

Milestone Cr.

MT. WHITNEY
14,495 △

Kaweah Pass

Kaweah Peaks

Kern River

Crabtree Cr.

Whitney Pass

Ranger Lake

Black Rock Pass

GREAT WESTERN DIVIDE

BIG ARROYO

CHAGOOPA PLATEAU

Rock Cr.

Army Pass

SEQUOIA

Sawtooth Pass

∧ □ Mineral King

LOST CANYON

Moraine Lake

Soda Cr.

Franklin Pass

Rattlesnake Cr.

BILL JONES

Odd-shaped ice cones *on the Kings-Kern Divide provide a fiendish footing for hikers.*

133

134   SEQUOIA and KINGS CANYON

IN A DEEP GROOVE *worn by the passage of thousands of hikers and pack animals over the years, the John Muir Trail swings across typical high country just below 12,000-foot Pinchot Pass.*

ON BIGHORN PLATEAU, *the gravelly rim of this tarn conceals the drop-off to Kern Canyon, but not the peaks of the Great Western Divide beyond it under the gathering clouds. Lakelets such as this dot the high country; some of them offer excellent trout fishing, but most are sterile and fishless because of the absence of minerals in the water needed to support algae and minute animals essential to the fish food-chain. Gravelled banks of high country tarns are formed by the frequent freezing and thawing of the water, which breaks up the rock around the edges and gradually converts it to pebbly beach.*

FROM THE TOP OF MOUNT WHITNEY, *highest point in the United States outside of Alaska, mountain peaks jut upward in all directions in this view to the northwest across the upper end of the vast Kern River basin. The peak was named in 1871 for J. D. Whitney, leader of the Geologic Survey party that first determined its exact height in 1864. For a brief time, the mountain carried the name Fisherman's Peak. First ascent: 1873.*

EAST-WEST SLICE THROUGH THE SIERRA

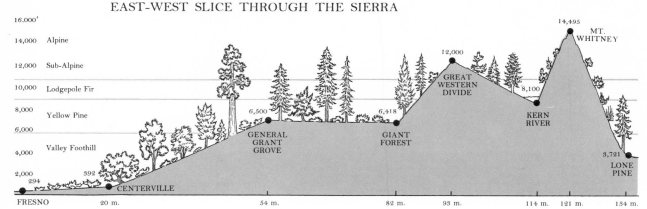

AN EAST-WEST SLICE THROUGH SEQUOIA *reveals the extreme range of altitude, terrain, and tree-cover encompassed within the park's boundaries. In a span of 67 miles the elevation ascends 8,000 feet to the top of Mount Whitney on the eastern border, then drops 11,000 feet in a brief 13 miles.*

LIKE BLEACHERS IN A GIGANTIC STADIUM, *sections of the western slopes of Mount Whitney ascend in a series of stair-like rock formations.*

SEQUOIA and KINGS CANYON 137

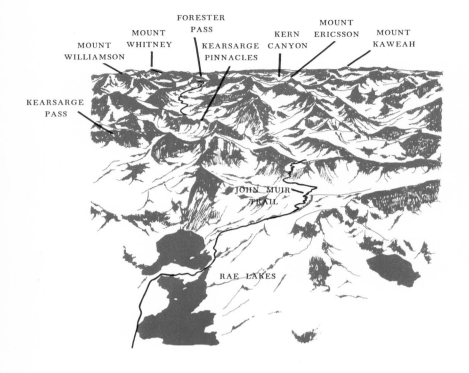

MOUNT
WILLIAMSON

MOUNT
WHITNEY

FORESTER
PASS

KEARSARGE
PINNACLES

KERN
CANYON

MOUNT
ERICSSON

MOUNT
KAWEAH

KEARSARGE
PASS

JOHN MUIR
TRAIL

RAE LAKES

SOUTHERN CLIMAX OF THE JOHN MUIR TRAIL *as viewed
from the air. The trail skirts Upper Rae Lake, disappears
over Glen Pass, climbs to Forester Pass and thence to
the top of Mount Whitney. This is true High Sierra, a
seemingly desolate and forbidding expanse of granite cliffs
and basins—oppressive to travellers who prefer
the friendlier forested mountains lower down—but when
viewed close-up, the high country becomes an inviting land of
small valleys, hidden forests and meadows, rushing streams
and imprisoned lakes, all seen in sharpened contrast to
the massive architecture of the great range that rises
on all sides.*

FAVORITE TRAIL COMPANION *of many hiking parties, the lowly burro adds a fascinating personality to any group. Yet, as one burro-wise hiker puts it "if the burro doesn't have a good time, you won't either." Their antenna-like ears swing in arcs to pick up unfamiliar sounds, listen to bird songs, or register disapproval of proceedings. Their melodious 5 A.M. reveille launches many a bleary-eyed hiking party on the trail.*

IN A SETTING OF RUGGED GRANDEUR *high above timberline, the John Muir Trail climbs out of treeless Evolution Basin and heads south along the 10,000-foot shoulders of the Sierra spine.*

MANY HIGH SIERRA RIVERS CASCADE *down deep, V-shaped gorges with few open valleys and scant elbow room for hikers. The Middle Fork of the Kings descends in a tumult of foaming cataracts.*

SEQUOIA and KINGS CANYON 141

GRAND CANYON

THE STORY OF THE EARTH ITSELF

PARK FACTS: *Discovered:* 1540. *Established:* February 26, 1919. *Size:* 1,100 sq. mi. *Altitude:* 2,000 to 9,000 feet. *Climate:* Progression of climate from that of Mexican desert at Canyon bottom to that of S. Canada at N. Rim. *Season:* S. Rim, all year; N. Rim, mid-May to late-Oct. *Visitors, 1964:* 1,575,737.

FROM EITHER NORTH OR SOUTH, you approach through rather flat, temperate country full of the familiar, friendly things of field and forest. The land is broken occasionally by picturesque minor gullies. Then, at the sudden edge of the Grand Canyon of the Colorado, you are confronted with one of the most sublime spectacles of this planet. Yet, standing on the brink for the first time, your impulse may be to turn away. It is not any fear of height, nor of the incredible wilderness gap in a land otherwise subdued by civilization. Rather it is disbelief, even saturation with the incredible size of it all.

A little knowledge of the canyon begets a craving for more. A great knowledge of it begets a greater craving for more. When you look into its depths you are looking back some twenty million centuries. Nowhere else can you do so. Nowhere else is geologic history, beginning with the oldest exposed rock on earth, so clear and orderly. When you look into the gorge you look over a bewildering array of plants and animals that in less awesome surroundings need this whole continent to find suitable homes. The sheer physical beauty of this place has defied the best descriptive efforts of men for 400 years. Photographs surpass words, but even they fall short.

Nobody has seen all of the Grand Canyon—and soon it may be too late to try. Human exploitation of the canyon has accelerated rapidly over the past century, and the builders of dams are eager to bend an already reduced Colorado River ever more to their purpose. If they succeed, the whole of the Lower Granite Gorge will be under reservoir water and mud.

"Ours has been the first, and will doubtless be the last, party of whites to visit this profitless locality," reported Lieutenant J. C. Ives, exploring the Grand

IT IS 3,000 FEET DOWN *from Toroweap Point to the roiling surface of the Colorado River. Visitors on the brink of this vertical wall look out over a spectacle so immense that no comparison will explain it. It has to be seen.*

PHILIP HYDE

143

Canyon region in 1857. Ives was no historian, and he was an even worse prophet. Thirteen men of Coronado's Spanish expeditions had entered the region in 1540, and the captain in command of the party had registered official dismay at the unbridgeable barrier posed by the chasm. Since Lieutenant Ives' cheerless pronouncement, the canyon has yielded profit in varying degrees to ranchers, miners, prospectors, horse thieves, hermits, and bootleggers, and has been visited by millions of parties of tourists.

In large measure, the Grand Canyon owes the beginnings of its fame as a natural wonder to the explorations of a one-armed major of artillery named John Wesley Powell. In 1869, the dauntless major set out with a small party in four boats to run the length of the Green River and the Colorado as far as the bottom of the Grand Canyon. It was a bucketing ride that cost the major two of his boats and collapsed the nerve of three men in the crew. But he prevailed. He proved the canyon explorable. The accounts of his adventure are still to be read today. River-runners, in fact, used his journals as a guide to their own journeys until the Glen Canyon Dam put an effective end to the Colorado's usefulness for this purpose.

The results of Powell's turbulent dash included widespread publication of accounts of the adventure. These led to greater awareness of the region, and this in turn led to much further exploration of a Southwest that was, before Powell, largely left blank by the mapmakers. Subsequent expeditions by Powell and others achieved two great results: Several branches of natural science found fertile new fields for study, and Powell's enhanced reputation won him the directorship of the fledgling Smithsonian Institution, which he put well on the way to its present eminent station.

This focus of attention also produced great optimism about the immediate tourist value of the Grand Canyon. Around 1880, an ex-miner named John Hance improved upon the Indian trails to some degree and upon the truth to an even greater extent to impress visitors. By the turn of the century there were hotels, tourist camps, orchards, and gardens at various levels all the way down to the river, and several aerial tramways across it. The Santa Fe Railroad built a spur line from Williams to the South Rim in 1901 and the famous El Tovar Hotel 3 years later, but for most operators the optimism proved short lived. The resorts failed, one by one; cable cars rusted in their moorings; the neglected trails disappeared (John Hance's name survives only on a few minor landmarks). For many years, only the Santa Fe and its subsidiary, Fred Harvey, were able to make a go of the tourist business, and the canyon was left mostly to the Indians whose ancestral homes are along its rims, or, in the case of the Havasupai, at the bottom of the great gorge. In time, substantial interests invested in tourism, and the park has for years served as a great magnet for thousands of tourists from all over the world. As early as 1915, 106,000 made their difficult way to the park; today 150 times as many crowd into the park in a year.

Efforts to preserve the canyon as a national park were begun soon after the establishment of Yellowstone but required 30 years of campaigning to take effect.

"WE ARE SWEPT BROADSIDE DOWN, *and are prevented, by the rebounding waters, from striking against the wall . . . We toss about . . . in these billows, and are carried past the danger." Powell wrote in 1869 of such scrapes again and again, and one was captured by his artist, R. A. Muilerse.*

On Jacob's Ladder, *a turn-of-the-century party of riders descends toward the river on mule and horseback. The trail is no longer used, and neither are horses, but woman's courage hasn't flagged at all. See page 163.*

WESTERN WAYS

ALTHOUGH HANDICAPPED BY THE LOSS OF AN ARM *in the Civil War, ex-artillery major John Wesley Powell daringly led an expedition down the unexplored Colorado River in 4 boats in 1869. Photographed 22 years later, he still looked hale and hearty, ready for further exploits.*

GRAND CANYON 145

FOR CENTURIES BEFORE WHITE MEN CAME *to the Grand Canyon, Indians lived in its depths and on its rim. One tribe, the Havasupai, still carries on the traditions of its ancestors relatively undisturbed by the rush of modern life. They live deep in the canyon on a small oasis where they raise grain, fruit, and vegetables as they have done since the 12th century. The 200 members of the nation support themselves with their produce and tend to the needs of the occasional vacationers who take the steep trail down to the reservation.*

The first protagonist, Senator Benjamin Harrison of Indiana, introduced a bill in the upper house in 1882 to make the area a national park. It failed. It was not until 1893 that Harrison, as President of the United States, was able to establish the Grand Canyon Forest Preserve, which could be and was exploited by mining and lumber interests. President Theodore Roosevelt took up the cause after his visit in 1903. He established Grand Canyon National Monument in 1908. An act of Congress, signed on February 26, 1919, established Grand Canyon National Park.

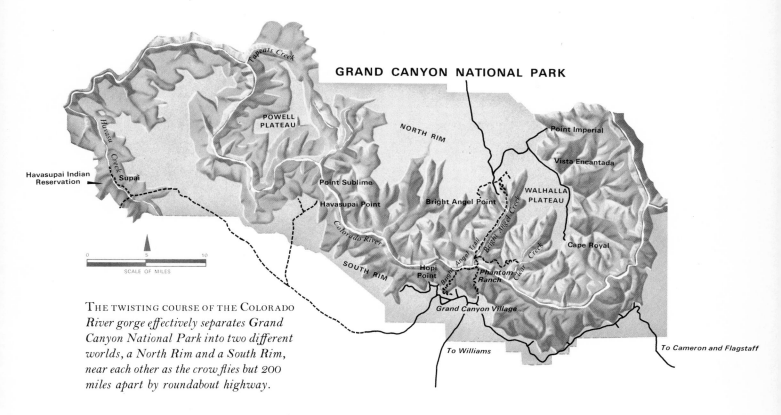

GRAND CANYON NATIONAL PARK

POWELL PLATEAU

NORTH RIM

Point Imperial

Vista Encantada

WALHALLA PLATEAU

Point Sublime

Bright Angel Point

Havasupai Point

Cape Royal

Havasupai Indian Reservation

Supai

Havasu Creek

Tapeats Creek

Colorado River

Bright Angel Trail

Bright Angel Creek

Clear Creek

SOUTH RIM

Hopi Point

Phantom Ranch

Grand Canyon Village

To Williams

To Cameron and Flagstaff

0   5   10
SCALE OF MILES

The twisting course of the Colorado River gorge effectively separates Grand Canyon National Park into two different worlds, a North Rim and a South Rim, near each other as the crow flies but 200 miles apart by roundabout highway.

HOW THE GRAND CANYON WAS FORMED

  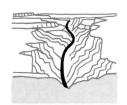 

Carved by the same forces as a roadside gully, *the Grand Canyon is an awesome example of the work of erosion. 1. First, a lazy river meandered through a gently sloping plain, cutting a shallow channel into the earth. 2. Pressure within the earth slowly tilted the surface, causing the river to run faster, cut deeper. As the channel deepened, land on both sides was gradually eroded into the river and the canyon took on a V shape instead of forming a straight-sided trench. 3. Sides of the V-shaped canyon began to break down as forces of erosion attacked them. Rain sluiced soil down into the canyon bottom where it was carried away by the river. Water from melting snow froze in cracks in rocks, splitting them and further crumbling canyon walls. 4. Over the ages, the river continued to cut deeper, ever following its original configuration, and as it cut, the break-up of the canyon walls became accelerated, disintegrating in an ever-widening gap. In time, the canyon walls will disappear, leaving a flat plain again.*

GRAND CANYON
History of the Earth

I IN THE ROCKS, a billion years.

Possibly, the first spark of life on earth came to be while the rock of the Vishnu Schist formed the surface of this region, instead of the bottom layer of the Grand Canyon.

This black rock of the inner gorge is the oldest man has seen exposed on this planet. Its age is two billion years, an incomprehensibly long span. The youngest rocks in this canyon, only 235 million years old, were deposited as sand by an encroaching sea long before the first dinosaur roamed the land.

The story is written in layers deposited so tidily that geologists use the canyon as a primer. There are missing chapters. Nothing remains of the Ordovician and Silurian geologic periods, which followed the Cambrian, and there is very little left of the Devonian period, which came after the Silurian and before the Carboniferous.

Later chapters are written at Bryce and Zion.

II DOWN THE CANYON WALLS,
a continent's range of life.

What is in the rock tells a long story. What is on it does too, in miles rather than time.

A sturdy man can hike down to the bottom of the Grand Canyon and back out again in two days. The experience lets him see plant and animal life that he could also see by walking from Mexico's Sonoran desert to the shore of Hudson's Bay in Canada.

The great depth of the canyon plays tricks with temperatures and precipitation to such a degree that the local range of climate equals the natural range of the entire continent. Mostly, the life zones occur in their logical order; but in some sections, the desert is higher than the Canadian zone, where the canyon's topography makes a high area hot and a lower one cool.

The Merriam Life Zones used on this chart are explained in greater detail on pages 308-309, where the Grand Canyon can be compared to other parks.

PERMIAN PERIOD
235,000,000 years ago

The highest rim rocks, the Kaibab Limestone, hold fossils of the last trilobites, which swam in a shallow sea. The Coconino Sandstone, a buff layer below, is dune sand. On it walked the early reptiles. Red rocks of the Hermit Shale and Supai Formation are next down, and mark the beginning of the period.

CARBONIFEROUS PERIOD
315,000,000 years ago

Mostly eroded away, these layers represent the time during which the coal of the earth had its beginnings as living plants. The fossil record is slim.

CAMBRIAN PERIOD
550,000,000 years ago

Trilobites dominated a sea floor that was beginning to teem with life, after countless eons struggling up from simple, one-celled beginnings. Top to bottom, the rocks of this period are: Muav Limestone, Bright Angel Shale, Tapeats Sandstone.

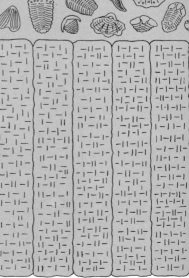

PRECAMBRIAN ERA
1,200,000,000 years ago

Longer than all time since, PreCambrian time witnessed somewhere in its dim recesses the first life. Life was earlier than the Grand Canyon Series that ends the era, or than the Chuar Group. It may have begun in the Vishnu Schist that is the bottommost layer known. No fossil remains to tell us what life was like.

BLUE SPRUCE

MT. MAPLE

BLUE GROUSE

**SUB-ARCTIC
LIFE FORMS**

*Above 9,000 feet, in the forests above the
North Rim of the canyon, the cold of
Hudson's Bay prevails.*

DOUGLAS FIR

WHITE FIR

ASPEN

GROUND
SQUIRREL

BLUE GROUSE

**CANADIAN
LIFE FORMS**

*This life zone occurs between 8,000 and
9,000 feet, on both rims of the Grand
Canyon. The great chasm's higher side
lies on the North Rim, hence the zone is
more extensive on that side.*

FERN
BUSH

PONDEROSA PINE

MT. CHICKADEE

GAMBEL'S
OAK

KAIBAB SQUIRREL

STELLAR JAY

**TRANSITION
LIFE FORMS**

*Most of the rim areas on each side fall
in this life zone, which also extends some
distance down along the Bright Angel
and Kaibab trails.*

CLIFF ROSE

**HIGH DESERT
LIFE FORMS**

*Life in this zone is much like that of the
high desert in Mexico. The accepted name
is "Upper Sonoran," and many of the
park's large mammals roam in this zone,
but they also inhabit the Transition and
Canadian Zones, and do not serve as
accurate indicators. The zone ranges
from 2,500 to 6,000 feet elevation.*

SAGEBRUSH

UTAH JUNIPER

PIÑON JAY

PIÑON PINE

BLUE
GRAMA

COTTONTAIL

PIÑON MOUSE

YUCCA

BIGHORN

**LOW DESERT
LIFE FORMS**

*This is the hot, dry desert. Also called
the "Lower Sonoran," this zone is
near the level of the river, at about
2,000 feet elevation.*

RATTLESNAKE

SPINY LIZARD

NORTH RIM

THERE ARE TWO CENTERS OF TOURIST INTEREST in the park—the North Rim and the South Rim of the great canyon. They are a mere 10 miles apart to a crow, or two days' hard hiking to men of stout heart and strong limb, or 215 road miles distant from each other. A great many enchanted visitors prefer to see one rim one year, the other the next.

ON THE NORTH RIM, altitudes run a thousand feet or so higher than on the South Rim. There is a greater variety in nature, and somewhat less diverse evidence of man's hand in the landscape.

Snow falls early and deep on the North Rim. The end of the tourist season is in sight by October, when the aspens put on a great, golden show of color. When the snow flies, as many as 200 inches may blanket the ground by May. Then warming updrafts from the canyon encourage wildflowers to bloom just at the rim. As snowbanks melt before a warming sun, the bright flowers spread ever more widely.

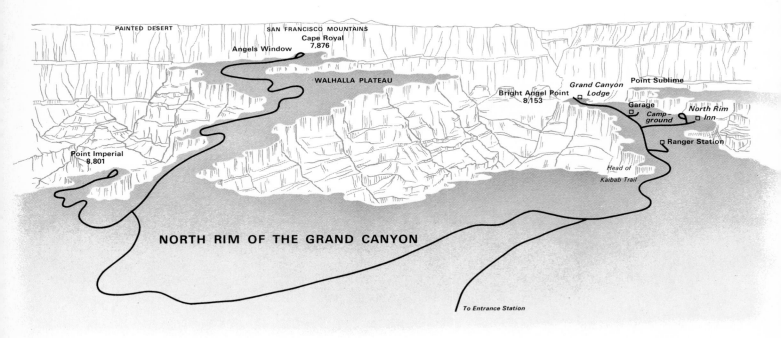

NORTH RIM OF THE GRAND CANYON

MARTIN LITTON

THE ANGEL'S WINDOW *is a hole through a thin point of rock projecting into the canyon near Cape Royal, a stark contrast to tranquil woods nearby.*

152   GRAND CANYON

On the lofty North Rim, flaming autumn *colors light the quaking aspens after September.*
Beyond, for as far as the eye can see, the canyon provides pastel counterpoint to its vivid rim
country. The show ends its brief life beneath the first snowy mantle of winter.

ANSEL ADAMS

FROM THE NORTH RIM, *looking east, south, and west, William H. Holmes produced this 22-mile panorama for science in 1880, transcending mere diagrams with an eye sensitive to composition.*

FROM POINT IMPERIAL (LEFT), *the camera sees only a fraction of the linear sweep of the South Rim that artist Holmes was able to capture on his drawing board.*

AT CAPE ROYAL, A TOUCH OF LIFE *is introduced on the lip of the canyon by a cluster of prickly pears in brave blossom regardless of the awesome backdrop. The spring show of wildflowers follows melting snow away from the rim.*

GRAND CANYON 155

JOSEF MUENCH

156   GRAND CANYON

STARK SHAPES AND BRILLIANT COLORS *fill the canyon in an afternoon of intense sunlight. In the softer light of morning the views from the South Rim are colored in the pastel hues of blue, purple, and gold. On a stormy day the colors go dull, even sullen; then, in the mists afterward, a new brightness shines forth.*

SOUTH RIM

"No matter how far you have wandered hitherto, or how many famous gorges and valleys you have seen, this one, the Grand Canyon of the Colorado will seem as novel to you, as unearthly in the color and grandeur and quantity of its architecture, as if you had found it after death, on some other star." So wrote John Muir, after he had visited the South Rim in the 1890's, eloquently summarizing the emotional response that this vast spectacle evokes in the traveler when he first sees it.

It is at the South Rim that the great majority of travelers experience this emotional impact. For nearly a century, tourists have converged here to soak in the unbelievable view. Being closer to major population centers and trunk highways than its counterpart across the canyon, the South Rim is easily accessible by bus, train, plane, or car, and it has always drawn the heavier volume of tourists. As a consequence, it is well provided with facilities for travelers: a half dozen hotels, two large campgrounds with 600 campsites, information centers, and gift shops bulging with Navajo and Hopi handicrafts.

Crowded as it is in season, the South Rim still offers ample opportunities to view the ever-changing canyon. Nine turnouts along the rim road permit motorists to drive right to the brink; and for a more intimate view, travelers can stroll along the 2½-mile trail that follows the lip of the canyon. Even in winter, when snow is deep on the ground (the elevation is 7,000 feet), the rim is accessible and the visitor can enjoy the unforgettable sight of the canyon walls frosted with snow.

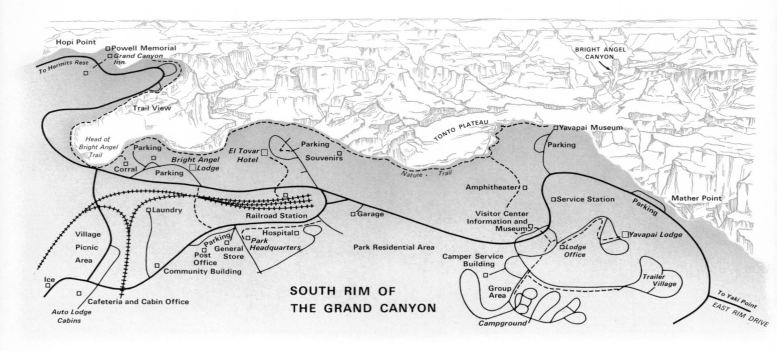

SOUTH RIM OF
THE GRAND CANYON

THE USUAL FIRST LOOK, MATHER POINT, *is where the entrance road first meets the South Rim. Across the chasm, Bright Angel Canyon extends 19 miles northward.*

GRAND CANYON   159

NAVAJO TOWER (ABOVE), *at Lipan
Point, offers startlingly long views over
the canyon. It duplicates prehistoric
watchtowers built by the Indians.*

IN ITS OVERWHELMING VASTNESS, *the
Grand Canyon befuddles the eye ·
Bright Angel Bridge is a tiny thread
across the Colorado River in the
lower right quarter of the photograph.
It is a thousand feet to the top of the black
cliff above the bridge. Bright Angel
Canyon points toward the North Rim,
7 miles away from this overlook.*

GRAND CANYON 161

INNER CANYON

IF YOU PAUSE FOR AN HOUR OR TWO somewhere along the rim and let the Grand Canyon soak into your soul, you will feel some of the lure that turns men into explorers. You will get enough of the big view and will want to get a closer look at the working parts. Sooner or later you will be tugged down one of the trails into the inner canyon.

From either rim, you can hike down or you can ride a mule. At the bottom is a desert, hot and dry and relieved only by the river. It is no place for Sunday strollers to wander aimlessly.

From the South Rim, the mule trips go down the Bright Angel and Kaibab Trails; from the North Rim, they descend the North Kaibab Trail. In summer, the methodical beasts plod their memorized routes in such numbers that a certain air of the barnyard arises from the wide, sun-drenched trails. Users of this service will gain a new appreciation of the width of a mule. Hikers would do well to allow two days to get from the rim to the river and back. Experienced hikers with respect for the effects of heat and dehydration, and with full knowledge of topographic map-reading, may prefer the less traveled Clear Creek, Thunder Spring, or Supai trails.

JOSEPH WAMPLER

A HALF DOZEN DASHING creeks flow out of tributary canyons. Most issue from the Redwall Limestone, from which many gather the mineral wealth to build high monuments to themselves out of travertine. A welcome by-product to dusty hikers is a natural bathtub safe for swimming, at Havasu.

IN THE TYPICAL AUTUMN CALM, *as the mule string maintains its methodical pace along memorized zigzags of the Bright Angel or Kaibab trail, you hear above the hoofsteps the jet-like swish of white-throated swifts flying close to the cliffs. You look sometimes out to the panorama of the canyon, sometimes at the edge of the trail to see Indian paintbrush, or gilia, or penstemon thriving where there is soil for a root to cling to. A few novices hike down, ignore the warning signs, and come out on the back of a mournful-looking mule that costs as much as $40 when he is called in for a "drag-out."*

163

CARVING A SINUOUS WAY *through brown Tapeats sandstone, crystal-clear Deer Creek hastens to its 125-foot fall into the Colorado River.*

THE ONLY SAFE CROSSING *of the Colorado River is on the suspension bridge at the bottom of the Kaibab Trail. To see the river closely, you have to "run" it. No trail stays with it. With the Glen Canyon Dam operating, it can be run only in certain seasons. Even at its best, it isn't the test that it once was.*

BRYCE CANYON

A TOUGH PLACE TO FIND A COW

Park facts: Discovered: 1800's. *Established:* June 7, 1924. *Size:* 56 sq. mi. *Altitude:* 6,600 to 9,105 feet. *Climate:* March to November, warm days and cool nights. Winters cold with snow. Air is thin due to high elevation. *Season:* All year; main road kept open in winter. *Visitors, 1964:* 300,311.

THE PAIUTE INDIANS CALLED IT "UNCA-TIMPE-WA-WINCE-POCK-ICH," which means Red-rocks-standing-like-men-in-a-bowl-shaped-canyon. Ebenezer Bryce, the canyon's first resident, had a saltier phrase. In his words, it was "a tough place to find a stray cow." Both descriptions are accurate.

Bryce Canyon is the result of erosive forces. For millions of years, wind, rain, sleet, and frost have worked relentlessly on the multicolored limestone of this great amphitheater. They have shaped countless columns, spires, walled windows, and figures of every description in soft reds, yellows, oranges, greys, and whites. These fantastic forms, filling a huge half-bowl 15 miles across, defy the imagination—or stimulate it, for here is an astonishing variety of shapes, some grotesque, some beautiful.

Just as the forces of nature created the landscape, so do the vagaries of the day alter it for the viewer. The domes and temples and spires never seem twice the same. With every cloud shadow, with every change of light, with every summer shower, the scene is new, and newly exciting. No matter how familiar one may be with this fairyland of form and color, some new formation or some undetected tone is always to be discovered.

It is possible, if you wish, to see Bryce Canyon National Park by car. A paved road skirts the western rim for 20 miles, terminating at Rainbow Point. You can look into a dozen minor amphitheaters, each with a character of its own. From Rainbow Point unfolds a sweeping view not only of the canyon but of the country beyond. On a clear day you can see the Henry Mountains, 90 miles away, the Tushars, 60 miles to the north, and, 80 miles to the southeast on the Arizona border, Navajo Mountain, sacred as the home of their war god.

"THE WILDEST AND MOST WONDERFUL SCENE *that the eye of man ever beheld," is the way an enraptured surveyor described the eroded fantasy of the Pink Cliffs in 1876. But early settlers were not so bemused: they considered this a hostile place for raising crops or grazing cattle.*

167

ANSEL ADAMS

"THE STUNNINGEST THING OUT OF A *picture, a perfect wilderness of red pinnacles,"* noted the member of a *scientific survey team in 1872. The Pink Cliffs, still considered the finest of Utah's eroded landscapes, stretch for 30 miles along the eastern edge of the Paunsaugunt ("home of the beaver") Plateau. The bright colors, fused into the native rock, are derived from iron—the more iron content the deeper the red. Bands of different colored and textured rock are layers of ancient sands compressed into rock by the immense weight of the thick layer of earth that once covered them but has long since eroded away. Within the brightly colored cliffs are bones of dinosaurs and other fossils of the Age of Reptiles.*

DAVID MUENCH

169

But to experience the park adequately, to capture its true grandeur and its varied moods, walk or ride into its heart over one of the fine trails; only in this way can you appreciate the beauty of the formations. The trails vary in length, from ½ mile to 5½ miles, and in gradient from nearly level to steep (those that lead into the canyon itself).

The colorful formations are geologically young—a mere million years of age. They overlie more ancient rocks of the strata exposed today in the walls of Zion Canyon to the west and Grand Canyon to the south. Thus one can trace a fascinating sequence in earth history from the oldest rocks of Grand Canyon, through the more recent walls of Zion, to the comparatively young strata of Bryce Canyon.

Bryce is an all-year park, and although access to some sections is limited, the road to certain of the major points is kept open throughout the winter. The beauty of the spires and minarets is no less breathtaking when the delicate colors stand out in contrast to a blanket of snow and frost.

Bryce has been a tourist destination only since the automobile made access possible. Before then, the area was familiar only to trappers and farmers, and before them, to the Indians, who lived in nearby caves or entered the canyon to hunt or to gather herbs, seeds, and berries. Trappers visited the locality in the early 1800's, Mormon scouts explored it between 1850 and 1870, and the first awe-struck descriptions of the fantastic landscape came from geologists and surveyors who explored the canyon in the 1870's. The first settler, Ebenezer Bryce, for whom the park is named, pastured cattle in the labyrinth from 1875 to 1880. Small settlements grew up nearby, but the area was too remote from railroads and wagon routes to grow. It was not until the first automobiles began to push their way through the sands after 1915 that the area gained recognition as a potential park. It was made a national monument in 1923 and a year later was established as Utah National Park, a name that was changed to the present one in 1928.

HOW THE ERODED FANTASY WAS FORMED

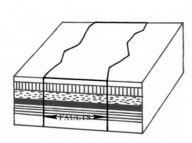 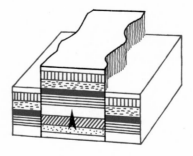 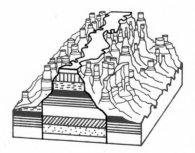

1. DEEP FAULTS FORM IN EARTH'S *crust made of layers of silt, sand, and lime deposited under an ancient inland sea.*

2. MASSIVE PRESSURE FROM BELOW *slowly forces up block of earth between major faults and forms flat-topped mesa.*

3. RAIN, WIND, AND FROST ACTION *gradually wear away edges of mesa; differences in layers produce odd shapes.*

WHO ARE THESE? *Viewed close-up, the forms seem to take on identities. Left to right: two-faced Janus; Nebuchadnezzar, with crown, mustache, beard; caped Florence Nightingale; and King Neptune.*

BRYCE CANYON   171

QUEEN VICTORIA HOLDS COURT, *surrounded by her entourage of nobles and ladies-in-waiting. The grotesque figures are the work of wind and rain, shaping stone of varying degrees of hardness. In time (an eon or two), these forces will wear down the jumbled land into a smooth plain.*

BRYCE CANYON NATIONAL PARK

The Triangle

Shakespeare △Point

● *Rubys Inn*

COPE CANYON

ENTRANCE
Park Headquarters □

△Boat Mesa

CAMPBELL CANYON

Crescent Castle

Inn

Sunrise Point
8,017 *Lodge*

Oastler Castle
Queens Garden

Tropic

Sunset Point
8,000

The Cathedral

Navajo Loop Trail

BRYCE CANYON

△ Bryce Point

Paria View

PINK CLIFFS

△ Swamp Canyon Butte

Noon Canyon Butte

Natural Bridge

Yovimpa Point ○ Rainbow Point
△The Promontory

Yovimpa Pass

Mutton Hollow

PARK STRETCHES ALONG EASTERN EDGE *of a plateau; 23 miles of trail run 500 feet below and parallel to rim; vast amphitheater to southeast, outside park.*

LEGEND
Paved Roads ———
Trails ------
Campsites ∧

0 1 2 3
SCALE OF MILES

LONE PINE TREE, *started against great odds in semi-darkness, now flourishes, its crown in the sunshine above, where the narrow cleft in the rocks widens out. Located on Navajo Loop Trail, it passes through Wall Street.*

BRYCE CANYON   173

DAVID MUENCH

DAVID MUENCH

Mixed in with the *eroded landforms is a pygmy forest of trees and shrubs that grow in poor soil, need little water. Juniper, piñons, and stray yellow pine share a precarious footing with manzanita, mountain mahogany, squaw bush, service berry, and other low growing shrubs. In cool canyons, cottonwoods, maples, birches, and willows grow. Here at Queens Garden sparse forest softens harshness of spectacular cliffs.*

SNOWSHOES WOULD BE NEEDED *for the hike down the Navajo Trail in winter. Snow piles deep on the rim by mid-December and covers the ledges of the Pink Cliffs, brightening the warm-hued filigree with contrasting white. Though accommodations are closed, roads are open to main view points.*

BRYCE CANYON   **175**

ANSEL ADAMS

ZION

"YOSEMITE VALLEY IN COLOR"

PARK FACTS: *Discovered:* 1776. *Established:* November 19, 1919. *Size:* 230 sq. mi. *Altitude:* 3,950 to 8,740 feet. *Climate:* Warm summers, mild winters. Temperature range from 0° to 115°. *Season:* All year. Facilities closed but main road open in snowy months. *Visitors in 1964:* 705,230.

ZION CANYON IS A COLORFUL JEWEL set in a land famed for color. It is a serene canyon, majestic with sandstone cliffs which at times rise more than 3,000 feet above its floor. Without the color—the delicate pinks and reds and whites of the sandstone and the fresh green of the cottonwoods, ash, and maples that border the river—these walls and domes might be overpoweringly stern. But the color softens the scene and casts a special aura over the canyon.

Zion has been called a Yosemite done in oils, for without color the sheer cliffs would resemble the California park in many ways. Zion Canyon is a narrow, curving gorge, 8¾ miles long; the upper end is so narrow that two men standing abreast can touch both walls with their outstretched arms. The canyon is cut by the Virgin River, a Jekyll-and-Hyde sort of stream that is usually clear and peaceful, reflecting the cliffs in its calm pools. But a storm in the higher country can transform it into a relentless torrent, tearing savagely at its banks, and carrying boulders and trees like pebbles and twigs.

Such storms are not frequent, but when they come they have their rewarding aspects. Visitors present at such a time will marvel at the power of the river and perhaps be loath to turn their eyes from the racing waters. But during a hard rain, a look up the walls of the canyon reveals waterfalls springing to life and plunging over the usually dry cliffs, some dropping 2,000 feet in a single leap. More than 50 large waterfalls and hundreds of smaller ones have been counted at one time during a heavy rain. It has been estimated that each year the Virgin carries three million tons of sediment from the park—an average of 180 carloads each day. Thus the river works as it has worked for centuries, cutting the canyon deeper and deeper through the strata of stone.

GREAT WHITE THRONE, *towering 2,400 feet above the canyon floor, is most majestic of the assembly of blocky peaks that form walls of Zion Canyon. Shading upward from red at base through pink to white, the monolith is crowned with forest.*

177

An excellent road traverses the canyon along the bank of the river and terminates at the Temple of Sinawava. Glorious in daylight hours, the Temple is even more impressive in the soft light of the moon.

There are many good trails, some that penetrate delightful side canyons and others, more strenuous, that climb to the rim on either side. One of the most popular and beautiful is the mile-long walk along the river beginning at the Temple of Sinawava and ending at the entrance to The Narrows. Here the trail passes the Hanging Gardens, where water trickles down the wall to moisten the flowers, ferns, and vines that trail from cracks in the rock.

Zion is an all-year park and each season has its own charm. Spring is fresh with flowers and new foliage. During the hot summer the park is its busiest. In autumn the trees glow brilliantly and tongues of red and yellow flame seem to creep up the ravines. Winter snows seldom linger in the lower part of the canyon, but in the upper portions, a fresh fall converts the landscape into a white fairyland.

Zion was for many years a retreat and a place of special reverence for the Mormon pioneers, who discovered the canyon and named the region "Zion," meaning "the heavenly city of God," and bestowed religious names on many of the rock formations. The area had been originally discovered by Spanish padres in 1776, explored 50 years later by Jedediah Smith and his fur-trappers, and then developed by the Mormons a decade after the founding of Salt Lake City in 1847. The area was not set aside for public use until 1909, when it was designated Mukuntuweap National Monument. Ten years later it was enlarged and changed to Zion National Park.

ROCKY MOUNTAIN MULE DEER *come out of the side canyons in late afternoon to feed in the river valleys.*

COLOR IN THE CLIFFS *is in the rock itself, not in the vegetation, surface stains, or lichens. Hues change with the hour as sun shifts, are intensified or fused with other colors when reflections from nearby peaks are set aglow by the sun, and look their best after a rain. Dominant color is red, derived from iron and magnesium in the sandstone.*

IT IS HARD TO REALIZE *that the innocent-looking little river below could have carved this profound gorge. But carve it it did, and the work is still going on. Like a river of sandpaper, the Virgin carries away 3 million tons of parkland each year, ever deepening its channel and disposing of the rocky debris washed down the canyon walls by rains. In this view, the Great White Throne dominates the West Rim at a bend in the river.*

SO TORTURED IS THE ZION TERRAIN *that it was not completely mapped until 1930, when it was systematically photographed from the air.*

THE GRANDEUR OF ZION CANYON *has inspired a feeling of reverence and worship in those who have seen it, ever since it was homesteaded in the 1860's by Mormon pioneers. They named the area Zion (The Heavenly City of God) and bestowed religious names on the peaks, canyons, plateaus. The view here is south from Angels Landing.*

PHILIP HYDE

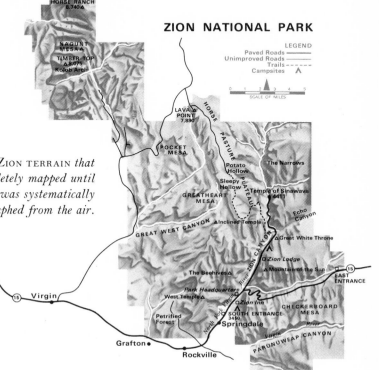

ZION NATIONAL PARK

LEGEND
Paved Roads ————
Unimproved Roads ————
Trails – – – – –
Campsites ∧

0 1 2 3 4 5
SCALE OF MILES

ZION **181**

Like a huge topographic map, *contour lines of ancient sand dunes are solidified into a massive stairway on eastern edge of the park, just off highway.*

Criss-cross crevicing *of the sandstone in Checkerboard Mesa, near the east entrance, presents a striking linear pattern. Cracks run both vertically and horizontally, slicing the rock into great blocks and making the stone vulnerable to erosion. Water seeps down the crevices, slowly dissolving soluble sandstone, and in winter when it freezes, it widens the cracks by fracturing the rock along edge.*

RAY ATKESON

QUIET-RUNNING VIRGIN RIVER *becomes a raging torrent when cloudbursts swell it to flood stage. Named by explorer Jedediah Smith in 1827 for Thomas Virgin.*

WEEPING ROCK *sheds its tears on visitors who step into cave behind falling water. Surface water on rim seeps down through porous cliffs and emerges as curtain of falling drops. Seepage is evident throughout the park and dozens of waterfalls spring to life after each rain.*

THE WATER OUZEL

Water ouzels live along the river, fly in and out of the water, swimming and walking under surface in search of food.

FROM JOHN MUIR'S "MOUNTAINS OF CALIFORNIA," 1894

185

PETRIFIED FOREST

ALCHEMY IN THE DESERT

PARK FACTS: *Discovered:* 1851. *Established:* Put under Forest Preserve 1896, made national monument 1906, national park December 9, 1962. *Size:* 147 sq. mi. *Altitude:* 5,300 to 6,235 feet. *Climate:* Area receives less than 10 inches of moisture per year. *Season:* All year. *Visitors in 1964:* 884,000.

THE FASCINATION OF PETRIFIED WOOD seems almost universal. Its attraction is more than a matter of beauty; it is partly the mystery of a magic transformation.

Mineralized wood is found in many places, but nowhere in such abundance as on the high plateau of northeastern Arizona. There, in six distinct forests, great logs of jasper and agate are interspersed with smaller sections and fragments that glisten in the sun like a ground cover of gems.

Explorers reported these "stone trees" in 1851, but it was another 30 years before there were enough settlers and travelers in the area to affect the forests seriously. Then the depredations of souvenir hunters and commercial exploiters reached the point where great quantities of petrified wood were being carried off. Logs were blasted in search of the amethysts that some contained; a stamp mill was even erected nearby to crush the trees into abrasives.

The aroused citizens of Arizona, through the territorial legislature, finally won federal protection for the area, and in 1906 the Petrified Forest National Monument was established. In 1962 it was designated a national park.

Petrified wood is manufactured by nature under rather special circumstances. The mineralized logs started as living trees in a prehistoric forest. When they died and fell, they were washed down from the hills by flood waters and covered, before they could decay, with sand, mud, and volcanic ash. Eventually some geologic upheaval lifted the land, and wind and rain began to wear away the overlying sediments. After millions of years, the trees were exposed. But the wood had been replaced, cell by cell, by silica borne in the water filtering down through the overlying strata. Oxides of iron and magnesium, carried in the same water, gave the logs the red, green, and black hues we see today.

THE PROFILE OF BLUE MESA *changes little by little as wind and rain erode it. Petrified logs cap small ridges until they are undercut and fall all a-tumble. As the old ridges crumble, new ones begin beneath the fallen log fragments.*

DARWIN VAN CAMPEN

187

ON AGATE BRIDGE *a stroller of 1899 takes a wonder of nature in stride.*
Soft sandstone eroded to form the 40-foot log arch, which is still intact.

The forests of petrified trees are the prime attractions at this national park, but there are other reasons to visit. One is the Painted Desert. This great expanse of colored sand stretches for many miles across northern Arizona, and a splendid sampling is included within the park boundaries. The colors are richest after a rain, but they are impressive in any light, and they change in tone and intensity as the day passes. A rim road, with parking areas at the best viewing points, skirts this portion of the park.

The main road through the stone forests also takes you past Puerco Indian Ruin, the remains of an ancient pueblo occupied until about 600 years ago, and Newspaper Rock, a great block of sandstone inscribed with petroglyphs. Another partially restored pueblo, Agate House, can be reached by trail from the Rainbow Forest parking area.

TREES THAT FELL *200,000,000 years ago are preserved*
by silica, to the interest of scientists, and dyed beautifully
by iron oxide and magnesium, to the delight of all.

DAVID MUENCH

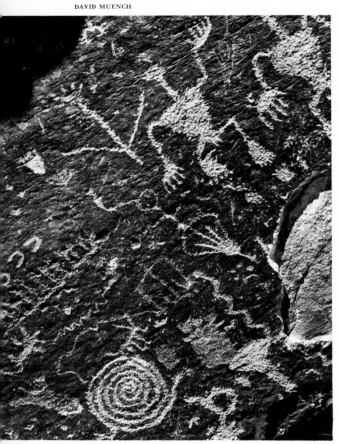

INDIANS KNEW THIS AREA *long before
advent of white explorers. Their notes
on Newspaper Rock can't be read today,
but the petroglyph is probably the
illustrated daily news of nearby villages.*

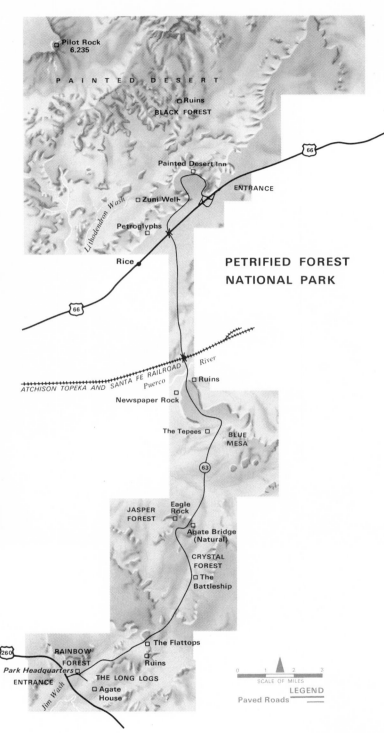

Pilot Rock
6,235

P A I N T E D   D E S E R T

☐ Ruins
BLACK FOREST

66

Painted Desert Inn

ENTRANCE

☐ Zuni Well

☐ Petroglyphs

Lithodendron Wash

Rice ■

66

PETRIFIED FOREST
NATIONAL PARK

River

ATCHISON TOPEKA AND SANTA FE RAILROAD

Puerco

☐ Ruins

☐
Newspaper Rock

The Tepees ☐

BLUE
MESA

63

JASPER
FOREST

Eagle
Rock

☐ Agate Bridge
(Natural)

CRYSTAL
FOREST

☐ The
Battleship

☐ The Flattops

260

RAINBOW
FOREST

☐ Ruins

Park Headquarters ☐

ENTRANCE

THE LONG LOGS

Jim Wash

☐ Agate
House

0   1   2   3
SCALE OF MILES

LEGEND

Paved Roads

SIX SEPARATE FORESTS *of petrified wood
flank the 27-mile-long road through the
neck of the park. At its north end, the
Painted Desert duplicates in sandstone
the fiery colors of petrified wood.*

DAVID MUENCH

IN THE CRYSTAL FOREST, *soft sandstone is weathering away from beneath a huge petrified log. The long section will fall and break, slowly by man's clock, rapidly by nature's.*

THE FOREST LOOKED LIKE THIS *when the trees were living in the Triassic Period. The globe-topped trees, related to pines, are called* Araucarioxylon. *They dominate the petrified forest.*

PETRIFIED FOREST **191**

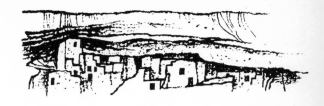

MESA VERDE

AMERICA'S OLDEST ABANDONED APARTMENTS

PARK FACTS: *Discovered:* Area discovered by Spanish 1765; Indian dwellings first discovered in 1870's. *Established:* June 29, 1906. *Size:* 80 sq. mi. Estimates indicate more than 500 dwellings within park boundaries. *Altitude:* 6,964 to 8,572 feet. *Season:* All year. *Visitors, 1964:* 344,400.

AFTER A MILLENIUM OF REMARKABLE PROGRESS, the people of the Mesa Verde gave up in A.D. 1300 and moved away. They dissolved a sophisticated culture without learning to write the record. And the question is unanswered after 700 years: Why did they go?

They had come as nomadic hunters in the time of Christ. Within two centuries they had learned to raise corn, and to weave with such consummate skill that they are known to history as the Basket-maker People.

They became the earliest of the pueblo Indians when they learned to cover their storage-pit homes on cave floors with crude huts of logs plastered over with adobe. By A.D. 750 they had come up out of the canyons to the mesa top, where they built connecting rows of rooms close to their farm fields. These were forerunners to the remarkable cliff dwellings. And they had turned from baskets to pottery, which has artistic merit today. They were outstandingly successful farmers.

Some archaeologists think their success was their ruin as well, that their wealth attracted raiders from hostile tribes. They say the evidence points to a retreat return to the cliff caves from which they had started, and not a willing move from the mesa. Whatever the reason, the people continued to farm on the mesa top while they cultivated their skills as masons on those incredibly difficult sites.

An average life span was 30 years; a man worked from the time he was 12 until he was too old at 25. He learned to haul talus up from the bottom of the cliffs and to lay the rock in careful courses, with a minimum of adobe mortar. He learned to string beams of piñon pine to make roofs. He learned to slope walls inward so he could build to a height of four stories. He figured out com-

CLIFF PALACE, *more than 700 years after abandonment, remains a most impressive monument to the skills of its builders, who continually added to it during the 200 years of its busy occupation. Peak population was about 400.*

193

FAR BELOW THE MESA TOP, *Mancos Valley of southwestern Colorado spreads flat and open. The peaceful Indians who farmed on mesa's 2,000-foot height chose remote area because it was easily defended. When hostile tribes threatened the mesa, its occupants retreated into inaccessible canyons to build defensive bastions in the cliff caves.*

plicated ventilating systems for the underground ceremonial room called the kiva, so he could use fire in his ceremonies without choking on the smoke.

While he was mastering these skills, he lived in a society with complex religious practices, a diverse agricultural knowledge, and a trading system that brought goods from as far away as the coast of southern California and the gulfs of Mexico and California.

Then, in about A.D. 1300, it all ended. The land may have worn out. Drought may have come. Enemies may have become too powerful. The social order may have broken down. The cause may have been a combination of all these. Whatever it was, the results were permanent.

The untenanted ruins endure in Mesa Verde National Park. From May 15 to October 15 ranger-guides conduct tours of some of the outstanding ruins. During the remainder of the year, visitors can look down into the great villages and the small ones from vantage points along the roads on the mesa. A great many artifacts were discovered by members of the ranching Wetherill family in 1888 and before the area became a park in 1906. A representative collection is in the fine park museum.

Hiking is not encouraged at Mesa Verde; there are only a few short trails. There are special horseback trips to dramatic view points far from the roads. The campgrounds near the park headquarters operate from May 1 to about November 1.

DAVID MUENCH

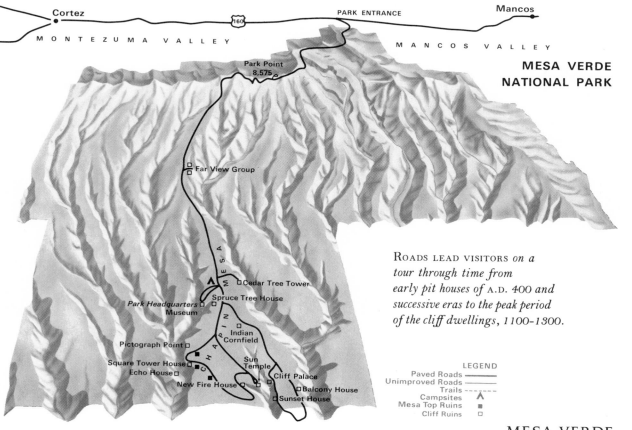

Cortez

PARK ENTRANCE

Mancos

M O N T E Z U M A   V A L L E Y

M A N C O S   V A L L E Y

Park Point
8,575

**MESA VERDE
NATIONAL PARK**

Far View Group

Cedar Tree Tower

Spruce Tree House

Park Headquarters
Museum

Pictograph Point

Indian
Cornfield

Square Tower House

Sun
Temple

Echo House

Cliff Palace

New Fire House

Balcony House

Sunset House

ROADS LEAD VISITORS *on a
tour through time from
early pit houses of* A.D. *400 and
successive eras to the peak period
of the cliff dwellings, 1100–1300.*

LEGEND
Paved Roads
Unimproved Roads
Trails
Campsites
Mesa Top Ruins
Cliff Ruins

MESA VERDE   195

IN THE HUGE, MULTI-FAMILY DWELLINGS *such as Cliff Palace, families added rooms as need arose, and without plan, spreading laterally until they ran out of space, then adding second, third, and even fourth stories to original apartments. Tiny rooms were for storage and sleeping. Daily activity went on in open courts, on kiva or apartment roofs.*

MESA VERDE BLACK-ON-WHITE POTTERY

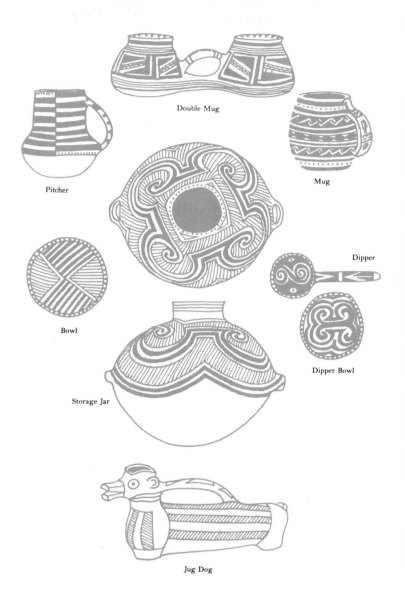

Double Mug

Pitcher

Mug

Bowl

Dipper

Dipper Bowl

Storage Jar

Jug Dog

MESA VERDE INDIANS MASTERED POTTERY *before they excelled at architecture. These pieces might have been made before the move from the mesa top or might have been fashioned by the village women while their men built the cliff dwellings. Artisans formed the pieces with spiral coils of clay, smoothing the surfaces with extra clay and finger pressure. Black paint is an iron oxide gathered by crushing a commonly found pebble to fine dust. The pieces were fired in nearly smothered ovens. Dippers ranged from 8 to 10 inches long. The double mug is slightly more than 10 inches wide. Pitchers ranged from 8 to 10 inches tall; mugs were in the 6 to 9-inch size. Water storage jugs (and the effigy figure of the dog) were usually more than a foot tall. Bowls were 6 to 9 inches in diameter.*

MYSTERIOUS SUN TEMPLE (*a name of none but poetic significance*) *sits atop mesa. It was built long after Mesa Verde Indians had retreated to cliff caves, and its purpose was probably religious. Nobody knows its exact function, but the D-shaped building is a maze of rooms and corridors. Small dwellings in canyon below could not have supplied enough people to build it. Archaeologists think many family groups shared in its construction and use.*

PIT HOUSES WERE FIRST *attempts at construction by the Mesa Verdes. The rude huts covered storage pits and apparently inspired the later ceremonial room called the kiva. Their sites were eventually covered by the cliff dwellings.*

PIT HOUSES

KIVAS WERE ALWAYS *circular at Mesa Verde. They were used by the men, who banded together in what probably were fraternal-religious groups. Kivas were the outer rim of the large villages. Their massive walls helped form defensive barriers.*

BALCONY HOUSE, *not as large as Cliff Palace, shows signs of even finer workmanship. Cantilevered "porches" were for access and extra storage at upper levels.*

FOR ONE GIDDY MOMENT, *contemporary visitors to the cliff dwellings can experience life as the original inhabitants lived it. They must climb a long ladder into Balcony House.*

TO THE NARROW LEDGES ON WHICH THEY BUILT, *the Mesa Verde Indians hauled thousands of stones
gathered from talus at the bottoms of the cliffs, and they felled and dragged hundreds of
piñon pines to serve as roof beams. They couldn't move large boulders, or change the shapes
of the caves, so they devised ingenious ways to get around these obstacles. They did it all in
places chosen because they were difficult to reach, as the example of Square Tower House shows.
They paid for their security with more broken limbs than any other society known to modern times.*

MESA VERDE 201

CARLSBAD CAVERNS

FANTASY BENEATH THE DESERT

PARK FACTS: *Discovered:* Settlers knew of caves in 1880's. *Established:* nat. mon., 1923; nat. park, May 14, 1930. *Size:* 77 sq. mi. Explored caverns cover 23 mi.; open to public: 3 mi. *Altitude:* 4,400 ft. at surface. *Climate:* Surface temps. from 0° to 100°. *Season:* All year. *Visitors, 1964:* 588,000.

AN INFINITY IN TIME AND THE INFINITE POWER of trickling water have hollowed at least 23 miles of caverns out of the limestone beneath the southeast corner of New Mexico. During the latter part of the 60 million years this has been going on, the oozing drops have left mineral trails behind them in the myriad rock sculptures that give the Carlsbad Caverns their eerie charm.

Nobody knows how extensive these caverns are. More than 23 miles have been explored, at depths ranging down to 1,100 feet below the surface. As many as 5 million bats share one mile of cavern. Known side tunnels and disconnected caverns amount to at least another 18 miles. At present, only three of the most amazing miles are open to park visitors.

The easily walked tour trail passes through great vaults with names like Green Lake Room, King's Palace, and Queen's Chamber, where the rock formations support even more picturesque names: Iceberg, Bone Yard, Totem Pole, and the Rock of Ages are examples. The biggest of these chambers (the Big Room) is 2,000 feet long and 200 feet from floor to soaring ceiling. The walls are hung with rock draperies. (The stalagmites grow from the floor up, the stalactites from the ceiling down.)

The full tour starts at the natural entrance to the caves and gives visitors a fine look at the caverns as the trail winds along the floor then high along a comfortingly wide ledge on one wall. Improbable as it may seem, a box luncheon is served at a restaurant located halfway along the trail, 750 feet below the surface. A shortened tour starts with the elevator ride down to the central area of the caverns, where it joins the other visitors for a stroll around the Big Room. Every tourist returns to the visitor center on the surface by elevator.

EACH DROP OF WATER *passing through the caverns deposits minute cargo of mineral. Where drops come slowly, a needle stalactite forms. Where they come faster, a fluted column like this one is the usual result.*

ANSEL ADAMS

203

The caverns are 56° the year around, whether the desert above is enduring the 0° winds of winter or the 100° heat of summer.

There is a surface side to the park, which supports a busy desert life community. Most of it is nocturnal, and the star attraction is the evening bat flight. The bat caves themselves are not open to touring; although bats are quite clean, their quarters are not. The best views of this striking spectacle are near the cavern mouth, where a ranger naturalist gives a short explanation of what is about to happen, just before the swirling storm erupts, within a few minutes of sundown. The greatest flights are in summer, when the whole colony is in residence and actively pursuing night-flying insects. A great number of the bats migrate south for the winter; in the coldest season the remaining ones go into a state of suspended animation, and the flights dwindle to nothing.

The park also has an abundance of small mammals, desert reptiles, and birds living in its scrub vegetation. Careful observation will reveal ground squirrels, skunks, raccoons, ringtails, kit foxes, many types of lizards, turkey vultures, and an occasional golden eagle.

The presence of the caverns has been known for a thousand years. Some wandering Indians used the cavern mouth for shelter but they did not test the temper of any god of the underworld by penetrating far inside. That was left to the turn-of-the-century bat guano miners. One of them, a young resident of the area, named James Larkin White, found himself drawn to serious explorations. His interest grew to passion, and his passion led to the establishment of the caverns as a national monument in 1923, and a national park in 1930. White's reward was a term as chief ranger of the park he helped establish.

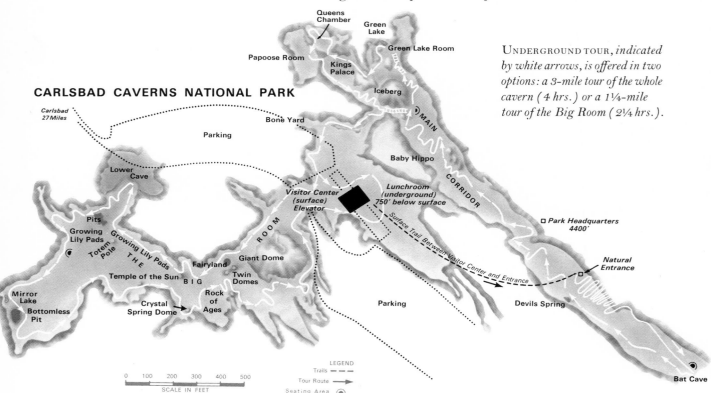

CARLSBAD CAVERNS NATIONAL PARK

UNDERGROUND TOUR, *indicated by white arrows, is offered in two options: a 3-mile tour of the whole cavern (4 hrs.) or a 1¼-mile tour of the Big Room (2¼ hrs.).*

THE GIANT DOME BULKS *massively beside its lesser neighbors in the cavern. The column rises 62 feet above figure-dotted floor of the Big Room; its diameter approaches 20 feet.*

Frozen waterfall is a rock model *of a waterfall formed by trickling water rather than by instant refrigeration. It is near the center of the main cavern. Above is a grotto on one wall of the Big Room. Its knobbled appearance owes to an incredibly slow drip of water, too slow to form a needle stalactite.*

HOW THE CAVERNS WERE FORMED

200 MILLION YEARS AGO

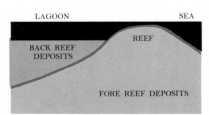

ABOUT 200 MILLION YEARS AGO, *dome of the cavern formation was a reef in a Permian sea. The sea deposited sediments in the lagoon, then rose and covered whole reef with deep deposits. Two succeeding uplifts of the earth's crust (which formed the Rocky Mountains then the Guadalupes) raised the formation above water table. Fractures in the limestone allowed seepage that formed the caverns, then seepage of ground water from rain and snow fashioned rock sculptures.*

3 MILLION YEARS AGO

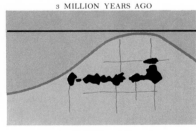

1 MILLION YEARS AGO

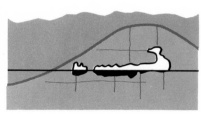

RECENT

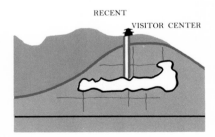

CARLSBAD CAVERNS   207

IN THE DOLL'S THEATER *the curtain is a gossamer web of stalactites. These crystalline limestone forms are incredibly brittle, breaking at a touch.*

THE BEAUTIFUL HUES *can be explained in scientific terms. The rock is calcite or aragonite—crystalline forms of limestone—colored by iron oxide or other minerals in the same way as is the Petrified Forest or Bryce Canyon. But their rich luster when they are wet defies chemical analysis and awes all who come to see them.*

JOSEF MUENCH

208   CARLSBAD CAVERNS

MEXICAN FREE-TAILED BAT

THE REMARKABLE RADAR OF BATS

A BAT CAN NAB A MOSQUITO *on the wing, dodge a wind-whipped tree limb, and wing merrily on his way through the blackest night of the year. How? The bats that live in these caves are in effect tiny FM transmitters. They emit a high-frequency note that covers twice the range of a human voice, yet lasts a thousandth of a second or less. They hear the minute portion of their sound that is reflected by prey— or an obstacle—and "lock in" with ever-faster beeps until they nab the food or dodge the obstacle with a daring bit of aerobatics. Scientists find it very difficult to jam the emissions, but impaired hearing or muting renders a bat nearly helpless in flight.*

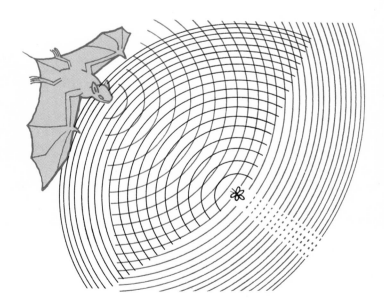

MILLIONS OF BATS FLY OUT *of their cavern in the span of half an hour, starting right at sundown. In-flight collision is unheard of. They fan out over a 50-mile radius to catch and eat several tons of winged insects before dawn, then return to sleep the day away, hanging head down in dense clusters. Fourteen species share the space. The Mexican free-tailed bat is commonest. Others: fringed myotis, western pipistrel, lump-nosed, and pallid.*

CARLSBAD CAVERNS   211

ROCKY MOUNTAIN

ASTRIDE THE CONTINENTAL DIVIDE

PARK FACTS: *Discovered:* 1859. *Established:* January 26, 1915. *Size:* 410 sq. mi. *Altitude:* 7,640 to 14,255 feet. *Climate:* Cool, pleasant; perpetual snows mantle highest summits and valley walls. *Season:* All year, but main cross-park highway, Trail Ridge Road, closed in winter. *Visitors in 1964:* 1,885,900.

THIS IS THE HIGH COUNTRY. The skyline is saw-toothed with jutting granite, unsoftened by vegetation, for timberline is at 11,000 feet. From one spot you can count 84 peaks that rise above that height. Seventeen soar to more than 13,000 feet. Snow covers the crags year-round in protected spots, and high cirques preserve the remnants of glaciers.

Rocky Mountain National Park has been called a primer of glacial geology. Even the most casual observer must notice the great rock amphitheaters where the glaciers formed, the U-shaped valleys carved when the ice began to move, the terminal moraines where the loose rocks collected. Only a few small glaciers are found here now, but the marks left by ice are all around.

Guardian of all is lofty Longs Peak, whose summit rises to 14,256 feet. It dominates the range and can be seen from far out on the plains to the east.

The park takes in about 410 square miles of the most scenic part of north-central Colorado. Below the towering peaks is a high vacationland of quiet lakes and plunging streams, grassy meadows and rugged gorges. Thick forests shelter countless wild creatures.

One of the remarkable aspects of the park is its widespread alpine tundra, that dense carpet of miniature plants that thrives in cold climate. Another is the large number of bighorn sheep, among the rarest of wild animals in North America. You may also see golden eagles, industrious beavers, herds of elk.

Despite the rugged terrain, the park is easily accessible. Much of its splendor can be viewed at a distance from main roads. The most famous, Trail Ridge Road, reaches an altitude of 12,183 feet and stays above timberline for 11 miles.

"ABOVE TIMBERLINE" *is a phrase that takes on real meaning in Rocky Mountain National Park. Most of the park's 400 square miles lie well above the ceiling of tree growth. Here, looking across Forest Canyon, the trees fill a canyon but do not ascend the slopes.*

DARWIN VAN CAMPEN

213

To enjoy this park to the fullest, to experience both its grandeur and its quiet peace, you must penetrate it by trail. Such exquisite spots as Loch Vale, Dream, Fern, and Odessa lakes are reached only by those willing to walk. There are more than 300 miles of trails leading to such rewarding destinations.

The park is open all year. Spring is shy and waits until late April or early May to display its finery. The long days of summer, when the sun is warm and the lakes and sky rich blue, are followed by the spectacular advent of the Colorado autumn. The mountain foliage blazes scarlet and gold, the days grow crisp, and through the clear air you may hear the trumpeted challenge of the big bull elk as he gathers his harem. Then the snows come again, a white blanket settles over the Rockies, and the skiers and snowshoers come back into their own.

Those who today enjoy the bounties of this mountain playground can thank one man for preserving it for their pleasure. Enos Mills, writer and naturalist, sometimes called the "John Muir of the Rockies," campaigned for the park for years against strong opposition. When at length it was established in 1915, its creation was universally credited to the persistence of Mills and his followers.

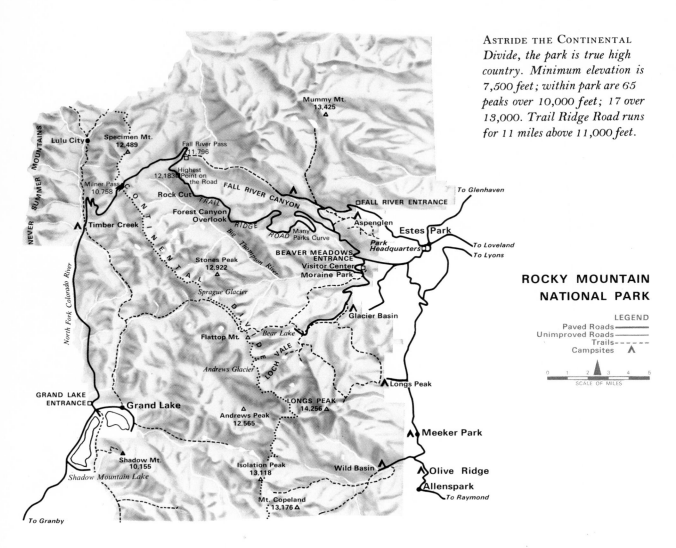

ASTRIDE THE CONTINENTAL *Divide, the park is true high country. Minimum elevation is 7,500 feet; within park are 65 peaks over 10,000 feet; 17 over 13,000. Trail Ridge Road runs for 11 miles above 11,000 feet.*

ROCKY MOUNTAIN
NATIONAL PARK

LEGEND
Paved Roads
Unimproved Roads
Trails
Campsites

0 1 2 3 4 5
SCALE OF MILES

EASY OF ACCESS BY TRAIL OR ROAD, *the mountain lakes such as Lake Helene are within range of every traveler. Most of the lakes were glacier-formed; some were engineered by beavers.*

THE QUEST FOR BEAVER *by fur trappers opened much of the Rocky Mountain area to exploration in the early 1800's. Beavers are still active within the park, where they dam quiet streams and lake margins, fell willow and aspen saplings for food, and build snug shelters.*

ROCKY MOUNTAIN   215

ANSEL ADAMS   SNOW-MANTLED NEVER SUMMER RANGE, *along the northwestern boundary of the park, was the setting for the first rough-and-ready settlements within the park in the 1880's. Towns named Lulu City, Teller, and Dutchtown sprang up as miners poured into the range to extract copper. The ore proved low in value, the mining boom collapsed, and the towns were abandoned.*

GLACIAL ODDITY, *a chunk of hard rock stands poised on a pedestal of softer stone that was almost worn away by glacial action. The Rockies in this area are composed of a mixture of hard volcanic and soft sedimentary stone.*

NEARLY EXTINGUISHED BY HUNTERS *before the park was established, the elk (wapiti) are a common sight now. Importation of elk from Yellowstone helped restore the herd.*

ROCKY MOUNTAIN   217

ANSEL ADAMS

GOAL OF MOUNTAIN CLIMBERS SINCE 1868, *Longs Peak (14,255 ft.) still draws mountaineers to its perpendicular cliffs. First recorded conquest was by Major John Wesley Powell and party during exploration of the Colorado River. Now, every year, dozens of mountaineers who have satisfied park authorities as to their fitness and technical skill scale this peak (the highest in the park) and others of equivalent challenge. A mountaineering school in the park trains novices in the techniques of mountain climbing.*

DEBONAIR, PIPE-SMOKING MOUNTAINEER *gets ready to rappel down from an ascent of Eagle Cliff. By paying out rope, he will lower himself gently to the ground below. Rope is run through a loop secured to piton driven into the rock; it permits quick and safe descent after the laborious climb. In distance: Longs Peak.*

FIRST MOUNTAINEERS IN THE PARK, *bighorn sheep are native to the higher elevations. Group of rams would not be so friendly in mating season. Then, they conduct butting bouts over their chosen mates. Ram with most endurance wins the ewe.*

ROCKY MOUNTAIN 219

GLACIER

THE INTERNATIONAL PARK

PARK FACTS: *Discovered:* 1800's. *Established:* Nat. park, May 11, 1910; made part of Waterton-Glacier International Peace Park, May 22, 1932. *Size:* 1,600 sq. mi. *Altitude:* 3,154-10,488 ft. *Climate:* Summers warm days, chilly nights. *Season:* All year, but passes closed Oct.-May. *Visitors, 1964:* 642,184.

THE MOUNTAINS OF GLACIER ARE NOT HIGH, compared with those in some national parks, but there is something distinctive about their sheer faces and angular contours that led the early French explorer Pierre Verendrye to call this "the land of shining mountains." There is something hospitable about them, too; their flanks are covered by heavy forests that descend to the edge of sapphire lakes and seem to welcome visitors. Above timberline their upper reaches are multicolored—blue-grey, buff, green, red, purple.

Straddling the Continental Divide in northwest Montana, Glacier contains an accessible but unspoiled wilderness penetrated by a thousand miles of trails. Here you can travel alone for an hour or a week, or you can take a guided trip without charge. There are saddle horses for those who want to rent them, and shelter cabins for those who reach the remote back country.

It is a land of colorful place names: Gunsight and Two Medicine are mountain passes, and Rising Wolf, Scalplock, and Going-to-the-Sun are mountains. And there are Indian names like Kintla and Appekunny, for this is Blackfoot country. The eastern part of the park was reservation until the Blackfeet sold it in 1896. They are still in evidence, for their present home adjoins the park on the east, and often in summer they perform their dances in costume at Glacier Park Lodge.

This is a park that deserves ample time—time to meditate and relax, to hike and ride, to study and observe, to fish and camp. John Muir was emphatic: "Give at least a month to this precious preserve. Time will not be taken from the sum of your life. Instead of shortening, it will indefinitely lengthen it and make you truly immortal."

Glacier's northernmost boundary is on the 49th parallel, and even though its mountains reach a height of only 10,448 feet, the northern latitude means

SPECTACULAR GOING-TO-THE-SUN ROAD *crosses The Continental Divide at Logan Pass (6,664 ft.) within sight of pyramidal Clements Mountain (8,764 ft.). The Mayan-temple shape of this peak is typical of mountains in park, which were carved by glaciers from soft, layered rock.*

221

222   GLACIER

EARLY SNOW COMES TO TWO MEDICINE LAKE *before the autumn colors have left the aspens. Two Medicine is one of many long, finger lakes that occupy the glaciated valleys in the park. In such settings of scenic grandeur, fishermen try for trout, Dolly Varden, kokanee, grayling, whitefish, and pike.*

223

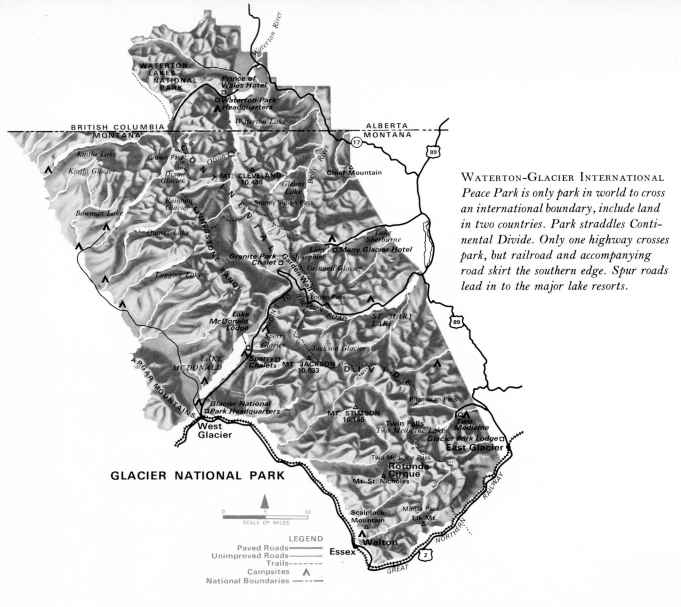

GLACIER NATIONAL PARK

0   5   10
SCALE OF MILES

LEGEND
Paved Roads —————
Unimproved Roads ————
Trails - - - - - -
Campsites ∧
National Boundaries — · — · —

WATERTON-GLACIER INTERNATIONAL *Peace Park is only park in world to cross an international boundary, include land in two countries. Park straddles Continental Divide. Only one highway crosses park, but railroad and accompanying road skirt the southern edge. Spur roads lead in to the major lake resorts.*

abundant snow. The snowfall and the 60 glaciers within the park feed more than 200 lakes and rushing streams. Water seems to be everywhere, in lush verdant valleys, in meadows ablaze with wildflowers, along highways, and nestling in glacial cirques at the base of sheer rock walls. Water is so abundant that the visitor is seldom out of sight of a lake or out of hearing of a waterfall or stream.

Although this is a trail park of the first magnitude, the roads are excellent and the scenic Going-to-the-Sun Highway is one of the most spectacular in America. The roads within the park are not generally passable before June 15, but if weather permits they are kept open until mid-October.

Adjoining Glacier on the north is Canada's Waterton Lakes National Park, and together they form the Waterton-Glacier International Peace Park, dedicated in 1932 to the permanent peace and friendship of the two neighboring nations. By all means, cross the boundary for a visit to the Canadian park. There are no border complications, and the boat trips, fine food, and English shops will remain in your memory as a pleasant adjunct to your Glacier trip.

FROM THE 10,000-FOOT SUMMIT *of Mount Jackson (left),
a class-3 mountain climb, an extensive sea of peaks is
visible for a hundred miles in all directions. The peak
stands on the Continental Divide. Rain falling on the
western slopes of the Divide eventually runs into the
Pacific Ocean; that falling on the eastern side runs
off into Hudson Bay, some reaches Gulf of Mexico.*

BE-WHISKERED MOUNTAIN GOAT, *native to this craggy
domain, may be encountered near trails or resorts. Tolerant
of tourists, goats often come within camera range. These
nimble animals rely on their agility to elude predators
that seek them out in their rocky lairs. Profile of this park
native decorates the boxcars of the Great Northern.*

GLACIER 225

GLACIER EXPLORING, HORSEBACK *riding, fishing are some of the attractions that make the Many Glacier area popular. (ABOVE) Rock-strewn surface of Grinnell Glacier lies just ahead of hikers, 7 miles out of Many Glacier. Stones fall from cliffs behind, are gradually carried to melting snout. Note crevasses along edge. (BELOW) Assembly of saddle horses awaits riders at Many Glacier Hotel. Chalet-style architecture typical of resorts throughout park.*

CLEAR, COLD WATER OF JOSEPHINE LAKE *reflects the bulky form of Mount Gould (9,541 ft.). Mountains within park look as big as they really are because the wide horizontal bands and strong lines of vertical joints give scale that viewer can relate to scene close by, far away.*

ANSEL ADAMS

HALF IN CANADA, HALF IN THE UNITED STATES, *Waterton Lake occupies a long glacial trench between towering crags. At the Canadian end, town of Waterton offers shopping and resort facilities, crowned by the striking Prince of Wales Hotel* (ABOVE), *perched on a promontory with a commanding view of the lake. Waterton is accessible by trail, launch, sightseeing bus, or family car. The motor launch* International (ABOVE RIGHT) *runs from Waterton to Goathaunt Camp in Montana, stops along the way to pick up hikers, let passengers explore. Here, boat is docked opposite Olson Creek, 3 miles inside Montana. Launches also run on all the major resort lakes.*

SHOWIEST OF THE PARK'S WILDFLOWERS, *beargrass is often considered the park's flower. Member of the lily family, it starts blooming in June in valleys, continues into August in high country. Like other alpine parks, Glacier puts on an extraordinary display of color after snows melt.*

GLACIER 229

YELLOWSTONE

THE GRAND OLD PARK

PARK FACTS: *Discovered:* 1807. *Established:* Mar. 1, 1872. *Size:* 3,472 sq. mi. *Altitude:* 5,314 to 11,360 ft. *Climate:* Mild summer days, cool nights, rain in June. Winter temperatures from below freezing; heavy snowfall. *Season:* All year (official season May 1-Oct. 31). *Visitors in 1964:* 1,929,316.

YELLOWSTONE IS THE "TYPICAL" NATIONAL PARK of anecdote and caricature, of plentiful over-friendly bears, of elbow-to-elbow fishermen and hopelessly tangled trout lines, and of incredible summer hordes of wandering tourists.

On the other side of the coin, Yellowstone works a magic spell in return for nothing but time and attention. It is not a place that jibes with personal time-tables. Travelers go to Yellowstone to witness things happening more than to look at static scenery, and seldom—at any site—will nature's performance coincide with one's arrival. So the visitor moves along, trusting to luck, or settles down and waits. In good time, sunlight reaches the bottom of a golden canyon and a waterfall's spray rises through rainbows. An osprey finally alights on the pinnacle-top nest in the telephoto viewfinder. The bull moose emerges from forest shadow and wades out into a marsh. A family of playful young grizzlies comes wrestling and tumbling through a wind-rippled prairie. A brown trout—big enough to feed a whole family—takes the lure and then sounds. The Sapphire Pool belches a brief alert and then explodes into snowy jets that climb for the sky.

There is hot-spring activity of one kind or another in many countries. But nowhere is there so much of it, nowhere is it so spectacular, and nowhere has it been so considerately cared for.

Neither color illustrations nor postcards can memorialize the diverse beauty of the countless ways hot water comes out of the ground in Yellowstone: the flooding colors of spectrum and algae, the transparence of bubble-starred pools dropping away into darkness, the echoed thumping of unheralded distant geysers in the night, the smell of hydrogen sulfide, the sky-flung plumes of water.

As IT HAS FOR THREE CENTURIES, *Old Faithful sends its towering plume of 12,000 gallons of boiling water into the thin mountain air. Famous the world over, the great geyser has attracted travelers to Yellowstone since 1870, when its existence was first reported to a disbelieving public.*

231

ANSEL ADAMS

So unbelievable were the tales about Yellowstone *told by the first explorers that two expeditions were sent to the region to determine the truth, if any, in their reports. This photograph, taken in 1871 by photographer W. H. Jackson, shows the second fact-finding expedition, the Geological Survey's Hayden Expedition. Reports of this party plus Jackson's photographs helped convince Congress that Yellowstone country should be made a national park.*

Although the wonders of Yellowstone were discovered in 1807 and rumors about them circulated for decades, they were laughed off as tall tales, too fantastic to believe, until nearly 1870.

Actual discovery is credited to a member of the Lewis and Clark expedition named John Colter, who left the group to explore and trap on his own. By 1837, the story of his adventures was widely enough known to have reached novelist Washington Irving who noted that Colter had given such an account of Yellowstone's "gloomy terrors, its hidden fires, smoking pits, noxious streams, and the all-pervading 'smell of brimstone,' that it received, and has ever since retained among trappers the name of 'Colter's Hell'."

Trappers wandered throughout Yellowstone for 60 years after Colter's visit, and tales about its marvels were common among them. However, little of the information reached the general public. The mountain men were a close-knit and unlettered fraternity, and they were known as braggarts and liars, and their stories were accepted as typical frontier "roarbacks."

But as settlement advanced in the territories nearby, prominent citizens began to take an interest in checking into these preposterous tales. In 1869, a party of three men spent more than a month exploring the eastern geyser basins and reported their findings to a still skeptical public. Their observations, however, spurred a more famous group to follow the trail to Yellowstone. This was the Washburn-Langford-Doane expedition, whose exploits led to the founding of the national park system, as described in the opening chapter.

This party of 19 young men, full of exuberance and wonder, systematically explored the area, keeping careful records as they progressed. They named the thermal features—favoring the Devil and all his works—but by common agreement, they refrained from naming anything for themselves. (Their names were later bestowed on some of the peaks and rivers.) After completing their survey, they met at a famous campfire at the intersection of the Gibbon, Firehole, and Madison rivers and there reached the historic decision to work for legislation to protect the wonderland from exploitation.

After returning home, they lectured, published articles in magazines and newspapers, and campaigned to have the area set aside as a public preserve. As an early result of their pressures, United States Geologist F. V. Hayden led a scientific expedition to Yellowstone to authenticate their findings. His enthusiastic endorsement of their observations, coupled with a superb set of photographs by W. H. Jackson, helped to speed the enactment of the historic legislation that created the first national park in the world in 1872.

FROM FREEMAN TILDEN'S "FOLLOWING THE FRONTIER"

CARRYING UMBRELLAS AS BADGES OF LEADERSHIP, *Indian chiefs line up to receive President Chester A. Arthur in 1883. The presidential party traveled 350 miles on horseback to visit the park, catch fish, shoot buffalo, and pow-wow with Indians en route.*

PERCHED ON THE BRITTLE FORMATIONS *of Minerva Terrace,*
a touring party of women and children strike a formal
pose for photographer Frank J. Haynes in 1888.

Unfortunately, far-sighted as the legislators were for their day, they did not provide for all eventualities in the new law nor did they appropriate funds, and the park administration struggled for years sorely handicapped.

The park was located miles from nowhere and in the midst of territory still plagued by unfriendly Indians. Just four years after creation of the park, General Custer suffered his last stand a scant 130 miles away. In 1877, the Nez Perce in the closing days of their bloody 1,600-mile retreat from Oregon, captured a party of tourists camped on Firehole River and killed two from another party. A few days later, the warriors were defeated in their final battle just outside the park. When, two years later, the park superintendent's headquarters was erected, it was equipped with a gun turret on the roof.

Even after the Indians were quieted, tourists faced an arduous trek to reach the park. In 1878, they had a choice of two routes: a northern one from Bismarck

234   YELLOWSTONE

that was 1,052 miles long—820 miles by steamboat and 232 by stagecoach—and took 12 to 14 days. The southern access from Ogden required 1,183 miles of train travel followed by 472 miles of stagecoaching, a combination that consumed 10 days.

Even after the tourists began to flow into the park, there were sticky problems in abundance. Not enough rangers were on hand to protect the geysers from vandalism, politicians gave away lucrative concessions to friends, and the "protected" game was so wantonly slaughtered, even by early park officials, that some species were nearly extinguished, most notably the buffalo. In 1883 administration was turned over to the Army, which built roads and ran the park with quiet efficiency until 1916, when the Park Service took over. Since then, affairs of this vast, complex, and over-popular park have been carried on by the Park Service and its concessioners with consummate skill.

YELLOWSTONE NATIONAL PARK

LARGEST NATIONAL PARK, *Yellowstone covers 3,472 square miles of rolling land surrounded by mountains. Geyser basins occupy less than tenth of area.*

LEGEND
Paved Roads ———
Unimproved Roads ———
Trails - - - - - -
Campsites ⋀

235

THERMAL AREAS

THE EARTH'S INNER HEAT, close to the surface of the ground all the way across the wide plateau, is the why and wherefore of Yellowstone's renown. In many parts of the park, the ground is warm or hot to the touch, and while this heating is accomplished by heated water or gases coming up through the crust, there is every likelihood that the temperature of the rock itself reaches the melting point less than a mile below the surface. Ground water moves easily into and through the porous, fissured surface rocks, eventually working its way down to depths where temperatures far exceed the boiling point, and forming reservoirs of super-

FROM OBSERVATION POINT, *you seem to have Old Faithful's eruption all to yourself. It is almost supper time and the boardwalk up Geyser Hill is deserted. With reasonable faithfulness, the geyser erupts every 61 to 67 minutes for 4 or 5 minutes and then subsides. Its display is most spectacular in cool weather or early morning when the superheated water meets cold air and condenses into billowing clouds of steam.*

Observation Point, 100 feet above the geyser, is reached by a trail from the Visitor Center. Down below spreads the barren opening in the forest that is typical of geyser basins throughout the park. Beyond the basin and Old Faithful Inn (built 1902), the Madison Plateau rises in waves of lodgepole forest, the typical cover of 90 percent of Yellowstone's acreage.

MARTIN LITTON

heated steam. Under extreme pressure, the steam seeks a way out. It may reach the atmosphere again as a steady roaring jet that becomes visible only as it condenses to vapor some distance above the ground; then it is a steam vent, or fumarole. Or it may have its exit clogged by inflowing liquid water, which it must push out of the way; then it becomes a geyser.

A typical geyser eruption may begin with a flow, or an increase in flow, of water from the orifice, accompanied by deep-seated cannonading that seems to shake the ground and indicates that the restraining pressure is off. Then the column of water in the tube is thrown upward for a few seconds, or a few minutes, by steam that continues to rumble underground and roar skyward for some time after the water is expelled. The force of the steam jet dies down as the subterranean pressure is relieved, and water again begins to fill the exhaust tube, blocking the exit of the steam and setting the stage for the next eruption.

ENDLESS VARIETY CHARACTERIZES THE EXPULSION of hot water and steam from the heated depths of the earth in the geyser basins. Where heated water is free to move to the surface, it bubbles out in hot springs. At Grand Prismatic Spring (Midway Basin), a gentle, pulsing flow covers a large area with a shallow, terraced pond. Where steam finds an easy passage to the surface, it comes out as a steam vent, or fumarole, such as the marshmallow-like formation (ABOVE RIGHT) in the Firehole Lake area that gives off wisps of steam to the accompaniment of guttural boilings and thumpings.

A GEYSER'S UNDERGROUND PLUMBING SYSTEM

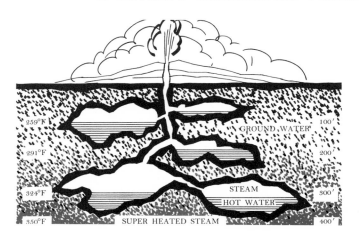

WHAT GOES ON INSIDE A GEYSER? *Water seeps down through porous volcanic soil and collects in chambers where it is turned to steam by superheated earth. The chambers all connect with a central vent which fills with water. Weight of the water in the main tube blocks escape of steam from the chambers. In time, steam is superheated to a point where it explosively expels the water in the tube into the air.*

Early in the morning *in Norris Geyser Basin, steam condenses in the cold air to form a forest of white, drifting plumes. A boardwalk safely conducts visitors through the active area. Twenty-seven geysers are located here, most of them minor performers that erupt only a few feet. Stars of the basin: Ledge Geyser, which rises 125 feet once a week; and the constantly erupting Steamboat Geyser that sometimes shoots up from its normal 20-30 feet to 380 feet.*

YELLOWSTONE 239

North of Old Faithful *is a series of geyser basins and thermal wonders close to the road to Mammoth. Castle Geyser (*above*), so-named because of its fancied resemblance to the ruins of an old castle tower, spouts 65 to 100 feet every 8 to 10 hours. It is located in Upper Geyser Basin next to the road.*

Steam rises constantly *from Fountain Geyser Pool (*right above*), one of a cluster of geysers and hot springs presumably connected by a common underground water system in Lower Geyser Basin. From the side of Roaring Mountain (*right*), steam rises from hundreds of vents. The mountain is named for a single vent that gave forth a loud roar for months in 1902 during a period of intense activity. After the opening became enlarged, the noise quieted down and the mountain now gives off its steam in relative quiet.*

YELLOWSTONE 241

242 YELLOWSTONE

HOT WATER SEEPING OUT A MOUNTAINSIDE *in the Mammoth Hot Springs area evaporates to leave level terraces of travertine. As the terrace edges grow upward, water may break through and flow down and outward to form new terraces, leaving old ones high and dry. Algae colors pools and terrace edges. In background: Mammoth, with hotel in center and former Fort Yellowstone (park headquarters) on right.*

BACK COUNTRY

HORSES AND HIKERS CAN GO over Yellowstone's gentle grades at speeds unheard of in the Sierra Nevada, Cascades, or Coast Ranges. The woods, waters, and wide open spaces beckon, yet the back-country trails are comparatively little used. Reasons are that many of Yellowstone's visitors are not used to Western mountains and would not feel at home in the wilderness; although guided horseback rides of short duration are available at several locations, there are no pack stations and there is no stock to be rented by overnight riding or hiking parties; and in the past, little or no information or encouragement has been offered to facilitate wilderness trail travel.

Most of the travel into the primitive corners of Yellowstone comes from outside the boundaries. Pack trips originating at dude ranches and pack stations around the perimeter often loop into the park, taking admirable advantage of its fine high country and productive fishing. Cooke City, 4 miles outside the Northeast Entrance, is a favorite jumping-off point for the high and rugged Absaroka Range along the east side of the park.

MARTIN LITTON

ONE OF THE ORIGINAL STAGECOACHES *that brought tourists into the park until 1917 heads for an evening cook-out in a quiet valley near Tower Junction. Here and there, wide-sweeping meadows push back the lodgepole forest and create spring wildflower parks and grazing land for antelope, deer, bison, and moose.*

BASALT COLUMNS FORM A BANDOLEER PATTERN *along the edge of the cliffs near Tower Junction. The dark band is in sharp contrast to the colorful, deeply eroded canyon wall. The basalt was deposited as a lava overflow in the dim geologic past on top of sandstones built up under an inland sea.*

A WATER WORLD FOR CANOERS *is an exclusive feature of Yellowstone National Park. Three arms of huge Yellowstone Lake and nearby Lake Shoshone are reserved for paddlers only. Motorboats that have the run of the big lake are denied entrance to these quiet bays. As these protected waters are game refuges, oarsmen can expect to see waterfowl, moose, and an occasional grizzly at the water's edge. A narrow channel between Shoshone and Lewis lakes permits portage of canoes from one to the other over a 1½-mile water trail.*

THE AWESOME GORGE OF THE YELLOWSTONE RIVER *is a stunning surprise to travelers when they first encounter it. The gentle, forested countryside scarcely prepares the visitor for such a spectacular sight. The precipitous walls glow with reds, ochres, and yellows (the park takes its name from this colorful canyon); at the head of the chasm, the river thunders over a 308-foot fall, casting rainbows in the morning sun; and small geysers jet into the turbulent water at the foot of the cliffs.*

THE PACKTRAIN PLODDING THROUGH THE WILDFLOWERS *is on its way to Cascade Corner, the mountainous southwest section of the park, noted for waterfalls, cascades, and fishing streams. An extensive trail system, originally developed by the Army for supply routes, leads to a magnificent, uncrowded backcountry.*

RIVERS MEANDER BETWEEN GRASSY
*banks in the park-like valleys of Yellow-
stone. The Firehole River snakes through
a half dozen geyser basins. In some
sections, its riverbed is warmed by
hot springs. (Oldtimers claimed the
bed was heated by fast-running water.)*

LONGER THAN ITS CARRIER, *a
3-passenger canoe is trussed down for
the ride to the lake country.*

THE ANIMALS

THERE IS TRUTH IN THE SAYING THAT Yellowstone National Park is the greatest wildlife sanctuary in the United States, but that is not so much a statement of abundance of wildlife in Yellowstone as of poverty elsewhere. Of large native animals summering on the park's 2,221,766 acres, only one species—the American elk or wapiti—is numbered in the thousands (the count has been fluctuating between 10,000 and 15,000 in recent years). The populations of black bear, moose, and pronghorn seldom if ever exceed 500 each; there may be nearly a thousand mule deer at times, but figures of 200 or so are probably tops for grizzly and bighorn. Yellowstone's "concentration" of bison amounts to an average of about one animal to 3½ square miles—proving that the thundering herd is indeed a thing of the past.

Beyond the range of the automobile, encounters with wildlife will be full of magic. If you recognize the deep, rolling call, you will pause to stalk a sandhill crane. If you see swans in the park in summer, you will know they are rare trumpeters; whistlers are spring and fall migrants only. If you have learned to handle a paddle efficiently and silently, the otter may let you come almost abreast of him before he dives. If you know how to stand or sit perfectly still, the curious antelope may move toward you instead of away from you. Small animals and birds are very much the same as in other mountain regions of the West.

FAWN, WITH SNOW ON ITS MUZZLE FROM *winter grazing, is member of the numerous clan of mule deer, beloved by the touring public for their grace and shy persistence around humans. Deer are most likely to be seen at Mammoth Hot Springs, Indian Creek, Chittenden Bridge, and West Thumb. Unlike its over-abundant cousins, the elk, the deer population within the park keeps in balance with its food supply.*

ELK PLOW THROUGH DEEP SNOW *on the winter range in search of food. The bulk of the 13,000-animal herd spends summer in the mountains and then crowds into the lowlands in winter in desperate competition for the available food. Grass is gone or covered with deep snow, trees are bare of leaves, and there is not enough food to keep all the elk alive. Hundreds die each winter, but the herd continues to grow because of absence of cougars and wolves that would keep it in balance.*

IN FEW PLACES IN THE UNITED STATES *can antelope be seen in their natural state. A herd of 350 ranges over the plains near Mammoth Hot Springs. Sharp-eyed and nervous, they are easily spooked, and if alarmed, they sweep over the fields in swift and graceful flight. Pronghorns of both sexes are armed with sharp, hollow horns that they shed each year.*

YELLOWSTONE 251

Belligerent cousins of familiar black bear, *grizzlies keep to themselves in wild areas; distinguished by shoulder hump, great size.*

Sent upstairs for safety, *cubs are taught to climb for self-protection. Black bears can "swim" up trees with ease; often perch on limbs.*

Judicial-looking bear *surveys the passing scene along the highway. The unconsciously comical poses that bears assume endear them to tourists but cause the poor beasts to receive more attention than they should for their own good.*

JOSEPH VAN WORMER

PEYTON MONCURE

CUBS STAY CLOSE TO MOTHER *for as long as a year. No bigger than a squirrel when born in early spring, they are capable of caring for themselves after a year of intensive training by the mother.*

PANHANDLING BEARS *set up shop along the main highways, take the same stations day after day to wheedle tidbits from soft-hearted tourists. Human food is unhealthful for them and dulls their appetite for natural fare. Although generally shy around people, they sometimes turn aggressive, particularly by fall when they have accumulated a summer's indignities and frustrations from dealing with the public. Dangerous when crossed or teased, they can move as swiftly as a cat.*

RAY ATKESON

BISON GRAZE IN GEYSER BASINS *in winter because warmth keeps snow melted and exposes the grass. Natural salt licks around mineral springs provide an essential part of their diet. Although a plains animal, bison have readily adapted to the park environment ever since the herd was started with an initial group of 27 purchased by Congress in 1902. There are now 400 in the park herd. Bison had nearly been exterminated by 1850 by ruthless hunting. First protective laws were passed in 1864.*

COW AND CALF IN LATE SNOW. *Cows usually give birth to one calf a year, which is born in late spring. Calves accompany their mothers to the mountains a month or two after they are born.*

AGE-LONG PARTNERS IN PLAINS LIVING, *bull and bird examine each other with respectful curiosity.*

GRAND TETON

RENDEZVOUS FOR MOUNTAINEERS

PARK FACTS: *Discovered:* 1807. *Established:* February 26, 1929; Jackson Hole added September 14, 1950. *Size:* 485 sq. mi. *Altitude:* 6,400-13,766 feet. *Climate:* Warm, dry summers with cool nights, occasional storms. Winter snows average 120 inches. *Season:* All year. *Visitors in 1964:* 2,456,836.

THE TETONS RISE FROM THE COUNTRYSIDE around them like a craggy island from the sea. Few American landscapes are more dramatic, more awe-inspiring, or more beautiful than these mountains of northwest Wyoming. From 100 or even 50 miles away, they seem little more than wisps of cloud. As you draw closer they begin to assume more substantial form, then suddenly their full impact strikes you, as if they had exploded from the level floor of Jackson Hole. Many ranges are more extensive and many mountains are higher, gradually ascending with foothills as stepping-stones. But there is nothing gradual about the Tetons in their sheer, 7,000-foot rise from the level plain.

Grand Teton National Park contains a little less than 500 square miles. It is smaller than many, but within it is packed more scenery, more history, more animals, more boating and fishing, more hiking and mountain climbing, more opportunity for enjoyment and relaxation than in many areas twice its size.

The scenic grandeur of the Tetons is that of the Sierra Nevada or of the Rockies telescoped into a range less than 40 miles long. The majesty of the Grand Teton, with its 13,766-foot summit and its companion peaks, Mount Owen, Mount Moran, and South and Middle Tetons, reflected in the placid waters of Jackson Lake, is almost overwhelming. Glaciers nestle in the cirques, streams tumble and cascade from high places, mountain lakes reflect the blue of a Wyoming sky, and in the valley below, the Snake River winds its way to Jackson Lake and on eventually to the Columbia.

Two hundred miles of trails beckon the hiker and horseman—trails that lead to lakes buried in virgin wilderness, through deep canyons, over high passes above timberline, and to mountaintops. There are trails for every mood and

ALWAYS IN VIEW FROM NEARLY EVERY PART OF THE PARK, *jagged Teton Range catches and holds the eye. "Mountains without foothills," the peaks rise straight from the valley. Here, viewed from a mountain trail, is Cathedral Group.*

257

THE MAGIC OF THE GRAND TETONS *has enthralled men ever since the range was first discovered. Indians, fur-traders, cattlemen, and tourists have in succession felt the spell of this dramatic country. The symmetrical mountains take on varying coloration, ranging from grey to blue to purple, their shadows softened by the configuration of the rock, often shading imperceptibly into the cloud-filled sky. In the foreground, the Snake begins its winding course to the Columbia River, 1,000 miles away.*

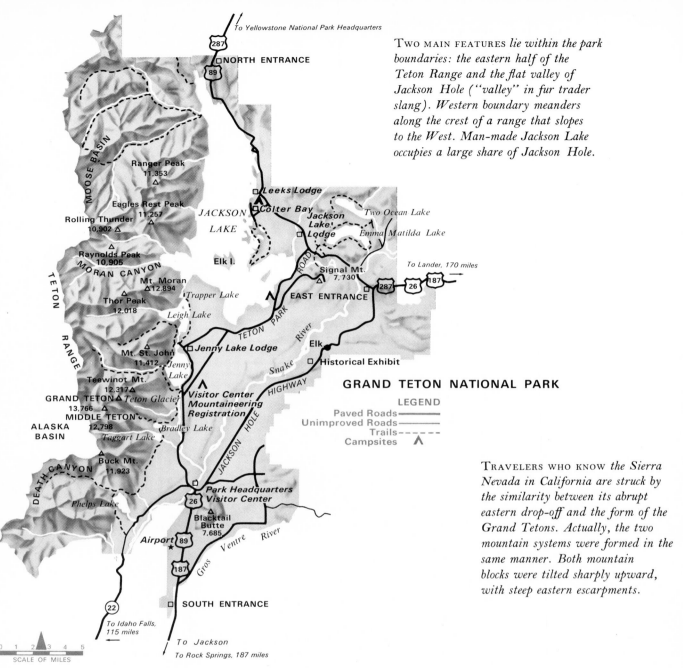

To Yellowstone National Park Headquarters

287

□ **NORTH ENTRANCE**

89

TWO MAIN FEATURES *lie within the park boundaries: the eastern half of the Teton Range and the flat valley of Jackson Hole ("valley" in fur trader slang). Western boundary meanders along the crest of a range that slopes to the West. Man-made Jackson Lake occupies a large share of Jackson Hole.*

MOOSE BASIN

Ranger Peak
11,353
△

□△ **Leeks Lodge**

Eagles Rest Peak
11,257
△

JACKSON LAKE

□ **Colter Bay**

Jackson Lake Lodge

Rolling Thunder
10,902 △

□

Two Ocean Lake

Emma Matilda Lake

Reynolds Peak
10,905
△

Elk I.

MORAN CANYON

Signal Mt.
7,730
△

To Lander, 170 miles

Mt. Moran
△12,894

Trapper Lake

EAST ENTRANCE

287 26 187

TETON RANGE

Thor Peak
12,018 △

Leigh Lake

River

Elk

TETON PARK

Mt. St. John
11,412 △

□ **Jenny Lake Lodge**

Snake

□ Historical Exhibit

Teewinot Mt.
12,317△

Jenny Lake

HIGHWAY

GRAND TETON NATIONAL PARK

GRAND TETON
13,766 △

△*Teton Glacier*

∧ **Visitor Center Mountaineering Registration**

LEGEND

Paved Roads ——————
Unimproved Roads ——————
Trails - - - - - -
Campsites ∧

MIDDLE TETON
12,798

Bradley Lake

ALASKA BASIN

Taggart Lake

JACKSON HOLE

DEATH CANYON

Buck Mt.
11,923 △

Phelps Lake

TRAVELERS WHO KNOW *the Sierra Nevada in California are struck by the similarity between its abrupt eastern drop-off and the form of the Grand Tetons. Actually, the two mountain systems were formed in the same manner. Both mountain blocks were tilted sharply upward, with steep eastern escarpments.*

□ **Park Headquarters Visitor Center**

26

Blacktail Butte
7,685

Airport
★ 89

Gros Ventre River

187

□ **SOUTH ENTRANCE**

22

To Idaho Falls, 115 miles

To Jackson

To Rock Springs, 187 miles

0 1 2 3 4 5
SCALE OF MILES

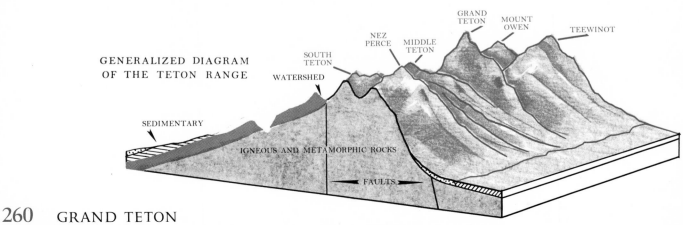

GENERALIZED DIAGRAM
OF THE TETON RANGE

SOUTH TETON

NEZ PERCE

MIDDLE TETON

GRAND TETON

MOUNT OWEN

TEEWINOT

WATERSHED

SEDIMENTARY

IGNEOUS AND METAMORPHIC ROCKS

← FAULTS →

every temperament, from short, level walks to long, strenuous hikes. The Tetons have long been the objective of serious climbers from this country and Europe—and few American peaks are more respected. Those who know are reluctant to rank the Alps above the Tetons in difficulty of ascent. It is little wonder that the last two peaks in this range were not conquered until 1930. Such climbs are not for the novice; for those who respond to the challenge, a mountaineering school operates here.

The history of the area has a fascination all its own. Probably the first white man to penetrate it was John Colter of the Lewis and Clark expedition in 1807. He was followed by the Astorians, who crossed Teton Pass in 1811. French-Canadian trappers in 1819 saw the three peaks from the west and referred to them as *Les Trois Tetons* (The Three Breasts).

From 1824 on, the area was a center of fur trade activity. Mountain men, among them Jim Bridger, William Sublette, Thomas Fitzpatrick, Jedediah Smith, Joseph Meek, knew the country well. One of the largest of the fur rendezvous, that of 1832, was held in Pierre's Hole across the range to the west. Still later in the 80's, it was cattle country; the town of Jackson yet retains a certain flavor of the days before tourists replaced steers in importance. Fictional characters, too, have furthered Jackson's fame. Here it was that the Virginian said, "When you call me that, *smile*," and it was to Honeymoon Island on Leigh Lake that he brought his bride. Owen Wister's book did much to publicize the romance of the Tetons.

As early as 1920, Jackson Hole was becoming known for its versions of the dude ranch, an institution that has grown in popularity over the years. Through it many an Easterner has fallen in love with the freedom and informality of Western life. It is here, for the first time, that many a tenderfoot has used a Western saddle and worn Western clothes; experienced the odors of sagebrush flats, pine forests, and a campfire; found luxury in falling asleep under the stars, and pleasure in the wash of windlashed rain in his face during a mountain storm.

Jackson Hole contains one of the largest remaining elk herds, but since it summers in the high country, the summer visitor will probably not see it. The Jackson Hole Wildlife Refuge is located within the park boundaries, however, and here both elk and bison can be viewed at close range.

No road penetrates the mountainous west side of this park, but on the east, good highways traverse it in a general north-south direction. One skirts the east shore of Jackson and Jenny lakes at the very foot of the peaks reflected in their mirrors. The Jackson Hole Highway, a few miles to the east, follows the Snake River and affords a better opportunity to view the range as a whole.

Excellent campgrounds and picnic areas, as well as boat ramps, are strategically placed, and lodges and guest ranches are numerous.

The season of greatest activity is from early June through Labor Day, although the highway from Jackson through the park and over Togwotee Pass to the east is kept open throughout the winter. The park is approached from all four directions by highway.

FROM ONE-DAY WALKS TO ONE-WEEK PACK TRIPS, *the Tetons offer a wide
choice of trail travel. Easiest trails run along the chain of lakes at
the foot of the mountains. Other, tougher ones climb up the glaciated
canyons separating the tall peaks to a high country similar to California's Sierra,
but more lonely. In this upland, few hikers come swinging along alone
with fishing rod and knapsack, for this is no land for the footloose explorers.
Serious campers engage a guide and arrange to have their supplies brought in
by packtrain. The pack string jogging along above is headed for a high camp.*

HIKERS' VIEW OF JACKSON HOLE *from the Glacier Trail, which zigzags up
from Jenny Lake through mountainside forest and steep-sloping meadows.
The whole sweep of Jackson Hole is in full view through every opening until
the trail flattens out on a high bench. Immediately below: Bradley
and Taggart Lakes and in the distance, Blacktail Butte.*

GRAND TETON   263

MAGNET FOR MOUNTAINEERS

THE JAGGED SPIRES OF THE TETONS *attract mountain climbers from all over the world. First attempts in the 1870's to scale the Grand Teton failed, but by now several thousand mountaineers have entered their names in the log on the summit.*

There are at least 16 basic routes up the "Grand," ranging in difficulty from third to fifth-class climbs, in mountaineering language. The third-class climb cannot be made alone, and the fifth-class routes are attempted only by expert teams. Permits are required and are issued only to climbers of proven ability. A school at Jenny Lake trains novices in the basic techniques. The post-graduate exercise is a climb up one of the easier routes on the Grand.

The essence of mountaineering is the calculated conquest of a peak, not harrowing acrobatics. A few climbing techniques made safe by the use of simple but reliable tools will get a man to his goal in these most difficult of American peaks.

BASIC TOOLS OF MOUNTAINEERING

BECAUSE THEIR LIVES *literally depend on their gear, mountaineers use only the topmost quality pitons and fresh, pretested nylon rope.*

1. PITONS *are driven into rock cracks to anchor ropes. Of high-test metal, can resist pull of 10G's or sudden strain of 5G's if properly driven.*
2. CARABINER *is snap ring that clips to piton, acts as pulley for rapelling, belaying.*
3. HAMMER *is prime tool. Blunt end for driving pitons; sharp end to test strength of fractured rock, chip away unsafe rock for solid hold.*
4. CLEATS *on boots assure secure grip on narrow ledges.*

RAPELLING IS QUICKEST MEANS OF DESCENT. *Climber secures himself to one end of doubled rope passed through carabiner, lowers himself to firm footing, and retrieves his rope. Used at X-points on climbing map on opposite page.*

BELAYING IS USED *to get past tough spots. Man edging around rock is attached by rope to leader above him who is firmly anchored and ready to belay the fall of the climber should he slip. (Used at Z-points on the map.)*

FINGER-AND-TOE WORK *like this calls for mastery of climbing art; used at Y-points on the map. Leader of climbing party chooses the route with all members of party in mind. When he reaches safe point, he becomes belayer for next man behind him.*

CLIMBING MAP OF THE
GRAND TETON, NORTH FACE

X—Rappel points
Y—Finger-and-toe climbs
Z—Difficult belays.

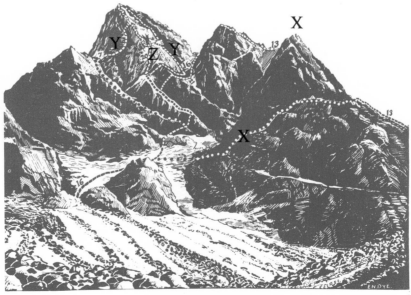

E. N. DYE, FROM SIERRA CLUB'S "CLIMBER'S GUIDE TO TETON RANGE"

PRECISE KNOWLEDGE OF SUCCESSFUL ROUTES *is set out in books on often-climbed ranges. Sixteen routes lead to the summit of Grand Teton, some are numbered on this map.*

GRAND TETON   265

Fur-trade rendezvousing, *cattle rustling, sheep wars are among the dramatic events that have taken place in tranquil looking Jackson Hole. Fur traders assembled here in the 1830's in wary company with the Shoshones; after the supply of fur-bearing animals declined, cattle were run here—initially by rustlers who capitalized on the remoteness of the area and later by European promoters who were nearly wiped out by blizzards in the 1870's; in 1892, sheep were slaughtered by cattlemen in an attempt to keep them out of the Hole. Now the valley is a peaceful setting for dude ranchers and tourists.*

ANSEL ADAMS

LEFT TO RIGHT: *Mount Moran (12,594 ft.), named for landscape painter Thomas Moran in 1872; Bivouac Peak (11,045 ft.), Eagles Rest Peak (11,257 ft.), and Ranger Peak (11,353 ft.). In foreground, Jackson Lake.*

5,000 ELK WINTERING IN SNOW-COVERED JACKSON HOLE. *Once nearly extinct, the elk (wapiti) are now almost more numerous than the winter range can support. The herds spend summer months in Yellowstone and migrate south in the fall, heading for lower and less forbidding area to spend the winter. En route between the two national parks, many are bagged by hunters who wait for them in the unprotected zone between.*

268   GRAND TETON

POWERFUL AND TRUCULENT BULL MOOSE *is best viewed from a reasonable distance. Moose usually summer in the higher mountains, but they may sometimes be seen browsing alder leaves around beaver ponds or grazing in the meadows.*

SPLIT-RAIL FENCING ALONG THE BYWAYS *emphasizes the "Western" atmosphere around Jackson Hole. This picturesque barrier keeps elk from invading nearby ranches.*

GRAND TETON 269

HAWAII VOLCANOES

HOME OF THE VOLCANO GODDESS

Park facts: *Discovered:* By missionaries in 1830's. *Established:* Hawaii Nat. Park, Aug. 1, 1916; and Haleakala separated from it, 1961; renamed Hawaii Volcanoes. *Size:* 344 sq. mi. *Altitude:* Sea level to 13,680 ft. *Climate:* From semitropical to subarctic. *Season:* All year. *Visitors in 1964:* 517,932.

The eighteen Hawaiian Islands are actually the tips of a massive range of volcanic mountains that rise from the bottom of the Pacific. They formed slowly, in the way of shield volcanoes: Liquid lava erupted and spread in broad sheets; as these hardened to build up successive layers, great inverted saucers or "shields" took shape. Thus over the ages the mountains grew up from the ocean floor, until their peaks finally rose above the surface of the sea.

They were not all created at the same time. The big island of Hawaii is the youngest, and on it are found the only volcanoes in the range that are still active: Mauna Loa and Kilauea. These two are among the most exciting in existence, and their crests are the principal features of Hawaii Volcanoes National Park.

Mauna Loa, "Long Mountain," is in fact the biggest mountain in the world, although most of it is hidden under the waters of the Pacific. Its base is on the ocean floor, and the lower 18,000 feet of its elevation lie below the water. The summit is 13,680 feet above sea level, so its total size is astonishing: a mass 100 times that of Mount Shasta, a height more than 2,000 feet greater than that of Mount Everest.

Mauna Loa has a large crater or caldera, called Mokuaweoweo: Island of Lurid Burning. Within this great basin are several summit craters that have erupted in the past and partially covered the caldera floor with lava.

Although smaller than Mauna Loa, Kilauea gets even more attention because it is so accessible. Visitors can park their cars within 200 feet of its summit or drive all the way around the top on good roads. At some time in the past the mountaintop collapsed to form a small caldera, or cauldron, and within this basin

Effervescent fountain of fire flares up 1,000 feet from the crater of Kilauea during the eruption of 1959. In the first stages of an eruption, fire fountains break through the crust, are followed by a flood of fiery lava.

271

ROBERT WENKAM

are several craters, largest of which is called Halemaumau: House of Everlasting Fire. Prior to 1924, a lake of molten lava constantly rose and fell inside Halemaumau; and within recent years, the crater has provided some of the most dramatic demonstrations to be seen anywhere. Wild fountains spray upward, and lava pours out of cracks in the floor.

This is the legendary home of Pele, the Hawaiian goddess of volcanoes. She is gone a good deal, visiting other islands of the Pacific; but Hawaiians always know when she returns, because of renewed activity in Halemaumau.

Eruptions within the craters of Mauna Loa and Kilauea are relatively harmless, extremely exciting, and fascinating to watch—and thousands of spectators have looked in on them from the crater rims. But the eruptions also break out in other areas. Both of the volcanoes have huge fissures in their flanks, and when underground pressures grow great enough to force the lava out these openings, it starts a slow and deadly advance down the slopes toward the sea, destroying crops and villages in its path. In 1960 the village of Kapoho was buried.

The active interest of Hawaiian citizens in protecting and preserving their volcanoes led to establishment in 1916 of Hawaii National Park. It included not only portions of Mauna Loa and Kilauea but also part of Haleakala, on the island of Maui. In 1961 the Haleakala section became a separate national park, and the Mauna Loa-Kilauea section was given its present name.

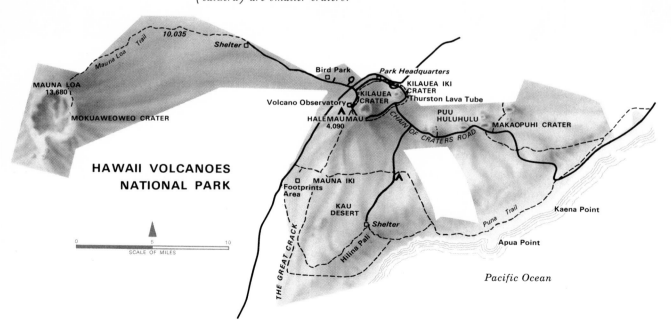

Two GREAT VOLCANOES *dominate the park's terrain: Mauna Loa and Kilauea. Formed by gentle outpourings of lava over the centuries, they are shaped like inverted saucers. Within each massive crater (caldera) are smaller craters.*

HAWAII VOLCANOES NATIONAL PARK

SCALE OF MILES

Long view across the caldera of *Kilauea, sunk deep in the restless earth, to the flattened dome of Mauna Loa 25 miles away. The summit of Mauna Loa is 10,000 feet higher than that of Kilauea.*

HAWAII VOLCANOES 273

A RIVER OF MOLTEN LAVA *once swept through this tube and poured out of Kilauea Iki (the "smaller"). As the lava streamed out of the side of the volcano, it baked its own conduit of rock. The Thurston Lava Tube is reached by a short trail from the road that passes through a lush jungle.*

A CRATER WITHIN A CRATER, *Halemaumau is the active part of Kilauea. From the floor of this oval-shaped vent, ½ mile across and several hundred feet deep, have roared spectacular fire fountains and lava flows, the most recent in 1954. Lava brims over the rim of the inner crater and flows onto the floor of the great caldera, whose encircling walls keep it contained.*

DEVASTATED BY THE ERUPTION OF 1959, *the skeletal remains of an ohia forest stand as bleak reminders of the destructive power of a volcano. The dead forest is located to the leeward of a cinder cone formed by this eruption.*

SOLIDIFIED INTO SWIRLING FLOW PATTERNS, *the lava that poured out of Kilauea in ages past covers a large area in the park. Best seen in the Kau desert where it is not covered with vegetation. The crust is brittle, collapses under foot.*

ANSEL ADAMS

ALONG THE SHORELINE HIGHWAY, *waves smash against the cliffs formed of chunks of lava and wrinkled layers of old lava flow. The rock wall and palm trees mark the site of an abandoned settlement at Kamoamoa.*

A TANGLE OF FERNS, *some as large as small trees, share a jungle luxuriance with the scrubby ohia trees in the eastern part of the park. The ohia blossoms are noted for their beauty. Known as* lehua, *these scarlet, feathery blooms are the official flower of the island of Hawaii.*

ROBERT WENKAM

HALEAKALA

THE MOON ON EARTH

PARK FACTS: *Established:* Part of Hawaii Nat. Park, Aug. 1, 1916; separate status, July 1, 1961. *Size:* 41 sq. mi. *Altitude:* 3,847-10,023 ft. *Climate:* Cool, windy. *Season:* All year. *Visitors, 1964:* 87,850.

Most of the eastern part of the Hawaiian island of Maui is a weirdly beautiful wasteland created by the fiery outpourings of a huge, now dormant volcano. The sleeping giant is called Haleakala: "House of the Sun."

At sea level the great mountain is 33 miles long and 24 miles wide. The elevation at its summit is 10,023 feet—high enough for snow flurries in winter. From the glassed-in Puu Ulaula Observatory at the top, visitors can see as far as 130 miles on clear days. In one direction the slope drops away to the sea; in another, the distant peaks of Mauna Loa and Mauna Kea, on the island of Hawaii, are visible. And in the foreground is the curious landscape of the vast Haleakala Crater, its floor 3,000 feet below the summit, its circumference 21 miles.

The bowl is pocked with numerous smaller craters and studded with cones formed of the cinders, pumice, ash, and spatter blown from volcanic vents. The tallest of these multicolored forms, Puu O Maui, rises 1,000 feet above the surrounding level.

Although Haleakala has not been active since the mid-eighteenth century, it is considered dormant rather than extinct; one indication that it is not dead is the earthquake activity recorded periodically on Maui.

There are several good vantage points along the rim drive to the summit, including Leleiwi and Kalahaku overlooks and the Haleakala Observatory. All look across to the peak called Hanakauhi, "Maker of Mists," which is often wreathed in clouds.

Most of the crater is nearly barren of plant life, but in the northeast corner is a surprise—an oasis of trees, grasses, and ferns. This spot receives 150 inches of rain a year, and the soil conditions are right for vegetation. A few plants

THE WEST WALL OF HALEAKALA CRATER, *viewed from the observatory, slopes 2,500 feet down into the caldera, its surface covered with smooth cinders, blown on top of the original rocky wall by trade winds. Clouds are billowing in from Koolau Gap, one of the two valleys within the caldera.*

exist elsewhere in the crater; one is the rare silversword, found only on the islands of Maui and Hawaii. When this odd plant matures (within 4 to 20 years) with a tall, fat stalk, it bears a hundred or more small, purplish flowers. After blooming, it dies.

Two main trails lead into Haleakala Crater, where they branch into a network that totals about 30 miles. Hikers and horseback riders will find many exotic formations, including lava tubes, and a colorful part of the trail called Pele's Paintpot. Stone monuments left by the early Hawaiians are also of special interest.

In the Hosmer Grove and Paliku areas of the park, there are birds in surprising number and variety. A dozen kinds of introduced birds share the sanctuary with natives; the rare nene (Hawaiian goose) is being reintroduced to the island. No mammals are native to the park, but there are some immigrant pigs, goats, and smaller animals.

Haleakala was included (along with Mauna Loa and Kilauea, on the island of Hawaii) in Hawaii National Park when it was established in 1916. In 1961, a division of that park resulted in redesignating the Mauna Loa-Kilauea section as Hawaii Volcanoes National Park and the Maui section as Haleakala National Park.

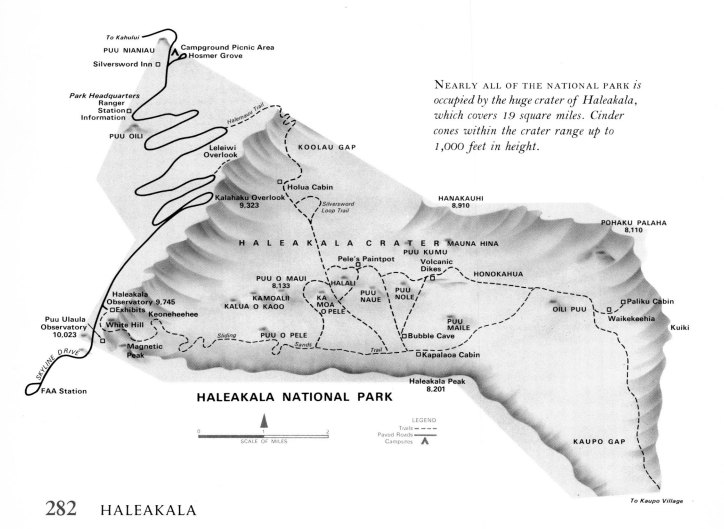

NEARLY ALL OF THE NATIONAL PARK *is occupied by the huge crater of Haleakala, which covers 19 square miles. Cinder cones within the crater range up to 1,000 feet in height.*

HALEAKALA NATIONAL PARK

SCALE OF MILES

LEGEND
Trails ---
Paved Roads ▬
Campsites ▲

THE FULL IMMENSITY OF THE CALDERA, *a great basin 7 miles by 3, can best be seen from the air.*
From its floor rise cinder cones that last erupted in the late 1700's—and may again some day.

ROBERT WENKAM

HALEAKALA   283

ONE OF THE THREE PARK SERVICE CABINS *that offer shelter to hikers or horseback riders in the crater is located in a green haven (150 inches of rain) in the barren waste.*

RARE SILVERSWORD PLANT *is found only in Haleakala and on the island of Hawaii. The small lavender blossoms are borne on the large single stalk only once in the plant's lifetime, and the plant dies immediately after blooming. Interval of bloom may be any time from 4 to 20 years.*

EERIE AND FORBIDDING, *cinder-strewn surface of the crater has the look of another planet. Fist-size cinders formed by sudden cooling of lava expelled into the air.*

MAN IS DWARFED BY THE MOON-LIKE *landscape within the vast crater. Nearly
30 miles of trail weave a path among the cinder cones and other volcanic
curiosities. Hikers can spend up to 3 days in the basin without retracing.*

GRAINS OF VOLCANIC GLASS *that form the cinder cones
reflect the sun in a changing array of color. Each grain
acts as a miniature prism and reflects the sun's rays
differently at different hours of the day, creating scenes
that range from monotonous to brightly colored landscapes.*

JOSEF MUENCH

STATE BIRD OF HAWAII, *the nene (Hawaiian goose) was reintroduced to the island in 1962 after becoming nearly extinct. This beautiful bird can be seen in the crater near the Paliku cabin near the western rim.*

PARK FACTS

DIGEST FOR THE TRAVELER, FACT COLLECTOR

ACCESS TO WESTERN PARKS

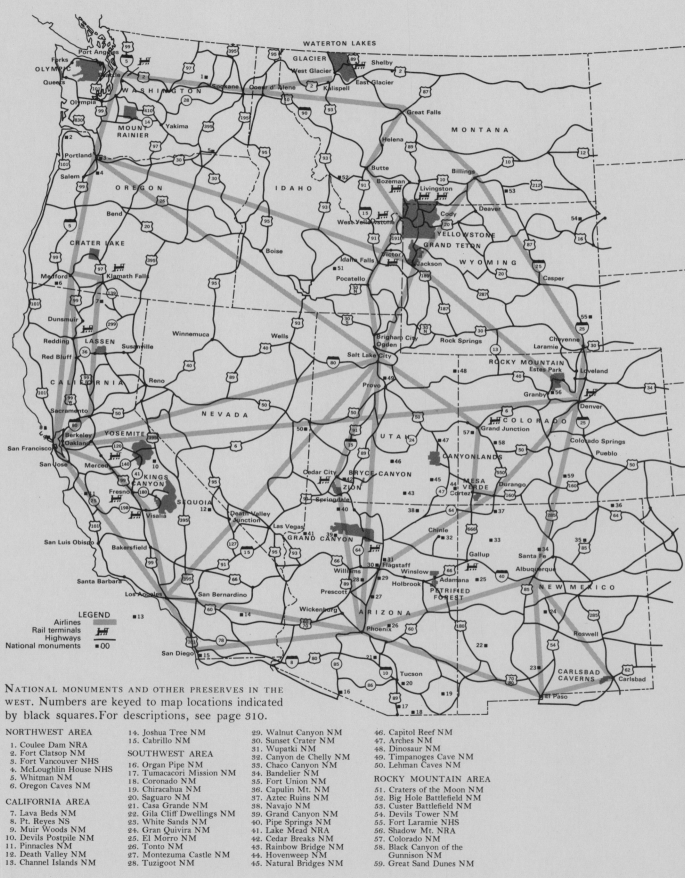

LEGEND
- Airlines
- Rail terminals
- Highways
- National monuments ■00

NATIONAL MONUMENTS AND OTHER PRESERVES IN THE
WEST. Numbers are keyed to map locations indicated
by black squares. For descriptions, see page 310.

NORTHWEST AREA
1. Coulee Dam NRA
2. Fort Clatsop NM
3. Fort Vancouver NHS
4. McLoughlin House NHS
5. Whitman NM
6. Oregon Caves NM

CALIFORNIA AREA
7. Lava Beds NM
8. Pt. Reyes NS
9. Muir Woods NM
10. Devils Postpile NM
11. Pinnacles NM
12. Death Valley NM
13. Channel Islands NM

14. Joshua Tree NM
15. Cabrillo NM

SOUTHWEST AREA
16. Organ Pipe NM
17. Tumacacori Mission NM
18. Coronado NM
19. Chiracahua NM
20. Saguaro NM
21. Casa Grande NM
22. Gila Cliff Dwellings NM
23. White Sands NM
24. Gran Quivira NM
25. El Morro NM
26. Tonto NM
27. Montezuma Castle NM
28. Tuzigoot NM

29. Walnut Canyon NM
30. Sunset Crater NM
31. Wupatki NM
32. Canyon de Chelly NM
33. Chaco Canyon NM
34. Bandelier NM
35. Fort Union NM
36. Capulin Mt. NM
37. Aztec Ruins NM
38. Navajo NM
39. Grand Canyon NM
40. Pipe Springs NM
41. Lake Mead NRA
42. Cedar Breaks NM
43. Rainbow Bridge NM
44. Hovenweep NM
45. Natural Bridges NM

46. Capitol Reef NM
47. Arches NM
48. Dinosaur NM
49. Timpanoges Cave NM
50. Lehman Caves NM

ROCKY MOUNTAIN AREA
51. Craters of the Moon NM
52. Big Hole Battlefield NM
53. Custer Battlefield NM
54. Devils Tower NM
55. Fort Laramie NHS
56. Shadow Mt. NRA
57. Colorado NM
58. Black Canyon of the
    Gunnison NM
59. Great Sand Dunes NM

PARK	BY CAR	BY PLANE	BY TRAIN	BY BUS
MOUNT McKINLEY	Via Denali Hwy. which connects with Richardson Hwy. at Parson (June 1–Sept 1).	3,000 ft. airstrip for small, private and non-scheduled aircraft. Airport serving flights from Fairbanks and Anchorage 10 mi. E of Nenana River. Rent-a-car.	Alaska Railroad has daily summer service from Fairbanks and Anchorage.	No bus connections.
OLYMPIC	From S: US 101 via Olympia or Grays Harbor area. Ferries across Puget Sound.	West Coast has daily round trip flights between Seattle and Port Angeles.	No service on Olympic Peninsula. Closest rail terminal: Seattle.	Western Greyhound from Seattle. North Coast Lines on Olympic Peninsula.
MOUNT RAINIER	All year: US 410 from Tacoma to Cayuse Pass, St. 5 Cayuse Pass to Ohanepecosh Hot Springs. St. 5 to Nisqually entrance, park road to Paradise. Other park roads closed in winter.	Closest airports: Seattle-Tacoma International: Yakima.	No service to park. Closest rail terminal: Seattle.	No bus connections. Closest bus terminal: Seattle.
CRATER LAKE	From W: St. 62 connects thru Medford with US 99, 199, 101. From S: St. 62 connects with US 97. From N: St. 230 connects with US 97 (closed winter).	West Coast Airlines and United Air Lines to Medford; West Coast to Klamath Falls; connecting concessioner buses serve both airports in summer.	Southern Pacific to Klamath Falls, connecting concessioner buses in summer.	Greyhound and Trailways buses to Klamath Falls. Buses to park in summer.
LASSEN VOLCANIC	From NW: St. 89 from Mt. Shasta City or St. 44 to Manzanita Lake. From SW: St. 36 via Red Bluff. From SE: St. 89.	Nearest airports at Redding and Red Bluff, served by Pacific Air Lines; concessioner buses meet plane in summer on request.	Southern Pacific to Redding; Western Pacific to Keddie.	Red Bluff and Susanville to Mineral, all year. Redding to Manzanita Lake, June 15–Sept 15.
YOSEMITE	From W: St. 140; St. 120 (closed winter). From S: St. 41. From E: St. 120 (closed winter).	Merced served by United Air Lines; Fresno by United, TWA, and Pacific. Concessioner buses serve Merced all year; Fresno, in summer only.	Southern Pacific and Santa Fe trains operate north and south to Merced and Fresno. Concessioner buses from Merced all year; from Fresno in summer.	Pacific Greyhound and Trailways operate north and south to Merced and Fresno. Concessioner buses from Merced all year; Lake Tahoe and Fresno in summer. Write for time tables.
SEQUOIA AND KINGS CANYON	St. 180 from Fresno or St. 198 and 65 from Visalia. Generals Hwy. connects the two parks.	United Air Lines serves Visalia; met by concessioner buses.	Southern Pacific and Santa Fe passengers met by concessioner buses at Visalia and Tulare. Santa Fe debarks at Hanford, sends Santa Fe buses to Visalia.	Greyhound to Visalia and Tulare. Concessioner buses meet stages. Write for schedule.
GRAND CANYON	North Rim: on paved road which leaves US 89A at Jacobs Lake, Ariz.; closed mid-Oct to mid-May. South Rim: paved road off US 66 via Williams and Flagstaff, Ariz.; US 89 via Cameron, Ariz.	South Rim: Flagstaff airport served by Frontier from Phoenix and other cities; bus to Grand Canyon Vill. Phoenix served by TWA, Western, American. North Rim: Nearest airport, Cedar City.	South Rim: local train makes daily round trip in summer. Connects with certain through trains.	North Rim: from Cedar City, Utah, June thru August. South Rim: service from Williams and Flagstaff.
BRYCE CANYON	From US 89 via Utah-12; all year.	Bonanza from Phoenix to Cedar City, connecting with Salt Lake City; Bryce Canyon airport for private planes.	Union Pacific trains met at Lund by concessioner buses.	Mainline buses met at Cedar City by concessioner buses.
ZION	US 89; from E and W connect with Utah-15.	Bonanza Airlines serves Cedar City, Utah.	Nearest terminal is Cedar City.	Regular concessioner bus service during summer, by arrangement at other times.
PETRIFIED FOREST	From E: US 66 crosses park near Painted Desert. From S, W, SW: US 180 to park road.	Frontier Airlines serves Flagstaff, Ariz., combines with bus to serve Gallup, New Mexico.	Nearest terminal at Holbrook, Ariz.	Taxi service from Holbrook and Winslow, Ariz.
MESA VERDE	US 160 (which connects to several major highways).	Frontier Airlines to Durango and Cortez; Colo.; daily flights. Rent-a-car service.	Nearest terminals are at Grand Junction, Colo. and Gallup, New Mexico.	Continental Trailways to park from Durango to Cortez.
CARLSBAD CAVERNS	US 62-180 via Carlsbad and El Paso.	Trans-Texas Airlines provides daily service to airport at city of Carlsbad.	Santa Fe serves Carlsbad; Texas and Pacific, Rock Island, and Southern Pacific serve El Paso.	Carlsbad Caverns Coaches serve the park from city of Carlsbad and El Paso.
ROCKY MOUNTAIN	From E: US 34 via Loveland; St. 66 via Longmont; St. 7 via Lyons and Raymond. From W: via Grand Lake on US 34 from junction with US 40 near Granby.	Major airlines to Denver; Frontier and Western Airlines to Cheyenne.	Major lines to Denver; way stations include Boulder; Fort Collins, Granby, Greeley, Longmont, Loveland.	Summer connection to park by Transportation Co. Write them at 1805 Broadway, Denver.
GLACIER	On US 2 and US 89; off US 91 and 93. Passes closed Oct-May.	West Coast Airlines to Kalispell (west). Airport transp. limited; arrange in advance.	Great Northern trains met at West Glacier and East Glacier by concessioner buses.	Mainline buses met by concessioner buses at Missoula, Mont. on west; at Shelby, Great Falls on east; concessioner buses connect with Canadian Greyhound to north.
YELLOWSTONE	From N: US 89 thru Gardiner, Mont., all year. From NE: US 12 via Cooke City, Mont.* From E: US 14/20 via Cody, Wyo.* From S: US 287 via Moran, Grand Teton N.P.* From W: US 191 via N. Yellowstone.* *Entrance closed winter.	Western Airlines direct service to West Yellowstone from Salt Lake City and connecting routes; taxi and car rental at airport. Frontier to Jackson, Wyo. from Billings, Salt Lake City. Northwest Orient to Billings, connect with Frontier; to Great Falls, to connect with Western.	Park buses meet Northern Pacific at Gardiner and Silver Gate, Mont.; Chicago, Burlington and Quincy Railroad at Cody, Wyo.; Union Pacific at W. Yellowstone, Mont. and Moran, Wyo.; Chicago, St. Paul and Pacific at Gallatin, Mont.	N. entrance served by Central Greyhound Lines to Livingstone, Mont., and Northern Pacific Transport to Gardiner, Mont. E. entrance served by Continental Trailways to Cody, Wyo. W. entrance served by Western Greyhound to W. Yellowstone. Park buses to all points in park. Write concessioner.
GRAND TETON	From SW: US 26 and 89 via Snake River Canyon; from W: Wyo-22 or Ida-33 from US 191 near Sugar City, Ida.; not rec. for trailers. From N: US 89 and 287 from Yellowstone (June-Oct).	Frontier Airlines to Jackson from Salt Lake City, Riverson, Wyo., Idaho Falls, Ida.; connects with mainliners at Denver, Cheyenne, Billings. Airport trans. available.	Union Pacific trains met at Victor, Ida. by concessioner buses.	From Yellowstone: daily bus to Jackson Lake Lodge; from Rock Springs, Wyo., stages to Jackson. Write to concessioner.

HAWAII VOLCANOES AND HALEAKALA:

Islands reached by airline or steamship from Los Angeles, San Francisco, and Seattle. Inter-island scheduled flights from Honolulu to Hilo and Kailua-Kona; from Honolulu to Maui. Taxi service, car rental at the airports. Unscheduled steamships from Honolulu. Information: Hawaii Visitors Bureau, 2051 Kalakaua Ave., Honolulu, Hawaii.

TRAVELERS' GUIDE

MT. McKINLEY

INFORMATION: Superintendent, McKinley Park, Alaska, 99755.

ACCOMMODATIONS—CAMPING: *Camps:* 7; sites: 106. *Season:* June 1-Sept. 1. *Limit:* None. *Trailers:* None over 15 ft. advised beyond Teklanika Camp. No utility hookups. *Private grounds:* Camp Denali (outside park).

ACCOMMODATIONS—RESORTS: *Reservations:* May 15-Sept. 30: Mgr., McKinley Park Hotel, McKinley, Alaska; Oct. 1-May 14: McKinley Natl. Park Co., 312 Valley Bldg., Tucson, Ariz. *Type:* Med.-priced rooms. *Season:* May 26-Sept. 10.

ACTIVITIES—SUMMER: *Hiking:* 8 mi. of trails. *Packing:* Outfitter in Lignite has permit. *Fishing:* Few streams— arctic graylings; Wonder Lk.—trout; ponds—Dolly Varden; no license reqd. *Boating:* No rentals; get permission for private boats, no motors. *Swimming:* Wonder Lk., Horseshoe Lk., some ponds for the hardy. *Rock climbing and ice climbing:* Both; permission reqd. for mountains over 10,000 ft. *Tours:* Buses daily from hotel to Eilson Visitor Center; Marino Loop trail. *Self-guiding trails:* Hotel to Horseshoe Lk., Nenana River. *Campfire Programs:* None outdoors; interpretive program in hotel, evenings.

ACTIVITIES—WINTER: No organized activities in winter. *Access:* Train or plane only. *Accommodations:* None in winter.

SERVICES: Telephone at hotel. Closest medical facility at Fairbanks. Service station—for gas, oil, tires, minor repairs. Supplies—groceries, first aid, fishing equipment. Restaurants—Full meals available at hotel.

OLYMPIC

INFORMATION: Superintendent, 600 East Park Avenue, Port Angeles, Washington, 98362.

ACCOMMODATIONS—CAMPING: *Camps:* 17; sites: 911. *Season:* Kalaloch and Elwha, all year; others, May-Oct. *Limit:* 14 days. *Trailers:* Small trailers at most camps; med. and lg. sizes at Fairholm, Mora, Kalaloch, Elwha and Altaire. No utility hookups. *Private grounds:* Long-fellows.

ACCOMMODATIONS—RESORTS: *Concessioner reservations:* Olympic Hot Springs, Mgr., Rt. 1, Port Angeles (May 27-Sept. 10; Housekeeping cabins); Lk. Crescent Lodge, Mgr., Star Rt. 1 Box 9, Port Angeles (May 1-Memorial Day; lodge rooms, cottages.); Lk. Crescent Log Cabin Lodge, Mgr., Rt. 1 Box 416, Port Angeles (mid-April-Oct. 31; housekeeping cabins, trlr. parking, camp space.); Kalaloch Beach Ocean Village, Mgr., Clearwater (all year; lodge rooms, cabins, housekeeping cabins.); La Push Ocean Park, Mgr., La Push (all year; motel units, housekeeping cabins.). *Non-concessioner:* For complete list of accommodations, write Olympic Peninsula Resort and Hotel Assn., Colman Ferry Terminal, Seattle, Washington, 98104.

ACTIVITIES—SUMMER: *Hiking:* 600 mi. of trails. *Packing:* Horses and guides at Forks, Pt. Angeles, Sol Duc Hot Springs. *Fishing:* Lakes, streams—Rainbow, brook, cut-throat, Dolly Varden trout; in winter steelhead trout. No license reqd. *Boating:* Rentals; launching at Lk. Crescent. *Swimming:* Olympic Hot Springs and Sol Duc Hot Springs. *Rock-climbing:* Peaks for novices and experienced climbers. Register with park ranger. *Ice-climbing:* On glacier-clad peaks for experienced climbers. Register with park ranger. *Tours:* Gray Line. *Self-guiding trails:* Alpine Wildflower Trail, Marymere Falls Trail, Rain Forest Trail, Spruce Trail. *Campfire programs:* Mora, Crescent Lk., Heart O' the Hills, Hoh, Kalaloch, Elwha.

ACTIVITIES—WINTER: *Season:* late Dec.-end of March. *Skiing:* Hurricane Ridge—tows, equipment rentals. *Cross country skiing:* Possible at Hurricane Ridge. *Ski tours:* No organized tours. *Other snow activities:* Sledding—Hurricane Ridge. *Access:* From Port Angeles via Hurricane Ridge Road. *Overnight accommodations:* In Port Angeles.

SERVICES: Post offices in Quinault, La Push, and towns on edge of park. Medical facilities in Port Angeles, Forks, Sequim. Service stations at regular intervals on Hwy. 101; Supplies—numerous general stores in and near park. Restaurants—variety of small restaurants, coffee shops, dining rooms.

MT. RAINIER

INFORMATION: Superintendent, Mt. Rainier National Park, Longmire, Washington, 98397.

ACCOMMODATIONS—CAMPING: *Camps:* 10; sites: 887. *Season:* June-Sept.; Sunshine Pt. all year. *Limit:* 14 days. *Trailers:* Where space permits in camps. No utility hook-ups. *Private grounds:* None in park.

ACCOMMODATIONS—RESORTS: *Concessioner Reservations:* Rainier National Park Co., Box 1136, Tacoma. *Type:* Med. priced rooms. *Season:* Paradise Inn—mid-June-Labor Day; National Park Inn—May-Oct. *Non-concessioner:* None in park.

ACTIVITIES—SUMMER: *Hiking:* 300 mi. of trail. *Packing:* Concession. *Riding:* Guided trips at Paradise. *Bicycling:* Permitted on roads only. No rentals. *Fishing:* Lakes, July 4-Sept. 30; Streams, conform with state of Wash. Trout. No license reqd. *Boating:* At designated open lakes only. Permits reqd. No rentals. *Swimming:* None. *Rock-climbing:* (Schools in mountaineering techniques.) *Ice-climbing:* May 30-Labor Day. Ingraham Glacier most popular. Register with park ranger. *Tours:* Hikes, naturalists walks, auto caravans. Guide service to Paradise Ice Cave and Glacier. *Self-guiding trails:* Trail of the Shadows, Kautz Creek Mudflow, Emmons Vista. *Campfire programs:* Ohanapecosh Amphitheater, Ipsut Creek.

ACTIVITIES—WINTER: *Season:* Dec.-May. *Skiing:* Paradise (weekends only)—rope tows. *Cross country skiing:* Several trails. *Ski tours:* None organized by Park. *Other snow activities:* Snowshoeing. *Access:* S.W. entrance (Nisqually-Paradise Road.) *Overnight Accommodations:* Just outside park.

SERVICES: Post office at Longmire (all year); Paradise (summer). Medical facilities at Morton, Enumclaw, Eatonville; nurse at Paradise Inn in summer. Service stations at Longmire (all year); Sunrise (summer). Supplies—limited camping supplies; souvenirs. Restaurants—Table d'hote, a la carte at Paradise; cafeteria in summer at Longmire, Sunrise.

CRATER LAKE

INFORMATION: Superintendent, Crater Lake National Park, Crater Lake, Oregon, 97604.

ACCOMMODATIONS—CAMPING: *Camps:* 4; sites: 241. *Season:* July 1-Sept. 30. *Limit:* 14 days. *Trailers:* Accepted in all camps. No utility hookups. *Private grounds:* None in park.

ACCOMMODATIONS—RESORTS: *Concessioner reservations:* Crater Lake Lodge, Inc., Crater Lake, Oregon, 97604. *Type:* Rooms in lodge, cottages and housekeeping cabins. *Season:* June 15-Sept. 10.

ACTIVITIES—SUMMER: *Hiking:* 6 mi. of trails (roads lead to most places of interest.) *Packing:* No packers (for stock); back packing as desired. *Riding:* None. *Bicycling:* On roads. No rentals. *Fishing:* Streams, June 15-Sept. 10; Crater Lake when trail is open. Rainbow trout, kokanee. No license reqd. *Boating:* Rental rowboats only. Private boats prohibited. *Swimming:* None. *Rock-climbing, ice-climbing:* None. *Tours:* Garfield Park, Discovery Point trails; Launch trips; Scenic bus trips. *Self-guiding trails:* Castle Crest Wildflower Garden. *Campfire programs:* Mazama Campground, Rim Village, and Crater Lake Lodge.

ACTIVITIES—WINTER: *Season:* Oct.-May. *Skiing:* Cross country (2 trails). *Ski Tours:* None. *Other Snow Activities:* Limited sledding and tobogganing. *Access:* So. or W. entrance (Hwy. 62) to Rim Village. *Overnight Accommodations:* Outside park.

SERVICES: Post office at park hq.; telephones. No medical facilities in park. Gas station open summer only. Supplies—some groceries, fishing tackle. Restaurants—summer: cafeteria; winter: coffee shop.

293

TRAVELERS' GUIDE

LASSEN VOLCANIC

INFORMATION: Superintendent, Lassen Volcanic National Park, Mineral, California, 96063.

ACCOMMODATIONS—CAMPING: *Camps:* 8; sites: 569; group campgrounds: 2. *Season:* May-Oct., depending on weather. *Limit:* 14 days. *Trailers:* Permitted in all camps but 2. *Private grounds:* None in park.

ACCOMMODATIONS—RESORTS: *Concessioner reservations:* Lassen National Park Co., Manzanita Lake, California. *Type:* Manzanita Lake Lodge: hotel rooms, deluxe housekeeping cottages, cabins; Drakesbad Guest Ranch: hotel rooms, cottages. *Season:* Manzanita, June 10-Sept. 20; Drakesbad, July 1—Labor Day.

ACTIVITIES—SUMMER: *Hiking:* 150 miles of trails. *Packing:* Summit Lake; Drakesbad. *Riding:* Summit Lake, Drakesbad. *Bicycling:* None. *Fishing:* Most lakes; rainbow, brown, brook trout; License reqd. *Boating:* Rowboat rentals at Manzanita and Butte Lakes. No power boats. *Swimming:* Most lakes, esp. Manzanita, Summit. *Rock-climbing and ice-climbing:* None. *Tours:* Naturalist walks and hikes; concessioner bus tours. *Self-guiding trails:* Manzanita Lake, Sulphur Works, Bumpass Hell, Butte Lake, Warner Valley. *Campfire programs:* Summit Lake, Manzanita Lake and Butte Lake campgrounds.

ACTIVITIES—WINTER: *Season:* Mid-Dec.-mid-April; some late skiing. *Facilities:* Lassen Park ski area, tows, winter use building, lunch counter, equipment rentals. *Cross-country skiing:* winter, spring, early summer. *Ski tours:* on request. *Other snow activities:* ice skating at Manzanita Lake, late autumn, early winter. *Access:* via California 36 and 89. *Overnight accommodations:* outside park, in and around Mineral.

SERVICES: Post office, May 16-Sept. 30, Manzanita Lake; telephone. Nearest medical facilities are at Redding, Red Bluff, Burney, and Chester. Service station at Manzanita Lake for gas, oil, minor repairs. Supplies—groceries, drugs, souvenirs, fishing and photo supplies at Manzanita Lake. Restaurants—dinning room and soda fountain at Manzanita Lake.

YOSEMITE

INFORMATION: Superintendent, P.O. Box 577, Yosemite National Park, California, 95389.

ACCOMMODATIONS—CAMPING: *Camps:* 20; sites: 3,876. *Season:* Valley open all year, high country summer only. *Limit:* 14 days (except June, July in Yosemite Valley, 10 days). *Trailers:* Permitted in most camps. *Private grounds:* None in park.

ACCOMMODATIONS—RESORTS: *Concessioner reservations:* Yosemite Park & Curry Co., Yosemite, California, 95389. *Type:* Luxury rooms, deluxe units at Ahwahnee Hotel, Wawona Hotel, Yosemite Lodge. Other hotels and lodges have med.-priced rooms, cabins, bungalows, housekeeping canvas cabins, tents. *Season:* All year; High Sierra camps summer only. *Non-concessioner:* Motel and cabins at El Portal.

ACTIVITIES—SUMMER: *Hiking:* Over 700 miles of trails. *Packing:* High Sierra Loop; John Muir Trail. *Riding:* Yosemite Valley, Tuolumne Meadows, Wawona and White Wolf. *Bicycling:* Rentals at Yosemite Lodge and Camp Curry. *Fishing:* Lakes, rivers, streams; Rainbow, brook and brown trout. License reqd. *Boating:* At these lakes only: Benson, Kibbie, Many Islands, May, Merced, Tenaya, Tilden, Twin. No motors. *Swimming:* Pools at Camp Curry, Yosemite Lodge, Wawona, Ahwahnee Hotel. *Rock-climbing:* Climbers must check out at park headquarters or ranger stations. *Ice-climbing:* None. *Tours:* Naturalist walks and hikes; Concessioner saddle and hiking trips. *Self-guiding trails:* Yosemite Valley, Wawona, Glacier Point, and Tuolumne Meadows. Self-guiding auto tours in Valley and through whole park. *Campfire programs:* Yosemite Valley: Camps 7 and 14, Yosemite Lodge, Glacier Point, Wawona, Bridalveil Creek Camp, White Wolf Camp, Crane Flat Camp, and Tuolumne Meadows.

ACTIVITIES—WINTER: *Season:* mid-Dec.-mid-April. *Facilities:* Badger Pass ski area, T-bar lifts, ski school, ski house, cafeteria, equipment rentals. *Cross-country skiing:* Marked trails maintained by National Park Service. *Ski Tours:* For information write Yosemite Park & Curry Co. *Other snow activities:* Ice skating and snowshoeing. *Access:* South entrance from Fresno; west from Merced. *Overnight accommodations:* Wawona or Yosemite Valley. None at Badger Pass.

SERVICES: Post office all year at Wawona and Yosemite Lodge; summer offices at Tuolumne Meadows and Camp Curry. Telephones and telegraph. Medical and dental facilities in Yosemite Valley; First Aid at Badger Pass during ski season. Filling stations, towing, garage and repair. Supplies—Rental camp equipment, gifts, laundry and baby-sitting services, groceries, photo supplies. Restaurants—Dining rooms and cafeterias.

SEQUOIA

INFORMATION: Superintendent, Sequoia and Kings Canyon National Parks, Three Rivers, California, 93271.

ACCOMMODATIONS—CAMPING: *Camps:* 10; sites: 820. *Season:* June 1-Oct., lower elevations open all year. *Limit:* 14 days June 15-Sept. 15; 30 days rest of the year. *Trailers:* Lodgepole, Dorst Creek, Potwisha camps only. *Private grounds:* None in park.

ACCOMMODATIONS—RESORTS: *Concessioner reservations:* Sequoia & Kings Canyon National Parks Co., Sequoia National Park, California, 93271. *Type:* Giant Forest: cottages, cabins, canvas-top cabins; Camp Kaweah: motel units, housekeeping cabins, canvas-top cabins, cottages; Pinewood: housekeeping cabins, cottages. *Season:* May-June to Sept.-Oct. depending on location; Camp Kaweah all year. Non-concessioner: None in park.

ACTIVITIES — SUMMER: *Hiking:* 900 miles of trails. *Packing:* Pack station at Giant Forest and other places around borders of park. *Riding:* Rental horses at Giant Forest. *Fishing:* Streams, May 1-Oct. 31. License reqd. *Boating:* None. *Swimming:* Not advised, lake temperatures too low. *Rock-climbing and ice-climbing:* Check in with ranger at entrance station. *Tours:* Naturalists trips; Crystal Cave, mid-June to mid-Sept. *Self-guiding trails:* Congress Trail (Giant Forest). *Campfire programs:* Giant Forest, Lodgepole, Dorst amphitheaters.

ACTIVITIES—WINTER: *Season:* Dec.-April. *Facilities:* Wolverton ski area (Giant Forest), rope tows, warming hut. *Cross-country skiing:* Several maintained trails. *Ski Tours:* None. *Other snow activities:* Ice skating (rink at Lodgepole open Dec.-Feb.). *Access:* California 180 from Fresno via Grant Grove; 198 from Visalia via Ash Mt. *Overnight accommodations:* Camp Kaweah; Pear Lake Ski Hut by advance reservation with National Park Service.

SERVICES: Post office at Giant Forest in summer. Telephone, telegraph. No medical facilities in park. Service station: gas, oil all year; minor repairs, towing during summer. Supplies—groceries, camping gear, ski and ice-skating equipment. Restaurants—dining room (May-Sept.); coffee shops.

KINGS CANYON

INFORMATION: Superintendent, Sequoia and Kings Canyon National Parks, Three Rivers, California, 93271.

ACCOMMODATIONS—CAMPING: *Camps:* 8; sites: 900. *Season:* June 1-Oct.; Cedar Grove, May-Oct. *Limit:* 14 days. *Trailers:* Cedar Grove Camp 4 and Azalea Camp only. *Private grounds:* Summer homesites at Wilsonia (Grant Grove).

ACCOMMODATIONS—RESORT: *Concessioner reservations:* Sequoia & Kings Canyon National Parks Co., Sequoia National Park, California. *Type:* Grant Grove Lodge: cottages, canvas-top cabins; Meadow Camp: housekeeping cabins; Cedar Grove: canvas-top cabins. *Season:* Late May to late Oct. *Non-concessioner:* Wilsonia Village—Lodge and store.

ACTIVITIES—SUMMER: *Hiking:* 940 miles of trails. *Packing:* Pack stations at Grant Grove and Cedar Grove; east side of Sierra and many other places around borders of park. *Riding:* Rental horses at Grant Grove and Cedar Grove. *Fishing:* Mountain lakes, streams; Rainbow, brook, brown and California golden trout. License reqd. *Boating:* None. *Swimming:* Low lake temperatures make it inadvisable. *Rock-climbing and ice-climbing:* None. *Tours:* Grant Grove and Cedar Grove. *Self-guiding trails:* Big Stump Trail (Grant Grove). *Campfire programs:* Grant Grove; Cedar Grove.

ACTIVITIES—WINTER: *Season:* Nov.-April. *Facilities:* None. *Cross-country skiing:* During winter, early spring. *Other snow activities:* Snow play area at Grant Grove. *Access:* California 180 from Fresno; California 65 from Visalia to Big Stump entrance. *Overnight accommodations:* None in park.

SERVICES: Summer Post Office at Grant Grove. Telephone and Telegraph at Grant Grove, Cedar Grove. No medical service in park. Gas and oil at Grant Grove all year; minor repairs at Grant Grove, Cedar Grove in summer. Supplies—groceries, sundries, camping, fishing gear. Restaurants—coffee shops.

TRAVELERS' GUIDE

GRAND CANYON

INFORMATION: Superintendent, Grand Canyon National Park, Grand Canyon, Arizona, 86023.

ACCOMMODATIONS—CAMPING: N. Rim: *Camps:* 1; sites: 76. Inner Canyon: *Camps:* 4; sites: 32. Bottom: *Camps:* 2; sites 24. S. Rim: *Camps:* 3; sites: 578. *Season:* S. Rim all year; N. Rim May-Oct. *Limit:* 14 days. *Trailers:* Permitted at most grounds N. and S. Rims; None at Inner Canyon or bottom. Trailer Village with utility hookups at S. Rim Village. *Private grounds:* None.

ACCOMMODATIONS—RESORTS: *Concessioner reservations:* S. Rim: Fred Harvey, Grand Canyon, Arizona. N. Rim: Utah Parks Co., Cedar City, Utah. *Type:* Med-priced rooms, cabins; housekeeping cabins. *Season:* S. Rim all year. N. Rim Lodge: June 13-Sept. 8; Inn: May 9-Oct. 11. *Non-concessioner:* None in park.

ACTIVITIES—SUMMER: *Hiking:* 31 miles of maintained trails. Permit from ranger reqd. to use non-maintained trails. *Packing:* Mules available; reserve in advance. *Riding:* Horseback trips summer only. *Bicycling:* No paths, cycling on main roads only. *Fishing:* Streams. License reqd. *Boating:* None. *Swimming:* Phantom Ranch only. *Rock-climbing and ice-climbing:* None. *Self-guiding trails:* Canyon Rim (S. Rim); Bright Angel Pt. Trail (N. Rim). *Campfire programs:* Amphitheater (S. Rim); camp near Inn (N. Rim).

ACTIVITIES—WINTER: *Season:* Nov. 1-May 10. N. Rim closed in winter. No snow activities or facilities on either side. *Access:* S. Rim: All regular routes open (US 66, Ariz. 64); N. Rim road (Hwy 67) usually closed by snow. *Overnight accommodations:* S. Rim only.

SERVICES: *S. Rim:* Post office near park hdq., telephones, telegraph, American Express, bank. Hospital near park hdq. Service stations, garage. Supplies—supermarket, general store, ice, souvenirs. Restaurants—Dining rooms, cafeteria. *N. Rim:* Post office in Lodge, telephones. Nurse at Lodge. Gas station. Supplies—groceries, general supplies.

BRYCE CANYON

INFORMATION: Superintendent, Bryce Canyon National Park, Bryce Canyon, Utah, 84717.

ACCOMMODATIONS:—CAMPING: *Camps:* 2; sites: 222. *Season:* May 15-Oct. 15. *Limit:* 14 days. *Trailers:* Permitted at North Camp. *Private grounds:* None in park.

ACCOMMODATIONS—RESORTS: *Concessioner reservations:* Utah Parks Co., Cedar City, Utah. *Type:* Med.-priced deluxe and standard cabins, cottages. *Season:* Lodge: June 13-Sept. 8; Inn: May 9-Oct. 11. *Non-concessioner:* None in park.

ACTIVITIES—SUMMER: *Hiking:* 61 miles of trails. *Packing:* None. *Riding:* Corral below lodge; afternoon and morning horseback trips. *Fishing:* None. *Boating:* None. *Swimming:* None. *Rock-climbing:* Prohibited, crumbling limestone. *Ice-climbing:* None. *Tours:* Navajo Loop Trail; scenic bus tours of Rim Drive in summer. *Self-guiding trails:* Queens Garden. *Campfire programs:* North and South camps during summer.

ACTIVITIES—WINTER: *Season:* Dec. 1-May 1. *Facilities:* No ski area or snow play areas. *Access:* Road open to Sunset Point, Inspiration Point, Bryce Point. *Overnight accommodations:* None in park.

SERVICES: Post office, telephone. Hospital located 26 miles from park; registered nurse at lodge in summer. Service stations. Supplies—groceries, film, souvenirs, general supplies. Restaurants—dining room, soda fountain.

ZION

INFORMATION: Superintendent, Zion National Park, Springdale, Utah, 84767.

ACCOMMODATIONS—CAMPING: *Camps:* 2; sites: 206. *Season:* South camp, all year; Grotto camp, June 10 to Labor Day. *Limit:* 14 days, June 1-Sept. 15. *Trailers:* Permitted in both camps. No utility hookups. *Private grounds:* None in park; trailer courts adjacent to park.

ACCOMMODATIONS—RESORTS: *Concessioner reservations:* Utah Parks Co., Cedar City, Utah. *Type:* Deluxe cabins, standard cabins, rooms. *Season:* Lodge: June 15-Labor Day; Inn: May 14-Oct. 1. *Non-concessioner:* None in park. Accommodations all year at Springdale.

ACTIVITIES—SUMMER: *Hiking:* 155 miles of trails. *Packing:* None. *Riding:* Regular and special escorted horseback trips. *Bicycling:* None. *Fishing:* Permitted in streams but few fish to be found. License reqd. *Boating:* None. *Swimming:* Zion Lodge pool. *Rock-climbing:* All climbers required to register at visitor center. *Ice-climbing:* None. *Tours:* Ranger-naturalist trips; all-expense tours. *Self-guiding trails:* Weeping Rock, Canyon Overlook *Campfire programs:* Grotto camp.

ACTIVITIES—WINTER: *Facilities:* No winter sports areas. *Access:* All main roads. *Overnight accommodations:* None in park.

SERVICES: Post office at Zion Lodge in summer; Springdale, all year. Telephones, telegraph. Hospital 22 miles from park; registered nurse at lodge in summer. Service stations, garage, May 15-Oct. 15; Springdale, all year. Supplies—groceries, general supplies. Restaurants—Dining room, soda fountain, cafeteria.

PETRIFIED FOREST

INFORMATION: Superintendent, Petrified Forest National Park, Holbrook, Arizona, 86025.

ACCOMMODATIONS—CAMPING: *Special note:* Camping in park not allowed. Nearest campgrounds are in the national forest located to the southeast and southwest, 100 miles away. Designated picnic areas at Rainbow Forest and Chinde Point.

ACCOMMODATIONS—RESORTS: *Concessioner reservations:* Painted Desert Oasis and Rainbow Forest Lodge, located near park entrances, 26 miles apart. No resort accommodations in park. Motels are located along the highways that cross the park and in nearby towns.

ACTIVITIES—SUMMER: *Hiking:* Short trails lead into the main "Forests." Long hikes into the Painted Desert are not advised unless you are conditioned to it. Hikers must give prior notice of such a trip to a park ranger. *Packing, Riding, Bicycling, Fishing, Boating, Swimming, Rock-climbing and ice-climbing:* None. *Tours:* Naturalists on duty at key points. Impromptu tours start at main "Forests." All principal points of interest are located near a main road which runs north and south. *Self-guiding trails:* Long Logs section of Rainbow Forest.

ACTIVITIES—WINTER: *Facilities:* No winter sports areas. *Access:* All roads open. *Overnight accommodations:* None in park.

SERVICES: Public telephones at Painted Desert Visitor Center and Rainbow Forest Lodge. Nearest medical facilities (2 clinics and modern hospital) at Holbrook. Gasoline station at Painted Desert Oasis and Rainbow Forest Lodge. Supplies—souvenirs, film. Restaurants—refreshments, lunches at Painted Desert and Rainbow Forest.

297

TRAVELERS' GUIDE

MESA VERDE

INFORMATION: Superintendent, Mesa Verde National Park, Colorado.

ACCOMMODATIONS—CAMPING: *Camps:* 4; sites: 400. *Season:* May 1-November 15. *Limit:* 14 days from June 1 through September 7. *Trailers:* At designated camps only. No utility hookups. *Private grounds:* None in park.

ACCOMMODATIONS—RESORTS: *Concessioner reservations:* Mesa Verde Co., Mesa Verde National Park, Colorado. *Type:* Spruce Tree Lodge (cabins); tent cottages; housekeeping cabins. *Season:* May 15 to October 15. *Nonconcessioner:* None in park.

ACTIVITIES—SUMMER: *Hiking:* Few short trails. Permit must be obtained. *Packing:* None. *Horseback riding:* Mesa Verde Pack & Saddle Co. for rides of 1, 2, and 4 hours. Must use wrangler-guide. *Bicycling:* None. *Fishing:* None. *Rock-climbing:* None. *Tours:* Bus trips to ruins, sunset trip to park point, ranger-guided tours through some outstanding ruins of cliff dwellings. *Self-guiding trails:* No hikes. Self-guiding drive on ruins road. *Campfire programs:* Conducted by ranger-archaeologists and naturalists June to mid-September.

ACTIVITIES—WINTER: *Season:* October 15-May 15. No special activities. *Overnight accommodations:* None in park.

SERVICES: General delivery mail; telephone; telegraph. Registered nurse at first aid station daily in summer, weekdays in winter. Service station for gas, oil, towing, minor repairs. Major repairs can be arranged through lodge in summer. Supplies—groceries, souvenirs, magazines, newspapers, film, ice. Restaurants—dining room, snack bar at Spruce Tree Lodge.

CARLSBAD CAVERNS

INFORMATION: Superintendent, Carlsbad Caverns National Park, Box 1598, Carlsbad, New Mexico.

ACCOMMODATIONS—CAMPING: No campgrounds in park.

ACCOMMODATIONS—RESORTS: No resorts in park. *Nonconcessioner:* Small trailer camp adjacent to park entrance.

ACTIVITIES—SUMMER: *Hiking:* None. *Packing:* None. *Riding:* None. *Bicycling:* None. *Fishing:* None. *Boating:* None. *Swimming:* None. *Rock-climbing and ice-climbing:* None. *Tours:* Ranger-guided tour of caverns. Special photographic tours. Evening bat flight. *Self-guiding trails:* None. *Campfire programs:* Naturalist lecture before evening bat flight.

ACTIVITIES—WINTER: Same as summer.

SERVICES: Telephone. Nearest medical facilities are at town of Carlsbad, 29 miles away. Service station near park entrance. Supplies—curios adjacent to visitor center. Restaurant at visitor center; lunchroom in caverns.

ROCKY MT.

INFORMATION: Superintendent, Rocky Mountain National Park, Estes Park, Colorado, 80517.

ACCOMMODATIONS—CAMPING: *Camps:* 7; sites: 653. *Season:* May-Oct. *Limit:* 14 days, July and Aug. *Trailers:* Permitted most camps; prohibited by narrow access at Wild Basin, Endovalley. *Private grounds:* None in park; outside park near Estes Park Village.

ACCOMMODATIONS—RESORTS: *Concessioner reservations:* None in park under government supervision. Outside park write to chambers of commerce at Estes Park or Grand Lake, Colorado.

ACTIVITIES—SUMMER: *Hiking:* 300 miles of trails. *Riding:* Saddle horses by hour, day or week at Glacier Creek Livery or other stables. *Fishing:* Streams, lakes; Cutthroat, brown, brook and rainbow trout. License reqd. *Boating:* None. *Swimming:* None. *Rock-climbing and ice-climbing:* Rocky Mt. Guide Service and Mountaineering School for classes, summit climbs. Longs Peak Climb. *Tours:* All-expense tours; sightseeing bus trips; naturalist hikes. *Self-guiding trails:* Bear Lake; auto tour of Trail Ridge Road. *Campfire programs:* Glacier Basin, Aspenglen, Endovalley, Timber Creek, and Wild Basin camps.

ACTIVITIES—WINTER: *Season:* mid-Dec.-mid-April. *Facilities:* Hidden Valley ski area, tows, cafeteria, rental-equipment shop, bus service. *Cross-country skiing:* With ranger's permission. *Ski tours:* With ranger's permission. *Other snow activities:* Ice-skating, platter sliding, snowshoeing. *Access:* Roads from east—Hwys. 34 and 66. *Overnight accommodations:* Outside the park at Estes Park Village.

SERVICES: Post office at Estes Park, Grand Lake; telephones, telegraph. Medical doctors all year at Estes Park and Grand Lake villages. Car service. Supplies—groceries, photo supplies and developing, camping supplies. Restaurants—None in park; outside park at Estes Park, Grand Lake, Allenpark.

GLACIER

INFORMATION: Superintendent, Glacier National Park, West Glacier, Montana, 59936.

ACCOMMODATIONS—CAMPING: *Camps:* 16; sites: 1,034; shelter cabins: 5. *Season:* June 15-Sept. 10. *Limit:* 14 days during July, Aug. *Trailers:* Permitted in all camps except Sprague Creek. No utility hookups. *Private grounds:* None in park.

ACCOMMODATIONS—RESORTS: *Concessioner reservations:* Glacier Park, Inc., (June 1-Oct. 15) E. Glacier Park, Montana; (Oct. 16-May 31) P.O. Box 4250, Tucson, Arizona. B. Ross Luding, Martin City, Montana (chalets only) *Type:* Lake McDonald Lodge and Many Glacier Hotel, deluxe rooms; also available motel units, cabins. *Season:* June 15-Sept. 10. *Non-concessioner:* Privately operated accommodations at foot of and upper Lake McDonald.

ACTIVITIES—SUMMER: *Hiking:* 1,000 miles of trails. *Packing:* Rental stock, guides and packers, equipment; back country trips throughout park. *Riding:* Saddle horses for rent; guides reqd. for trips. *Bicycling:* Permitted but no rentals. *Fishing:* Streams, lakes; 22 kinds of fish. No license reqd. *Boating:* Regular launch service; rental rowboats; restrictions on motors in some waters. Private boats require permits. *Swimming:* Not recommended, waters too cold. *Rock-climbing and ice-climbing:* Not recommended. *Tours:* Ranger-naturalist hikes; all-expense tours—write concessioner. *Self-guiding trails:* Swiftcurrent Lake, Baring Falls, Avalanche Camp, Trick Falls, Hidden Lake Overlook. *Evening programs:* Lake McDonald Lodge, Many Glacier Hotel, most major camps.

ACTIVITIES—WINTER: *Season:* Sept. 10-June 15. *Facilities:* No ski areas. *Cross-country skiing:* Permitted but hazardous. *Ski tours:* None. *Other snow activities:* None. *Access:* One 12-mi. road open from W. Glacier to head of Lake McDonald. *Overnight accommodations:* None in park.

SERVICES: Post office at E. Glacier Park, W. Glacier, and (June 15-Sept. 10) Lake McDonald; telephones and telegraph. Medical doctors at Glacier Park Lodge during main season, nurses at hotels. Several service stations. Supplies—groceries, film, camping and fishing supplies. Restaurants—hotel dining rooms, coffee shops.

299

TRAVELERS' GUIDE

YELLOWSTONE

INFORMATION: Superintendent, Yellowstone National Park, Wyoming, 83020.

ACCOMMODATIONS—CAMPING: *Camps:* 18; sites: 2,569. *Season:* June 1-Sept. 15. *Limit:* 14 days (July 1 to Labor Day). *Trailers:* Permitted at most camps. No utility hookups. (Fishing Bridge Trailer Village has 365 sites, utility hookups, $2. per day.) *Private grounds:* None in park.

ACCOMMODATIONS—RESORTS: *Concessioner reservations:* Yellowstone Park Co., Reservations Dept., Yellowstone National Park, Wyoming. *Type:* Med.-priced cabins, motel units, rooms; camper's cabins. *Season:* Mid-May to mid-Oct. *Non-concessioner:* None in park.

ACTIVITIES—SUMMER: *Hiking:* 1,000 miles of trails. *Packing:* Dude rancher pack trips; backpacking—N. section, July-Sept., S. section, Aug.-Sept. *Riding:* Rental horses at Mammoth Hot Springs, Roosevelt, Old Faithful, Canyon. Guides reqd. for trips. *Bicycling:* Rentals at Canyon Village. *Fishing:* Streams, lakes. No license reqd. *Boating:* Rentals at Fishing Bridge, Bridge Bay, West Thumb. Private boats less than 40-ft. allowed by permit. No sailboats. *Swimming:* None. *Rock-climbing and ice-climbing:* None. *Tours:* Naturalist walks along the shore of Yellowstone Lake, in thermal areas along rim of Grand Canyon, up into the more interesting mountain areas. *Self-guiding trails:* Fountain Paint Pots. *Campfire programs:* Tower Fall, Old Faithful, Mammoth Hot Springs, Madison Jct., West Thumb, Fishing Bridge, Canyon Village, Bridge Bay.

ACTIVITIES—WINTER: *Season:* Dec.-March. *Facilities:* No ski area. *Cross-country skiing:* Excellent, but no shelters. Registration reqd. *Ski Tours:* None. *Other snow activities:* Snowmobile trips from W. Yellowstone to Old Faithful, Dec.-March. *Access:* North entrance open all year (Gardiner to Mammoth Hot Springs, Mammoth across northern part of park to northeast entrance). Northeast entrance closed Oct. 15-May 30. West, east, south entrances closed Nov. 1-May 1. *Overnight accommodations:* None in park.

SERVICES: Post offices at Mammoth Hot Springs, Old Faithful, West Thumb, Fishing Bridge, Canyon. Telephones, telegraph. Clinic at Mammoth Springs. Physicians at Old Faithful, Canyon; nurses at each hotel and lodge. Hospital at Lake. Gas stations, garages. Supplies—groceries, drugs, newspapers, sportswear, camping equipment, photo supplies, souvenirs. Restaurants—dining rooms, coffee shops.

GRAND TETON

INFORMATION: Superintendent, Grand Teton National Park, Moose, Wyoming, 83012.

ACCOMMODATIONS—CAMPING: *Camps:* 5; sites: 725. *Season:* May-Oct. *Limit:* 14 days (Jenny Lake, 10 days). *Trailers:* All camps except Jenny Lake. No utility hookups. (Concession operated trailer village at Colter Bay provides hookups.) *Private grounds:* None in park.

ACCOMMODATIONS—RESORTS: *Concessioner reservations:* Grand Teton Lodge Co. or Jenny Lake Lodge, Jackson Wyo.; Signal Mt. Lodge* or Leek's Lodge Inc.,* Moran, Wyo.; Triangle X Guest Ranch* or Elbo Guest Ranch,* Moose, Wyo. *Type:* Med.-priced rooms, cabins, housekeeping cabins, tent cabins. *Season:* *May 15-Oct. 15. Others May/June-Sept./Oct. *Non-concessioner:* Several privately owned accommodations.

ACTIVITIES—SUMMER: *Hiking:* 200 miles of trails. *Packing:* Pack trips incl. animals, equipment and wranglers. *Riding:* Horses at Jenny Lake, Jackson Lake Lodge, and Colter Bay. *Bicycling:* None. *Fishing:* Streams, lakes; license reqd. *Boating:* Rental boats at Jenny Lake, Colter Bay, Signal Mt. Lodge, Leek's Lodge. 18-person rubber rafts for trips down Snake River to Moose. *Swimming:* Beach at Colter Bay; pool at Jackson Lake Lodge. *Rock-climbing:* Exum School of Mountaineering, hdq. at Jenny Lake. Popular climbs: Mt. Owens, Mt. Moran, Grand Teton, etc. *Ice-climbing:* Indian Paintbrush Canyon. Permits reqd. for *ALL* climbs. *Tours:* Nature walks, naturalist-guided hikes, Jackson Lake cruise, sight-seeing bus tours. *Self-guiding trails:* Jenny Lake, Colter Bay. *Campfire programs:* Jenny Lake, Colter Bay, Jackson Lake Lodge, Jackson Lake camp.

ACTIVITIES—WINTER: *Season:* Dec.-March. *Facilities:* No skiing or snow play areas in park; developed area at nearby Jackson, Wyo. *Cross-country skiing:* winter thru early spring. *Ski tours:* None. *Other snow activities:* Snow planing, ice fishing. *Access:* US 89 open all winter. *Overnight accommodations:* None in park; accommodations in Jackson.

SERVICES: Post offices at Moose, Moran, Elk. Telephones. Nearest hospital in Jackson; registered nurse at Jackson Lake Lodge in summer. Service stations in park operate summer only. Supplies—groceries, film, souvenirs, camp supplies. Restaurants—grill, cafeteria during summer.

HAWAII VOLCANOES

INFORMATION: Superintendent, Hawaii Volcanoes National Park, Hawaii, 96718.

ACCOMMODATIONS—CAMPING: *Camps:* 3; hikers' cabins: 2. *Season:* All year. *Limit:* None. *Trailers:* Permitted in 2 camps. *Private grounds:* Kilauea Military Camp.

ACCOMMODATIONS—RESORTS: *Concessioner reservations:* Volcano House, Hawaii Volcanoes National Park, Hawaii, 96718. *Type:* Hotel rooms, housekeeping cabins. *Season:* All year.

ACTIVITIES—SUMMER: *Hiking:* 160 miles of trails. *Packing:* Horses available. *Riding:* Saddle horses rented. *Bicycling:* Permitted. *Fishing:* In the ocean. *Boating:* None from park lands. *Swimming:* None. *Rock-climbing and ice-climbing:* None. *Tours:* None. *Self-guiding trails:* Halemaumau trail, Kipuka Puaulu. *Visitor center programs:* 9:30 a.m., 12:45, 1:15, and 1:45 p.m.

ACTIVITIES—WINTER: No winter season to speak of. Same activities prevail as listed under summer. Times for visitor center programs: 9:30 a.m., 1:15, and 1:45 p.m.

SERVICES: Post office in Volcano House, telephone, telegraph, radio. Hospitals outside park at Hilo and Pahala. Gas and oil available 2 miles from park hdq. toward Hilo. Supplies—small general stores at Hilo entrance. Restaurants—Volcano House.

HALEAKALA

INFORMATION: Superintendent, Haleakala National Park, P.O. Box 456 Kahului, Maui, Hawaii, 96732.

ACCOMMODATIONS—CAMPING: *Camps:* 1; sites: 5; picnic area; 3 cabins, 12 bunks each, reserve in advance. *Season:* All year. *Limit:* 3 days during summer and holidays for cabins only. *Trailers:* No hookups but can be parked near camp. *Private grounds:* None.

ACCOMMODATIONS—RESORTS: No overnight accommodations, no meals are available in the park. Closest restaurant and lodge is 12 miles outside the park on way back to Kahului.

ACTIVITIES—SUMMER: *Hiking:* 32.5 miles of trails. *Packing:* Regular trails. *Riding:* 1, 2, and 3 day trips. Horses rented with guides only. No guides necessary for hikers or those riding their own stock. *Bicycling, Fishing, Boating, Swimming, Rock-climbing, Tours:* None. *Self-guiding trails:* Hosmer Grove.

ACTIVITIES—WINTER: No winter season to speak of. Same activities as listed under summer prevail.

SERVICES: Post offices, medical facilities, service stations, supplies, restaurants available in nearby towns. None in park.

301

HISTORICAL CHRONOLOGY

1400's   Apache Indian tribe moves into area of Carlsbad Caverns.

1500's   Pecos River area explored by Spanish conquistadores.

1540   Don Lopez de Cardenas discovers the Grand Canyon.

1720   Blackfoot Indians penetrate Glacier area, hold for a century.

·—·1700·—·

1700's   Paiute tribe claims Zion region.

1765   Don Juan Maria de Rivera leads first official Spanish expedition into Mesa Verde area.

mid-1770's   Spanish traders penetrate southwestern Colorado.

1774   Spanish sea Captain Juan Perez discovers Olympic Mountains; called them *La Sierra de la Santa Rosalia.*

1776   Zion area discovered by Escalante-Dominguez party of Spanish padres. Escalante and Dominguez camp at foot of Mesa Verde.

1778   English Captain John Meares names dominant Olympic peak Mount Olympus.

1790   Hawaiian volcano Kilauea has violent steam explosion.

1792   Captain Vancouver sights Mount Rainier while sailing in Puget Sound; names it for his friend Rear Admiral Peter Rainier.

·—·1800·—·

1800's   Ranchers in the Pecos River area venture into the mountainous area near Carlsbad Caverns; refer to caverns as Bat Cave.

1800-50   Trappers use Bryce Canyon.

1803   United States acquires Rocky Mountain area as part of Louisiana Purchase.

1806   Meriwether Lewis reaches point 30 miles from Glacier Park area.

1807   John Colter of Lewis and Clark party discovers Jackson Hole; leaves expedition to explore Yellowstone.

1811   Astorians cross Grand Teton range.

1819   Grand Teton Mountains named by party of French-Canadian trappers.

·—·1820·—·

1820's   First missionaries arrive in Hawaiian Islands.

1821   Mexico wins independence from Spain. Mesa Verde becomes Mexican territory.

1826   Jedediah Smith leads party of 16 through Zion's valleys to Virgin River.

1829   Lake and valley in Grand Tetons named for David Jackson, mountain man. Antonio Armijo blazes trail from Santa Fe to the Pueblo of Los Angeles through Mesa Verde.

1833   Captain Joseph Walker expedition party crosses Sierra, probably enters Yosemite. Dr. William Fraser Tolmie and party of five Indians explore Mount Rainier area.

·—·1840·—·

1840   Fur trade in Grand Teton area begins decline; ends in 1860's.

1843-44   John C. Fremont explores Zion.

1845   Fremont's third western expedition travels along Kern River in Sequoia-Kings Canyon area.

1847   Mormons migrate en masse to Great Salt Lake valley.

1848   United States signs Treaty of Guadalupe Hidalgo, takes possession of Mesa Verde and Grand Canyon.

1849   United States Department of Interior created to be responsible for national resources, including national parks.

WESTERN NATIONAL PARKS IN ORDER OF FOUNDING

1. Yellowstone, 1872	8. Glacier, 1910	15. Bryce Canyon, 1928
2. Sequoia, 1890	9. Rocky Mountain, 1915	16. Grand Teton, 1929
3. General Grant, 1890*	10. Lassen Volcanic, 1916	17. Carlsbad Caverns, 1930
4. Yosemite, 1890**	11. Hawaii, 1916***	18. Olympic, 1938
5. Mount Rainier, 1899	12. Mount McKinley, 1917	19. Kings Canyon, 1940
6. Crater Lake, 1902	13. Grand Canyon, 1919	20. Haleakala, 1961
7. Mesa Verde, 1906	14. Zion, 1919	21. Petrified Forest, 1962
		22. Canyonlands, 1964

*Incorporated into Kings Canyon, 1940.
**Established as a state-operated park in 1864.
***Became two national parks—Hawaii Volcanoes and Haleakala—in 1961.

1850

1850-70 Mormon scouts explore Bryce Canyon area. Hale Tharp settles at Three Rivers (Sequoia-Kings Canyon).

1851 Mariposa Battalion enters Yosemite Valley to subdue the Sierra Indian tribe. Lt. Lorenzo Sitgreaves explores northern Arizona, reports "stone trees."

mid-1800's Lassen Peak used as a landmark by Peter Lassen (California pioneer from Denmark) when he piloted emigrants from Humboldt, Nevada, into the Sacramento Valley.

1853 John Wesley Hillman is first white man to see what is now known as Crater Lake; names it Deep Blue Lake. Railroad survey party crosses Glacier mountain range.

1855 James Mason Hutchings leads first tourist party into Yosemite.

1856 Clark's Station—now known as Wawona—established in Yosemite by Galen Clark. Sketches of Yosemite from 1855 trip (drawn by Thomas Ayres) appear in *California Magazine* and attract visitors from all over the United States.

1857 First serious assault on Mount Rainier by Lt. A. V. Kautz, Dr. O. R. Craig, Indian guide, and four soldiers. Mormon settlements established in Virgin Rivers; Mormons discover Zion Canyon.

1858 Potwisha Indians lead Hale Tharp up to Indian Trail under Moro Rock to the big trees (Sequoia-Kings Canyon).

1859 Joel Estes and son Milton see Rocky Mountain park area. Prof. J. S. Newberry, geologist with the Macomb expedition, climbs Mesa Verde, provides first printed description.

1859-60 Brigadier General W. F. Reynolds leads exploration party into Yellowstone area; writes report complete with illustrated map.

1860

1860 Estes family settles in valley in Rocky Mountains.

1861 Canadian boundary party surveys Glacier area.

1862 Party of prospectors led by Chauncey Nye stumble on lake in a crater, name it Blue Lake. Joseph Thomas discovers General Grant Grove and General Grant Tree.

1864 National grant signed by Lincoln to make Yosemite a recreational area; becomes the first state park.

1865 Two soldiers "discover" Crater Lake, name it Lake Majesty.

1867 Griff Evans acquires Estes claim in Rocky Mountains.

1868 Major John Wesley Powell makes first successful ascent of Longs Peak in Rocky Mountains. John Muir comes to Yosemite area to herd sheep.

1869 Major Powell makes first successful transit of Grand Canyon. Visitors from Jacksonville see lake in a crater, name it Crater Lake. Reynolds report on Yellowstone published.

1870

1870 Nineteen men in Washburn, Langford, Doane expedition explore Yellowstone; return to Montana and propose area be made into a national park. Major Powell expedition explores Bryce Canyon. Crest of Mount Rainier reached by Hazard Stevens and P. B. Van Trump.

1871 Scientific and military expedition directed by Dr. Ferdinand V. Hayden explores Yellowstone.

1872 First known photographs of Grand Tetons taken from west by W. H. Jackson. Major Powell visits Zion, calls N. fork of Virgin River "Mukuntuweap" and E. fork "Parunuweap." Yellowstone National Park established.

1874 First photographs made of the Mesa Verde cliff dwellings by W. H. Jackson. First Mormon settlements established in Bryce Canyon.

1875 Ebenezer Bryce settles in Bryce Canyon.

1877 Chief Joseph and his Nez Perce Indians retreat through Yellowstone.

1878 Settlement of Arizona begins.

1879 Artist Thomas Moran paints the Grand Tetons. A trapper, James Wolverton, discovers General Sherman Tree.

1880

1880's Tourist travel to Grand Canyon begins. Muir writes in *Century Illustrated Monthly Magazine* on need to preserve Yosemite. Rocky Mountains mining boom is on; Lulu City, Dutchtown, and Teller established.

1881 Mauna Loa erupts; lava enters outskirts of Hilo.

1883 Atlantic and Pacific Railway (now Santa Fe) completed. James Longmire discovers warm mineral springs during summit climb of Mount Rainier.

1884 Longmire constructs first building (near present park headquarters) on Mount Rainier. First settlers arrive in Grand Tetons; villages of Jackson, Wilson, and Moran established.

1885 William G. Steel of Kansas sees Crater Lake and determines to preserve it.

1887 Senator Benjamin Harrison, Indiana, introduces a bill to make the Grand Canyon a national park.

303

1888 Richard Wetherill and Charles Mason discover the Mesa Verde's Cliff Palace, Spruce Tree House and Square Tower House. William Steel plants 37 fingerling rainbow trout in Crater Lake.

1889 Marias Pass, used by Great Northern, explored by John F. Stevens.

1889-90 First major exploration of Olympics by Press Party led by James Cristie and Captain Charles Burns.

1890 Sequoia National Park, General Grant National Park, Yosemite National Park are all established. Longmire and sons push crude road through and build small hotel at Longmire's Springs on Mount Rainier. Copper ore discovered in Glacier area; short mining boom collapses when ore found unprofitable.

1891 Town of Tropic founded in Bryce Canyon. Swedish scientist Gustaf Nordenskiold conducts first scientific excavations of the Mesa Verde. Sierra Club organized; John Muir and others determine to fight for big Kings Canyon.

1892 Hotel built at Grandview Point in Grand Canyon.

1893 Gun battle between settlers and horse thieves at Cunningham homestead in Grand Tetons. President Benjamin Harrison establishes Grand Canyon Forest Preserve.

1894 Efforts underway to preserve Mount Rainier area. Lacey Act passed to "protect the birds and animals in Yellowstone National Park and punish crimes in said park."

1896 Federal law enacted prohibiting removal of petrified wood from the Petrified Forest area. W. A. Dickey prospects in the region of Mount McKinley.

1897 Olympic Forest Reserve established.

1899 Mount Rainier National Park established.

————————•••1900•••————————

1900 Colorado Cliff Dwellings Association incorporates and starts work to get park bill in Congress.

1901 Santa Fe Lines completes track to South Rim of Grand Canyon.

1902 Crater Lake National Park established. Alfred H. Brooks and D. L. Raeburn of United States Geological Survey study geology of Alaska Range. Brooks is first white man known to set foot on slopes of Mount McKinley. First auto arrives at South Rim of Grand Canyon.

1903 President Theodore Roosevelt visits Grand Canyon.

1904 Bill to establish Elk National Park in Olympics fails.

1905 Paunsaugunt Plateau in Bryce Canyon set aside as a national forest.

1906 Mesa Verde National Park established. Idea to make Hawaii Volcanoes area a park promoted. Petrified Forest named a national monument.

1906-08 Charles Sheldon, noted hunter-naturalist, visits Mount McKinley to study Dall sheep and other wildlife; becomes proponent of preserving area.

1907 Cinder Cone and Lassen Peak named national monuments.

1908 President Theodore Roosevelt establishes Grand Canyon National Monument. First ranger-guided trips conducted to Mesa Verde's Cliff Dwellings: Spruce Tree House excavated by Dr. Jesse Walter Fewkes.

1909 Dr. Fewkes excavates Cliff Palace. President proclaims Mukuntuweap National Monument. Mount Olympus National Monument, 615,000 acreas, established.

————————•••1910•••————————

1910 Glacier National Park established. Automobile makes trips to Rockies practicable. First ascent of north peak of Mount McKinley (19,470 ft.) by Alaska sourdoughs. Dr. J. L. Nusbaum excavates Balcony House.

1912 American scientist Thomas Jagger and others set up Hawaiian Volcano Research Association with an observatory on Mount Kilauea.

1915 Mount Rainier National Park established. Glowing lava appears, spills through western notch of Lassen; destructive mudflows; vapor and ash rise 5 miles above crater. 124 Congressmen visit Hawaii to investigate possibilities for a national park.

1915-22 Dr. Fewkes excavates several cliff dwellings and mesa-top sites in the Mesa Verde.

1916 Lassen Volcanic National Park established. Hawaii National Park established. National Park Service created.

1917 Mount McKinley National Park established. Beginning of the 11-year administration of Steven T. Mather as NPS Director. Mather sought to make parks known to more persons, build park museums, preserve natural aspects; helped establish 12 national parks.

1918 Explorations by LeRoy Jeffers in Bryce Canyon publicize area. Mukuntuweap National Monument enlarged and name changed to Zion. Park service ranger force replaces soldiers in national parks.

1919 Grand Canyon National Park established. Zion National Park established. Utah legislature proposes to Congress that Bryce Canyon be made a national park.

————————•••1920•••————————

1920 Campfire lecture series and nature study trips instituted in Yosemite.

1922 43,000 acres, mainly the Kau Lava Flow in the Kau Desert, added to Hawaii National Park.

1923 Bryce Canyon National Monument established. Wagon road to Savage River Camp near Mount McKinley completed; Alaska Railroad completed. Explorations of Carlsbad Caverns by James Larkin White included in report by Robert Holley of the General Land Office, United States Department of Interior. Carlsbad Cave National Monument authorized.

1923-24 Exploration of Carlsbad Caverns by Dr. Willis T. Lee conducted by and reported by National Geographic Society.

1924 Bryce Canyon National Park authorized. Kilauea erupts; steam blast ends the lava lake phase in Halemaumau. Archaeological surveys, excavations begin in the Mesa Verde.

1926 Mauna Loa eruption destroys Hoopuloa.

1928 Bryce Canyon National Park established.

1929 Grand Teton National Park established. Beginning of 4-year administration of Horace M. Albright as Director, NPS. Previously Mather's assistant, Albright saw many important roads built providing access to parks: Zion-Mt. Carmel, Wawona Tunnel and Road, Grand Canyon Cape Royal Road, Paradise Valley, Yakima Park Hwy., and new road across divide in Rocky Mountains, among many. Three new parks added.

———————◆◆1930◆◆———————

1930 Carlsbad Caverns National Park established.

1932 Waterton-Glacier International Peace Park established.

1933 President Hoover proclaims additional 9,239 acres in Carlsbad Caverns National Park. Beginning of 7-year administration of Arno B. Cammerer as Director, NPS. He oversees complete study to get a plan for adequate park facilities. CCC does much park work during Depression era. Winter use of parks increases.

1935 Efforts renewed for an Olympic National Park.

1936 NPS gets Congress to provide for adequate water rights.

1937 Second Zion National Monument established. President Franklin Roosevelt visits Olympic Peninsula. Rocky Mountain irrigation tunnel authorized and begun despite opposition of NPS, NP Assn., and conservationists.

1938 Olympic National Park established. Mount McKinley park road built.

1939 President Roosevelt adds 39,488 acres to Carlsbad Caverns National Park

———————◆◆1940◆◆———————

1940 Kings Canyon (encompassing General Grant National Park) established. Addition made to Olympic National Park. Beginning of 11-year administration of Newton B. Drury as Director, NPS. Educational-Interpretive branch of NPS grows. War turns parks into

training areas. After war, tourist boom in national parks; Drury spends much time and energy fighting for funds. Regional offices of NPS set up in San Francisco, Richmond, Omaha, Santa Fe.

1941 Park appropriations cut in half during World War II. National Parks Concessioners, Inc. formed.

1942 Lava flow from Mauna Loa comes within 12 miles of the city of Hilo.

1943 Jackson Hole National Monument established. Addition to Olympic National Park.

1945 War over; tourists head for the parks.

1947-50 Dam threats to parks by Bureau of Reclamation, Army Engineers.

———————◆◆1950◆◆———————

1950 Jackson Hole added to Grand Teton National Park. Mauna Loa's eruption destroys village.

1951 Secretary of Interior Oscar Chapman issues order barring Bureau of Reclamation from surveys and investigations in national parks and monuments, wilderness areas and wildlife areas. Beginning of administration of Conrad Wirth as Director, NPS. During this time greater freedom accorded park service, more private land acquired, ambitious Mission 66 plan conceived and adopted.

1952 Kilauea eruption lasts 136 days.

1953 Queets Corridor and Pacific Coast area added to Olympic National Park.

1954 Brilliant eruption of Kilauea lasts 4 days.

1955 Kilauea erupts again, lasts 55 days.

1956 Monument added to Zion National Park. Mission 66 project begun by NPS—a 10-year conservation, and improvement program.

1957 Denali Highway completed to Mount McKinley.

1958 Archaeological survey and excavation in the Mesa Verde begun by the Wetherill Mesa Archaeological Project.

1959 Kilauea makes most spectacular eruption in its recorded history; fountains of molten lava 1,900 ft. high. Earthquake in Yellowstone destroys campground, creates new lake.

———————◆◆1960◆◆———————

1960 Kilauea's month-long eruption sends lava flowing to the sea; adds 500 acres

1961 Haleakala section made separate national park. Original park name changed to Hawaii Volcanoes.

1962 Petrified Forest National Park established.

1964 Yosemite celebrates centennial of Abraham Lincoln's proclamation setting aside the Valley and Mariposa Grove as a park under state of California; Pioneer History Center dedicated. Canyonlands National Park is established.

1965 Opening of West Yellowstone airport

305

PARK STATISTICS

MOUNTAIN PEAKS

The principal mountain peaks within the Western National Parks rank as follows:

Mount National Park	Elevation
McKinley, Mount McKinley	20,320'
North Peak, Mount McKinley	19,470
Foraker, Mount McKinley	17,400
Whitney, Sequoia	14,495
Rainier, Mount Rainier	14,410
Williamson, Sequoia	14,375
Longs Peak, Rocky Mountain	14,256
Langley, Sequoia	14,042
Muir, Sequoia	14,015
Grand Teton, Grand Teton	13,766
Mauna Loa, Hawaii Volcanoes	13,680*
Silverthrone, Mount McKinley	13,220
Lyell, Yosemite	13,114
Dana, Yosemite	13,053
Middle Teton, Grand Teton	12,798
South Teton, Grand Teton	12,505
Teewinot, Grand Teton	12,317
Mather, Mount McKinley	12,123
Hoffman, Yosemite	10,836
Lassen Peak, Lassen Volcanic	10,457
Cleveland, Glacier	10,448
Washburn, Yellowstone	10,243
Clouds Rest, Yosemite	9,926
Brokeoff Mountain, Lassen Volcanic	9,235
Scott, Crater Lake	8,926
Half Dome, Yosemite	8,842
Olympus, Olympic	7,965
West Temple, Zion	7,795
El Capitan, Yosemite	7,569
Glacier Point, Yosemite	7,214
The Watchman, Zion	6,555
Temple of Sinawava, Zion	4,411

And by way of comparison:

Everest	29,002

*If the below sea-level footage were added to the above sea-level elevation of Mauna Loa, it would top them all with 31,680 feet.

HIGHWAY PASSES

Pass National Park	Summit
Fall River, Rocky Mountain	11,796'
Milner, Rocky Mountain	10,758
Tioga, Yosemite	9,941
Dunraven, Yellowstone	8,859
Craig (over Continental Divide) Yellowstone	8,262
Logan, Glacier	6,664

CANYONS

Canyon National Park	Depth
Kings, Kings Canyon	7,000-8,000'
Kern, Sequoia	6,000
Grand Canyon, Grand Canyon	5,200
Tuolumne, Yosemite	4-5,000
Yosemite Valley, Yosemite	3,000
Grand Canyon of the Yellowstone, Yell.	1,200

WATERFALLS

Falls National Park	Height
Yosemite Falls, Yosemite	2,425'
Ribbon, Yosemite	1,612
Bridalveil, Yosemite	620
Nevada, Yosemite	594
Illilouette, Yosemite	370
Vernal, Yosemite	317
Lower Falls, Yellowstone River, Yell.	308
Tower, Yellowstone	132
Upper Falls, Yellowstone River, Yell.	109

And by way of comparison:

Niagara, American	167
Canadian	158

LAKES

Lake National Park	Square Miles
Yellowstone, Yellowstone	137
Crater, Crater Lake	20
Jackson, Grand Teton	40

And by way of comparison:

Tahoe	193

TREES

Dimensions of the General Sherman and General Grant Trees

	General Sherman	General Grant
Height above mean base	272.4 feet	267.4 feet
Circumference at base	101.6 feet	107.6 feet
Maximum diameter at base	36.5 feet	40.3 feet
Mean diameter at base	32.2 feet	33.3 feet
Diameter 60 feet above ground	17.5 feet	18.8 feet
Diameter 120 feet above ground	17.0 feet	15.0 feet
Diameter 180 feet above ground	14.0 feet	12.9 feet
Height to first large branch	130.0 feet	129.0 feet
Diameter of largest branch	6.8 feet	4.5 feet
Weight of trunk (approximate)	625 tons	565 tons
Total volume of trunk	50,010 cu. ft.	45,232 cu. ft.

Comparison with Other Giant Sequoias

Tree Location	Base diameter	Height
McKinley, Sequoia	28.0'	291.0'
Hart, Kings Canyon	26.5	277.9
Boole, Sequoia	33.2	268.8
California, Kings Canyon	30.0	260.0
Lincoln, Sequoia	31.0	259.0
President, Sequoia	29.0	250.0
Wawona (Tunnel Tree), Yosemite	27.5	231.0
Grizzly Giant, Yosemite	27.6	209.0

Comparison of Giant Sequoias with other Trees

Coast redwood (Libbey Tree)	14.0'	367.8'
Coast redwood (Founders Tree)	12.7	352.6
Mountain gum (eucalyptus regnans)	15.0	326.0
Douglas fir	12.0	324.0

NATIONAL PARK OR NATIONAL FOREST ?

In what ways do they differ?	NATIONAL PARK SERVICE	UNITED STATES FOREST SERVICE
BACKGROUND	Established by Congress as a bureau of the Department of the Interior in 1916. Initial idea resulted from an expedition in 1869-70 through what is now Yellowstone Park, when a Montana judge named Cornelius Hedges opposed private exploitation of the area and proposed instead that such wildernesses be kept in the public domain for the enjoyment of all.	Established under the Department of Agriculture in 1905, a direct descendant of the Bureau of Forestry that had functioned as part of the Department of the Interior after Congress first authorized forest reserves in 1891. Initially, government forest reserves were needed to safeguard the dwindling western timberlands still in public domain toward the end of the 19th century.
PURPOSE	Conservation and preservation of lands and sites which owing to their natural beauty historical significance are part of our natural heritage.	Preservation and development of all the resources in our national forests and the maintenance of these regions to prevent extinction of our natural reserves.
POLICY	Provide for public benefit and enjoyment without impairment of the wilderness or interfering with nature's cycle. Activities such as cutting timber, hunting and mining are not permitted but the control of plant and wildlife diseases, fire control and facilities for display and explanation of natural phenomena and historical features are provided.	Conservation of national forest areas by selective cutting of timber, regulated hunting of wildlife and mining of certain minerals, controlled grazing by domestic animals, study of plant growth and disease, reforestation, fire control, cooperation with state and private landowners in forestry programs and, as an adjunct to this program, public recreation.
JURISDICTION	Presently 201 areas including national parks, monuments and recreational areas, historical parks, battlefields, sites and memorials totalling over 26 million acres.	Presently 154 national forests and 18 national grasslands comprising 186 million acres of land in 41 states and Puerto Rico.
ORGANIZATION	Headquarters in Washington, D.C., and segmented into 6 regional offices, each having a regional director in charge; each park managed by a resident superintendent assisted by his staff of park rangers.	Headquarters in Washington, D.C., and 10 administrative regions, each headed by a regional forester; each national forest under a forest supervisor with a staff of technicians; each forest divided into ranger districts, usually composed of 50,000 to 300,000 acres each and headed by a district ranger who in turn supervises a staff of forest rangers.
LAW ENFORCEMENT	Rangers have authority to arrest for misdemeanors, e.g., traffic violations, disorderly conduct, etc., commited within park boundaries, as well as violations of park rules; cases tried before Federal Commissioner, often located within the park.	Rangers have authority to enforce laws effecting the land management, e.g., trespass, illegal timber cutting, poaching, etc., but call in sheriff for misdemeanors; violations of law tried in state courts.

307

PARK LIFE ZONES

THE MAIN IDEA OF THE MERRIAM LIFE ZONES is a fairly simple one: If the climate in one place is like the climate somewhere else, then the plants and animals in the two places will be as much alike as the climates are, because certain kinds of life exist in certain conditions.

C. Hart Merriam, the American naturalist, worked out a scale in 1898 which held that a gain of 1000 feet in elevation produces the same change in climate to be found by moving 200 miles northward from any established point in this continent. With this basic scale, Merriam defined six climatic regions or zones of life in North America. The names are appropriate and descriptive of the regions involved: the Arctic, Hudson's Bay, and the state of Sonora in Mexico. Each zone exists in its own latitude, but where elevation or topography result in climatic change the zones can be found north or south. So, for example, the Hudsonian Zone persists far south along the Rocky Mountains, at increasingly higher elevations on the lofty peaks.

In broad outline, Merriam's theory is as useful today as when he first advanced it. In close detail, the Merriam zones are hardly accurate to the expert botanist, taxono-

| | | NORTHWEST | | | CALIFORNIA | | |
LIFE ZONES (MERRIAM)	OLYMPIC	MOUNT RAINIER	CRATER LAKE	LASSEN VOLCANIC	YOSEMITE	SEQUOIA & KINGS CANYON
ARCTIC-ALPINE Above timberline to fields of perennial snow and ice.	Obstruction Pt.	On trails above Paradise, Sunrise areas		Lassen Peak	Crest of Sierra N. of Tioga Rd. from White Wolf to Tioga Pass	Everywhere above timberline
HUDSONIAN On high mountain slopes: thinning forest to timberline.	Hurricane Ridge	Paradise and Sunrise	Rim Vill.; Garfield Pk., Mt. Scott, and Watchman trails	Summit of Lassen Park Rd.	White Wolf, Tuolumne Meadows	Timberline down to main forest, at about 9,200'; includes white bark and foxtail pines and mountain hemlock
CANADIAN Generally forested slopes, with annual rainfall 25-30".	Olympic Hot Spr. Campgrnd.	Longmire, Ohanapecosh	Annie Spr. Sta.; Park HQ; junction N. entr. rd. with Rim Dr.	Summit Lake, Kings Cr. Meadows	Crane Flat, Chinquapin, Mariposa Grove, Glacier Pt.	Most extensive; main forest of the higher zones; includes lodgepole pines; highest of sequoias here above lower fringe of zone
TRANSITION Plateaulands of open, scrubby forest mostly.	Elwha Campgrnd., Lake Crescent, Hoh Rain Forest		From S. entr. to 4 mi. along park rd.	Manzanita Lk., Butte Lk., Warner Valley	Yosemite Valley	4,500-7,500' Giant Forest, Grant Grove Cedar Grove, Kern Canyon at low extreme
UPPER SONORAN Mesas; foothills on dry eastern slopes.					Arch Rock entrance	Park HQ at Ash Mountain
LOWER SONORAN Deserts.						

BY COMPARING INFORMATION about a park with which he is familiar with one that is unknown to him, the traveler can get a rough approximation from this chart of what plants and animals he can expect to see when he visits the unfamiliar park. Since this chart is highly generalized, its information should be amplified with a stop at the Visitors Center.

SPECIAL NOTE ON HAWAII VOLCANOES NATIONAL PARK: Because of the tropical nature of the island vegetation, habitats include Coastal Lowland Zone (rain forest, 0-2,000 feet on the

mist, or ecologist. They are only vague descriptions of life communities that can be broken profitably into dozens or even hundreds of far more specific communities. Climate, as Merriam's successors have found, is only one part of life associations and the tricks that Western mountains play with climates leave the Merriam Zones stacked upside down in places (e.g., Grand Canyon), or cause the upper Sonoran zone to run right into the Canadian at another place where the Transition Zone is absent altogether.

For all of the departures, similarities exist between the corresponding zones of widely separated parks. The alert traveller can take pleasure out of noticing which life forms prosper inland as well as by the sea. He can take equal pleasure from discovering which ones do not. The chart below lists some of the most widely distributed indicators.

Plants are the most reliable guides. They exist where they root, and conditions must be suitable or they cannot long endure. A few small animals must live in the presence of some one plant, but most large species can adapt to enough dietary differences to range out of one zone into another. Large mammals wander freely from Transition Zone to Hudsonian where seasonal diets encourage this. Birds serve best among animals in that they nest in the zone to which they are best adapted.

SOUTHWEST						ROCKY MOUNTAIN			ALASKA
GRAND CANYON	BRYCE CANYON	ZION	PETRIFIED FOREST	MESA VERDE	CARLSBAD CAVERNS	ROCKY MOUNTAIN	GLACIER	GRAND TETON	MOUNT McKINLEY
						11,500-14,255' Alpine Vis. Cent. Trail Ridge Rd.	Logan Pass; most high country trails	Much of pk. above timberline; best 7 mi. along trail from Lk. Solitude	Sable, Polychrome Hwy., and Thorofare passes; alpine tundra
Above 9,200' on trails from N. Rim						9,000 to 11,500' Bear Lk. area; also called Subalpine	This zone is nowhere well defined in the park	On trail 6 mi. above Jenny Lk.; 1 mi. av. Lake Solitude	All campgrnds.; all points where park road crosses rivers
8,200-9,200' Grand Can. Lodge area, N. Rim Inn, N. Rim camp Cape Royal road	Whiteman Bench, S. portions of park above the rim					6,000-9,000' "Montane Zone" is thorough mixture of materials from Can-	Nearly all developed areas in the park	Zone not clearly defined; but Douglas fir forest 2 mi. above Jenny Lake	
7,000-8,000 Along E. Rim Dr. and around Grand View Overlook	Above rim in N. portions of park	Lady Mt. trail, W. Rim trail, Taylor Cr. area, Kolob section		In moist draws and canyon heads		adian and Transition Zones. Endovalley Aspenglen campgrnds.	3100' W. to 4700' E.; near park HQ on W., St. Mary on E.; N. Fk., Polebridge		
5,000-7,000' S., W., and E. Rim Drs.; parts of Bright Angel Tr.	Boat Mesa, Tropic Can. Rd. below rim; most hiking trails	E. and W. rim trails, Emerald Pool trails	Entire park, but not wholly typical	Mesa top					
Phantom Ranch, Inner Canyon		Scoggans Wash, S. portion of Zion Canyon			Park HQ area in entirety				

windward side; coastal shrubs, 0-1,500 feet on leeward side). Transition Forest Zone (1,500-3,000 feet on leeward side); Mountain Forest Zone (2,000-4,000 feet on windward side and 2,500-6,000 feet on leeward side). Parkland Zone (up to timberline at 7,000 feet). Subalpine Zone (7,000 to 9-10,000 feet), and Alpine Zone (above 9-10,000 feet). HALEAKALA: Tropical Rain Forest (Paliku, 6,300 feet), Subalpine (park headquarters, 7,030 feet), Transition Forest (Hosmer Grove, 6,800 feet), and Semi-desert (6,000 feet).

NATIONAL MONUMENTS

There are 63 national monuments, recreation areas, historic sites, and memorials also administered by the National Park Service in the West. Each is briefly described below. The post office address, attractions, season (where applicable), facilities, and activities of each are listed, with a warning where hazards exist.

Further information about any of these areas may be obtained by writing to the superintendent at the address listed. Where dangerous conditions may prevail, prior advice should always be obtained from park rangers at the location. (For definition of "national monument," see page 20.)

NORTHWEST

COULEE DAM NATIONAL RECREATION AREA, Washington. Lake formed by dam. May-Oct. Thirty-eight developed areas around lake with picnic grounds, bathing beaches, campsites, boat docks, fuel; fishing, camping, swimming, boating, water skiing, picnics.

FORT CLATSOP NATIONAL MEMORIAL, Astoria, Ore. Historic site of encampment of Lewis-Clark Expedition during winter of 1805-6. Daytime visits only; picnic table.

FORT VANCOUVER NATIONAL HISTORIC SITE, Vancouver, Wash. Hudson's Bay Company's western headquarters, 1825-49, and former military reservation. Visitor center; daytime visits only.

GLACIER BAY NATIONAL MONUMENT, Juneau, Alaska. Tidewater glaciers, ice-capped mountains, glacial forests, rare wildlife. Approach only by cruise ship, chartered boat, or airplane. Hazardous to get within ½ mile of active glaciers by boat, in no case should boat without experienced pilot visit the monument.

KATMAI NATIONAL MONUMENT, Mount McKinley Park, Alaska. Active and inactive volcanoes; lakes, glaciers; brown bear, world's largest carnivore. June-Sept. Tent cabins, meals, fishing and camping equipment. Reach only by plane from King Salmon, 16 miles away.

MCLOUGHLIN HOUSE NATIONAL HISTORIC SITE, Oregon City, Ore. Former home of "Father of Oregon," Dr. John McLoughlin, who played major role in development of Pacific Northwest. Daytime visits only, closed Mondays.

OREGON CAVES NATIONAL MONUMENT, Crater Lake National Park, Medford, Ore. Remarkable marble cavern. Lodge, cabins, meals, nursery (June-Sept.), picnic area, campground 8 miles from monument; guided tours through cave, trail walks, campfire programs.

SITKA NATIONAL MONUMENT, Juneau, Alaska. Historic site of Indian stockade attacked in 1804 by Russian settlers. Totem pole exhibit. Reach via scheduled airline from Seattle, Wash., or Juneau.

WHITMAN NATIONAL MONUMENT, Walla Walla, Wash. Landmark on Oregon Trail, site where Dr. and Mrs. Marcus Whitman ministered to Indians. Picnic tables; self-guided trips, summer guide service.

CALIFORNIA

CABRILLO NATIONAL MONUMENT, San Diego. Memorial to discoverer and explorer of western U.S. Includes old Point Loma Lighthouse. Daytime visits only; historical talks.

CHANNEL ISLANDS NATIONAL MONUMENT, San Diego. Includes Santa Barbara and Anacapa Islands off coast of Los Angeles. Large numbers of sea lions, sea birds; unique plants and animals.

DEATH VALLEY NATIONAL MONUMENT, Death Valley. Vast desert in California and Nevada containing many salt beds, borax formations and other natural phenomena. The lowest point in Western Hemisphere. Visitor center, campgrounds, hotels, cabins, meals, fuel. Illustrated nature talks in winter, self-guiding auto tours; horseback trips, golf, swimming pool.

DEVILS POSTPILE NATIONAL MONUMENT, Yosemite National Park. Organlike pipes of blue-gray basalt rising 60 feet. July-Oct. Campground, cabins, meals, fuel, hot-springs baths, shops; hiking, fishing, pack and saddle trips.

JOSHUA TREE NATIONAL MONUMENT, Twentynine Palms. Desert country with magnificent examples of Joshua tree, cholla cactus, other desert flora, granite formations. Campgrounds, some water, no fuel; self-guiding trails. Stay on designated travel routes.

LAVA BEDS NATIONAL MONUMENT, Tulelake. Principal site of Modoc Indian War, 1872-3. Ice caves, lava tubes or caves, cinder cones, recent lava flows; museum, campground, picnic area; campfire programs and illustrated talks in summer, self-guided trips.

MUIR WOODS NATIONAL MONUMENT, Mill Valley. Superb examples of towering redwoods. Daytime visits only. Light meals, gift shop; self-guiding nature trail, picnic area.

PINNACLES NATIONAL MONUMENT, Paicines. Spires of rock 500 to 1200 feet high, caves and volcanic features. Campground, picnic area; hiking on trails.

POINT REYES NATIONAL SEASHORE, Point Reyes, Calif. Miles of unspoiled beaches, forested ridges and upland meadows with ocean views. Picnicking, fishing, hiking, swimming. Extensive future development.

SOUTHWEST

ARCHES NATIONAL MONUMENT, Moab, Utah. Longest stone span in the world; immense arches and windows in slabs of red sandstone. Visitor center, picnic areas; hiking, camping, prearranged pack trips. Scarcity of water sources, possibility of getting lost, and sudden road washouts hazardous.

AZTEC RUINS NATIONAL MONUMENT, Aztec, N.M. Ruins of 12th century prehistoric Indian town constructed of masonry and timber. Museum; self-guiding trips to ruins.

BANDELIER NATIONAL MONUMENT, Santa Fe, N.M. Late prehistoric cliff and pueblo ruins, awesome canyons. Lodging, meals, fuel, camping supplies (May-Sept), campground, museum; guided, self-guided trips, campfire programs, hikes.

CANYON DE CHELLY NATIONAL MONUMENT, Chinle, Ariz. Ruins of prehistoric Indian homes below sheer red cliffs, Indian caves, modern Navajo homes. Picnic area, campground, meals, lodging; canyon trips by special auto. Roads impassable in bad weather, quicksand in canyon.

CAPITOL REEF NATIONAL MONUMENT, Torrey, Utah. Long sandstone cliff, colorful formations. Small museum, small campground with water; scenic drives, hiking. Hikers, campers' register. Road sometimes difficult to travel.

CAPULIN MOUNTAIN NATIONAL MONUMENT, Capulin, N.M. Crater of extinct volcano, lava-covered mesas, view of four states. Picnic area, no fuel or water, only portable stoves permitted; self-guiding trips around crater rim.

CASA GRANDE NATIONAL MONUMENT, Coolidge, Ariz. Ruins of Indian tower and village. Museum, picnic area; guided trips.

CEDAR BREAKS NATIONAL MONUMENT, Zion National Park, Springdale, Utah. Natural amphitheatre cut into pink cliffs, colorful rocks, flora. June-Oct. Lodge, cabins, meals (June-Sept.), picnic area, campground, museum.

CHACO CANYON NATIONAL MONUMENT, Bloomfield, N.M. Prehistoric Indian pueblo ruins. Visitor center, picnic area, small campground. Approach roads impassable in wet weather.

CHIRACAHUA NATIONAL MONUMENT, Dos Cabezas, Ariz. Strange rock shapes, strata spanning almost a billion years. Exhibits, meals, lodging, campground; scenic drive, hikes, horseback.

CORONADO NATIONAL MEMORIAL, Hereford, Ariz. Expansive view of Coronado's route in 1540, memorial to his explorations. Visitor center, picnic areas; self-guiding trip.

DINOSAUR NATIONAL MONUMENT, Vernal, Utah. Semiarid plateau in Colorado-Utah with deep gorges, rapid waters, and rich skeletal deposits of prehistoric reptiles. All-year visitor center with dinosaur fossils; campgrounds. May-Oct. Self-guiding nature trips and campfires in summer, river boat and auto trips through canyons; back roads sometimes hazardous.

EL MORRO NATIONAL MONUMENT, Ramah, N.M. "Inscription rock" with hundreds of inscriptions by Spanish settlers and American emigrants. Prehistoric ruins; campground; self-guided trips. Roads bad in winter, wet weather.

FORT UNION NATIONAL MONUMENT, Watrous, N.M. Part of Santa Fe Trail, site of major fort in early Southwest. Visitor center; self-guiding trail trip.

GILA CLIFF DWELLINGS NATIONAL MONUMENT, Silver City, N.M. Well-preserved cliff dwellings. Access difficult.

GRAN QUIVIRA NATIONAL MONUMENT, Gran Quivira, N.M. Ruins of frontier Spanish mission and Pueblo Indian house mounds. Picnic area, museum; guided, self-guided trips.

GRAND CANYON NATIONAL MONUMENT, Grand Canyon, Ariz. Spectacular view of inner gorge of Grand Canyon, traces of lava cascade. Access only by primitive road.

HOVENWEEP NATIONAL MONUMENT, Mesa Verde National Park, Colo. Six groups prehistoric pueblos, cliff dwellings, towers. No facilities or water. Road conditions uncertain; check at headquarters.

LAKE MEAD NATIONAL RECREATION AREA, Boulder City, Nev. Lake Mead, formed by Hoover Dam, and Lake Mohave, formed by Davis Dam. Lodges, meals, cabins, trailer courts, campgrounds, boat ramps and service, moorings, fishing supplies, swimming; boat trips, water skiing, hiking, camping, fishing, swimming, illustrated talks.

LEHMAN CAVES NATIONAL MONUMENT, Baker, Nev. Limestone caverns with tunnels, galleries, huge stalagmites and stalactites. Meals, souvenirs, picnic area, 2 miles to campground.

MONTEZUMA CASTLE NATIONAL MONUMENT, Camp Verde, Ariz. Well-preserved prehistoric cliff dwelling, Montezuma Well, located in detached area. Several picnic areas, visitor center; self-guiding trail trips.

NATURAL BRIDGES NATIONAL MONUMENT, Arches National Monument, Moab, Utah. Three natural sandstone bridges, highest 220 feet. May-Sept. Campground; self-guiding trail trips. Access difficult.

NAVAJO NATIONAL MONUMENT, Tonalea, Ariz. Three remarkable cliff dwellings; Betatakin, Keet Seel, Inscription Rock. Campground, picnic area. Guided trips to ruins, self-guiding trail trips.

ORGAN PIPE CACTUS NATIONAL MONUMENT, Ajo, Ariz. Wild desert country with organpipe and other cactus, wild life, impressive scenery. Visitor center, campground; hikes, self-guided auto trips, winter campfire programs.

PIPE SPRING NATIONAL MONUMENT, Moccasin, Ariz. Historic 19th century Mormon fort. Picnic area; guided tour.

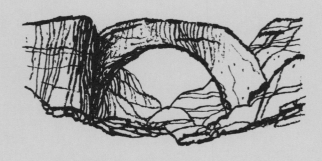

RAINBOW BRIDGE NATIONAL MONUMENT, Tonalea, Ariz. Most massive of world's known natural bridges, salmon-pink sandstone arching 309 feet above gorge. April-Nov. 15. Meals, lodging, guides, horses. Approach by boat trip only. A 10-mile round-trip hike from boat is necessary to reach bridge and return; hike is isolated, hot.

SAGUARO NATIONAL MONUMENT, Tucson, Ariz. Cactus desert containing superlative examples of unique giant saguaro. Picnic areas, small museum; self-guiding 9-mile loop drive, self-guiding geology tour, nature trails, hikes.

SUNSET CRATER NATIONAL MONUMENT, Wupatki National Monument, Flagstaff, Ariz. Prehistoric volcano with upper cinder cone sunset-colored. May-Sept. Self-guiding trail trip. Entrance road sometimes closed by snow.

TIMPANOGOS CAVE NATIONAL MONUMENT, American Fork, Utah. Cave noted for delicate helictite formations. May-Oct. Store, picnic area, small campground; guided cave tour, self-guided trail trips.

Tonto National Monument, Roosevelt, Ariz. Well-preserved 14th century Indian pueblo cliff-dwellings. Picnic area; guided and self-guided tours of ruins.

Tumacacori National Monument, Tumacacori, Ariz. Historic Spanish mission building. Museum, patio garden; self-guiding trips.

Tuzigoot National Monument, Clarkdale, Ariz. Excavated ruins of large prehistoric pueblo; museum; self-guiding trips.

Walnut Canyon National Monument, Flagstaff, Ariz. Early limestone cliff dwellings of Pueblo Indians. Picnic area; self-guiding trail trips.

White Sands National Monument, Alamogordo, N.M. Bright, white sand-forming dunes up to 45 feet high, small desert animals. Visitor center, museum, refreshments, gift shop, picnic area; self-guiding auto trip.

Wupatki National Monument, Flagstaff, Ariz. Ruins of red sandstone pueblos built by prehistoric farming Indians. Wayside museum; self-guiding trips to ruins. Road from Sunset Crater usually not passable in winter.

ROCKY MOUNTAINS

Big Hole Battlefield National Monument, Yellowstone Park, Wyo. Site of 1877 battle during famous retreat of Chief Joseph and his Nez Perce Indians. June-Oct 15. Museum.

Black Canyon of the Gunnison National Monument, Fruita, Colo. Spectacular gorge of river, noted for narrowness, shadowy depth, vast sheer walls. Late spring-early fall. Campgrounds on gorge rims, gift shop on south rim; light meals, self-guiding trails, campfire programs. Canyon descent hazardous and difficult.

Colorado National Monument, Fruita, Colo. Bone deposits of five dinosaur species. Highly colored and weirdly carved rock formations of towering proportions; campgrounds and picnic areas; canyon rim auto trip, self-guiding trails; campfire programs in summer.

Craters of the Moon National Monument, Arco, Idaho. Volcanic phenomena such as fissure eruptions, c nder cones, craters, lava flows, caves. Visitor center, picnic area, campground; scenic loop drive (May-Nov.), camping, hiking, guided tours.

Custer Battlefield National Monument, Crow Agency, Mont. Site of famous "last stand" along Little Bighorn River in 1876, in which Lt. Col. Custer and 261 men were slain by Indians. Museum; historian talks in summer, self-guiding trails.

Devils Tower National Monument, Devils Tower, Wyo. First U.S. national monument, an 865 foot rock pinnacle left by prehistoric volcanic activity. Museum at monument, campground, picnic area, cabin camp outside monument; trail hikes.

Fort Laramie National Historic Site, Fort Laramie, Wyo. Fur-trading post, major military guard post along westward covered-wagon trails, 1834-90. Temporary museum, picnic area; guided and self-guided trips through fort area.

Great Sand Dunes National Monument, Alamosa, Colo. Some of largest and highest sand dunes in U.S. Visitor center, picnic area, campground; self-guiding nature trail trip.

Shadow Mountain National Recreation Area, Rocky Mtn. National Park, Estes, Colo. Mountain lake and reservoir, beautiful scenery. Campgrounds, boat launch ramps, federally-operated; motels, restaurants, boat rentals, horses, mooring sites, shops privately owned nearby; boating, fishing, camping.

BIBLIOGRAPHY

THIS BIBLIOGRAPHY IS GENERALLY LIMITED to books, pamphlets, and articles that are likely to be found in a large library or a good bookstore. In addition to the titles listed, there is a wealth of material published within each park by a non-profit association from whom books, maps, films, and color slides may be ordered by mail. Addresses of these associations are listed under each park.

NATIONAL PARKS—GENERAL

Bolin, Luis A. *National Parks of the United States.* New York: Knopf, 1962.

Butcher, Deveraux. *Exploring Our National Parks and Monuments.* New York: Houghton Mifflin Co., 1956.

Heath, Monroe. *Our National Parks at a Glance.* Menlo Park, Calif.: Pacific Coast Publishers, 1959.

Ise, John. *Our National Park Policy, A Critical History.* Baltimore· Johns Hopkins Press, 1961.

Jensen, Paul. *National Parks.* New York: Golden Press.

Matthews, William H., III. *National Parks.* New York: Barnes and Noble, 1964.

Melbo, Irving H. *Our Country's National Parks.* 2 vols. New York: Bobbs-Merrill Co., Inc., 1963.

National Geographic Society. *America's Wonderlands, The National Parks.* Washington, D.C.: National Geographic Society, 1959.

Shankland, Robert. *Steve Mather of the National Parks.* New York: Knopf, 1954.

Story, Isabelle F. *The National Park Story in Pictures.* Washington, D.C.: Government Printing Office, 1957.

Sunset Magazine. *Western Campsite Directory.* Menlo Park, Calif.: Lane Books, 1965.

Tilden, Freeman. *The National Parks: What They Mean to You and Me.* New York: Knopf, 1951.

Udall, Stewart L. *The Quiet Crisis.* New York: Holt, Rinehart and Winston, 1963.

Yeager, Dorr. *National Parks in California—A Sunset Discovery Book.* Menlo Park, Calif.: Lane Books, 1964.

———. *Your Western National Parks.* New York: Dodd, Mead & Co., 1947.

NATURAL SCIENCE

Arnberger, Leslie P. and Jeanne R. Janish. *Flowers of the Southwest Mountains.* Globe, Arizona: Southwestern, 1962.

Bailey, Harold E. and Virginia L. *Forests and Trees of Western National Parks.* Washington, D.C.: Government Printing Office, 1941.

Brown, Vinson and David Allan. *Rocks and Minerals of California and Their Stories.* Healdsburg, Calif.: Naturegraph.

Burt, W. H. and R. B. Grossenheider. *A Field Guide to Mammals.* New York: Houghton Mifflin Co., 1959.

Dodge, Natt N. and Herbert S. Zim. *The Pacific Northwest, A Golden Regional Guide.* New York: Golden Press.

Fenton, Carol L. and Mildred A. *The Rock Book.* New York: Doubleday & Co.

Fryxell, Fritiof (ed.) *Francois Matthes and the Marks of Time.* San Francisco: Sierra Club Books, 1962.

Haines, Madge and Leslie Morrill. *John Muir, Protector of the Wilds.* New York: Abingdon Press, 1957.

Harrison, A. E. *Exploring Glaciers—With a Camera.* San Francisco: Sierra Club Books, 1960.

Hoffman, Ralph. *Birds of the Pacific States.* Boston: Houghton Mifflin Co., 1927.

Leet, F. and L. *The World of Geology.* New York: McGraw-Hill Book Co., 1961.

Loomis, Frederic B. *Field Book of Common Rocks and Minerals.* New York: Putnam, 1948.

Muir, John. *The Mountains of California.* New York: Doubleday & Co., 1962.

———. *Our National Parks.* Boston: Houghton Mifflin Co., 1916.

Murie, Olaus. *A Field Guide to Animal Tracks.* New York: Houghton Mifflin Co., 1954.

Olin, George and Jerry Cannon. *Mammals of the Southwest Deserts.* Globe, Arizona: Southwestern.

Palmer, Ralph S. *The Mammal Guide: Mammals of North America, North of Mexico.* New York: Doubleday & Co.

Patraw, Pauline M. and Jeanne R. Janish. *Flowers of the Southwest Mesas.* Globe, Arizona: Southwestern, 1959.

Patterson, Roger Tory. *A Field Guide to Western Birds.* New York: Houghton Mifflin Co., 1961.

Preston, Richard J., Jr. *North American Trees.* Ames, Iowa: Iowa State University Press.

Schultz, G. *Glaciers and the Ice Age.* New York: Holt, Rinehart and Winston, 1963.

Teale, Edwin Way. *Wilderness World of John Muir.* New York: Houghton Mifflin Co., 1954.

Zim, Herbert S. and Paul R. Shaffer. *Rocks and Minerals.* New York: Golden Press.

NORTHWEST PARKS

MOUNT McKINLEY

To secure pamphlets and books on local aspects of the park, write for catalog to Mount McKinley Natural History Association, McKinley Park, Alaska.

Anderson, J. P. *Flora of Alaska and Parts of Adjacent Canada*. Ames, Iowa: Iowa State University Press, 1959.

Dixon, Joseph S. *Birds and Mammals of Mount McKinley National Park*. Washington, D.C.: U.S. Government Printing Office, 1938.

Murie, Adolph. *A Naturalist in Alaska*. (American Nature Series, No. 302.) New York: Devin-Adair Co., 1961.

———. *Birds of Mount McKinley. A field handbook*. McKinley Park, Alaska: Mount McKinley Natural History Association, 1963.

———. *Mammals of Mount McKinley*. McKinley Park, Alaska: Mount McKinley Natural History Association, 1962.

———. *The Wolves of Mount McKinley*. Washington, D.C.: U.S. Government Printing Office, 1944.

Pearson, Grant H. and Philip Newill. *My Life of High Adventure*. Englewood Cliffs, New Jersey: Prentice-Hall, Inc., 1962.

Sheldon, Charles. *The Wilderness of Denali*. New York: Charles Scribner's Sons, 1960.

OLYMPIC NATIONAL PARK

To secure pamphlets and books on local aspects of the park, write for catalog to Olympic Natural History Association, Inc., 600 Park Avenue, Port Angeles, Washington, 98362.

Danner, Wilbert R. *Geology of Olympic National Park*. Seattle, Washington: University of Washington Press, 1955.

Kirk, Ruth. *Exploring the Olympic Peninsula*. Seattle, Washington: University of Washington Press.

———. *The Olympic Seashore*. Port Angeles, Washington: Olympic Natural History Assn., 1962.

Leissler, Frederick. *Roads and Trails of Olympic National Park*. Seattle, Washington: University of Washington Press, 1957.

Sharpe, Grant and Wenonah. *101 Wildflowers of Olympic National Park*. Seattle, Washington: University of Washington Press, 1957.

MOUNT RAINIER

To secure pamphlets and books on local aspects of the park, write for catalog to Mount Rainier Natural History Association, Longmire, Washington 98397.

Allen, Grenville F. *Forests of Mount Rainier National Park*. Washington, D.C.: U.S. Government Printing Office, 1916.

Brockman, C. Frank. *Flora of Mount Rainier National Park*. Washington, D.C.: U.S. Government Printing Office, 1947.

———. *Trees of Mount Rainier National Park*. Seattle, Washington: University of Washington Press, 1949.

Brower, David (ed.) *Manual of Ski Mountaineering*. San Francisco: Sierra Club Books, 1956.

Grater, Russell K. *Grater's Guide to Mount Rainier National Park*. Portland, Oregon: Binfords and Mort, 1962.

Haines, Aubrey L. *Mountain Fever: Historic Conquests of Mount Rainier*. Portland, Oregon: Oregon Historical Society, 1962.

Jones, George Neville. *The Flowering Plants and Ferns of Mount Rainier*. Seattle, Washington: University of Washington Press, 1960.

Meaney, Edmund S. *Mount Rainier, Record of Exploration*. Portland, Oregon: Binfords and Mort, 1916.

The Mountaineers. *The Freedom of the Hills*. Seattle, Washington: The Mountaineers.

Schmoe, Floyd. *Year in Paradise, Chronicle of Mount Rainier and Paradise Valley*. New York: Harper and Row, 1950.

Sharpe, Grant and Wenonah, *101 Wildflowers of Mount Rainier National Park*. Seattle, Washington: University of Washington Press, 1957.

CRATER LAKE

To secure pamphlets and books on local aspects of the park, write for catalog to Crater Lake Natural History Association, Crater Lake, Oregon 97604.

Lapham, Stanton. *Enchanted Lake*. Portland, Oregon: Gill Co., 1931.

Pernat, John F. *Forests of Crater Lake National Park*. Washington, D.C.: Government Printing Office, 1916.

Sharpe, Grant and Wenonah. *101 Wildflowers of Crater Lake National Park*. Seattle, Washington: University of Washington Press, 1959.

Williams, Howel. *Crater Lake: The Story of its Origin*. Berkeley, Calif.: University of California Press, 1957.

CALIFORNIA PARKS

LASSEN VOLCANIC

To secure pamphlets and books on local aspects of the park, write for catalog to Loomis Museum Association, Lassen Volcanic National Park, Mineral, California 96063.

315

Loomis, Frederic B. *Pictorial History of the Lassen Volcano*. Mineral, Calif.: Loomis Museum Association, 1953.

Schulz, James W. *Geology of Lassen's Landscape*. Mineral, Calif.: Loomis Museum Association.

————. *Indians of Lassen Volcanic National Park*. Mineral, Calif.: Loomis Museum Association.

Smith, Gladys L. *Flowers of Lassen Volcanic National Park*. Mineral, Calif.: Loomis Museum Association.

YOSEMITE

To secure pamphlets and books on local aspects of the park, write for catalog to Yosemite Natural History Association, P.O. Box 545, Yosemite National Park, California 95389.

Adams, Ansel and Nancy Newhall. *Yosemite Valley*. San Francisco: Sierra Club Books.

Adams, Ansel and Virginia. *Illustrated Guide to Yosemite*. San Francisco: Sierra Club Books, 1963.

Barrett, S. A. and E. W. Gifford. *Miwok Material Culture*. Yosemite, Calif.: Yosemite Natural History Association, 1933.

Bingaman, John W. *Guardians of the Yosemite*. Palm Desert, Calif.: Desert Printers, Inc., 1961.

Bunnell, Lafayette. *Discovery of the Yosemite*. New York: Fleming H. Revell, 1892.

Degnan, Laurence and Douglass Hubbard. *Yosemite Yarns*. Fresno, Calif.: Awani Press, 1961.

Garth, John S. and J. W. Tilden. *Yosemite Butterflies*. Arcadia, Calif.: The Lepidoptera Foundation, 1963.

Johnston, Hank. *Short Line to Paradise; Story of Yosemite Valley Railroad*. Long Beach, Calif.: Trans-anglo Books, 1962.

————. *Railroads of the Yosemite Valley*. Long Beach, Calif.: Trans-anglo Books, 1963.

Matthes, Francois E. *Incomparable Valley: a Geologic Interpretation of the Yosemite* (ed. Fritiof Fryxell). Berkeley, Calif.: University of California Press, 1956.

Muir, John. *The Yosemite*. New York: Doubleday & Co., 1962.

Muir, John and Ansel Adams. *Yosemite and the Sierra Nevada*. Boston: Houghton Mifflin Co., 1948.

Paden, Irene and Margaret Schlightmann. *Big Oak Flat Road to Yosemite*. Yosemite, Calif.: Yosemite Natural History Association, 1959.

Russell, Carl P. *One Hundred Years in Yosemite*. Yosemite, Calif.: Yosemite Natural History Association, 1959.

Sargent, Shirley. *Galen Clark, Yosemite Guardian*. San Francisco: Sierra Club Books, 1964.

Stebbins, Cyril A. and Robert C. "Birds of Yosemite." *Yosemite Nature Notes*, XXXIII (1954), No. 8, pp. 74–152.

Tressider, Mary Curry and Della Taylor Hoss. *Trees of Yosemite National Park*. Yosemite, California: Yosemite Natural History Association, 1963.

SEQUOIA AND KINGS CANYON

To secure pamphlets and books on local aspects of the park, write for catalog to Sequoia Natural History Association, Three Rivers, California 93271.

Brower, David. *Going Light with Backpack or Burro*. San Francisco: Sierra Club Books, 1960.

Carrighar, Sally. *One Day on Beetle Rock*. New York: Knopf, 1955.

Cook, Lawrence F. *Giant Sequoias of California*. Washington, D.C.: U.S. Government Printing Office, 1942.

Corle, Edwin. *Listen, Bright Angel*. New York: Sloane and Pearce, 1946.

Matthes, Francois E. *Sequoia National Park—A Geological Album*, Berkeley, Calif.: University of California Press, 1950.

Muench, Josef and Joyce. *Kings Canyon National Park*. New York: Hastings House, 1949.

Scoyen, E. T. and Frank Taylor. *Rainbow Canyons*. Stanford, Calif.: Stanford University Press, 1931.

Shirley, James C. *Redwoods of Coast and Sierra*. Berkeley, Calif.: University of California Press, 1937.

Starr, Walter A., Jr. *Starr's Guide to the John Muir Trail and the High Sierra Region*. San Francisco: Sierra Club Books, 1959.

Stewart, George W. *Big Trees of the Giant Forest*. San Francisco: A. M. Robertson, 1930.

Storer, Tracy I. and R. L. Usinger. *Sierra Nevada Natural History*. Berkeley, Calif.: University of California Press, 1963.

Sumner, Lowell, and Joseph S. Dixon. *Birds and Mammals of the Sierra Nevada: With Records from Sequoia and Kings Canyon National Parks*. Berkeley, California: University of California Press, 1953.

Voge, Hervey. *A Climber's Guide to the High Sierra*. San Francisco: Sierra Club Books, 1956.

White, John R. and Samuel J. Pusateri. *Illustrated Guide, Sequoia and Kings Canyon National Parks*. Stanford, Calif.: Stanford University Press, 1952.

Wilson, Herbert E. *Lore and Lure of Sequoia*. Los Angeles: Wolfer Printing Co., 1928.

SOUTHWEST PARKS

GRAND CANYON

To secure pamphlets and books on local aspects of the park, write for catalog to Grand Canyon Natural History Association, Box 219, Grand Canyon, Arizona 86023.

Dellenbaugh, Frederick S. *Canyon Voyage*. New Haven: Yale University Press (rev. ed.), 1962.

Farquhar, Francis P. *Books of the Colorado River and the Grand Canyon, a Selective Bibliography*. Los Angeles: Dawson's, 1953.

Krutch, Joseph Wood. *Grand Canyon: Today and All its Yesterdays*. New York: Sloane, 1958.

————. *Grand Canyon*. New York: Doubleday.

Powell, John Wesley. *Exploration of the Colorado River*. Chicago: University of Chicago Press, 1957.

————. *Exploration of the Colorado River*. New York: Doubleday & Co. (Reprint of the 1895 report.)

Tillotson, M. R. and Frank J. Taylor. *Grand Canyon Country*. Stanford, Calif.: Stanford University Press, (rev. ed.), 1954.

BRYCE AND ZION

To secure pamphlets and books on local aspects of the parks, write for catalogs to Bryce Canyon Natural History Association, Inc., Bryce Canyon, Utah 84717; or to Zion Natural History Association, Springdale, Utah 84767.

Burt, Olive. *Cave of Shouting Silence*. New York: John Day Co., 1960.

Grater, Russel K. *Grater's Guide to Zion, Bryce, and Cedar Breaks*. Portland, Oregon: Binfords and Mort, 1950.

Woodbury, A. *A History of Southern Utah and Its National Parks*. Utah Historical Quarterly, Nos. 3 and 4.

PETRIFIED FOREST

To secure pamphlets and books on local aspects of the park, write for catalog to Petrified Forest Museum Association, Holbrook, Arizona 86025.

Ransom, Jay Ellis. *Petrified Forest Trails: Field Guide*. Mentone, Calif.: Gembooks.

————. *Petrified Forest Trails: Guide to the Petrified Forests of America*. Spokane, Washington: J. D. Simpson and Co., 1955.

MESA VERDE

To secure pamphlets and books on local aspects of the park, write for catalog to The Mesa Verde Museum Association, Mesa Verde National Park, Colorado 81330.

Fewkes, J. W. "Antiquities of Mesa Verde National Park: Cliff Palace," *Bureau of American Ethnology Bulletin*, No. 51 (1911).

————. "Antiquities of Mesa Verde National Park: Spruce Tree House," *Bureau of American Ethnology Bulletin*, No. 41 (1909).

Watson, Don. *Cliff Dwellings of the Mesa Verde*. Mesa Verde National Park, Colorado: The Mesa Verde Association ,1950.

————. *Indians of the Mesa Verde*. Mesa Verde National Park, Colorado: Mesa Verde Museum Association.

CARLSBAD CAVERNS

To secure pamphlets and books on local aspects of the park, write for catalog to Carlsbad Caverns Natural History Association, Box 1599, Carlsbad, New Mexico 88220.

Anderson, A. W. *Carlsbad Caverns of New Mexico*. Carlsbad, New Mexico: Cavern Supply Co.

Lee, Willis T. "A Visit to Carlsbad Cavern," *National Geographic Magazine*, XLV, No. 1, (1924), 1–40.

————. "New Discoveries in Carlsbad Cavern," *National Geographic Magazine*, XLVIII No. 3 (1925), 301–320.

ROCKY MOUNTAIN PARKS

ROCKY MOUNTAIN NATIONAL PARK

To secure pamphlets and books on local aspects of the park, write for catalog to Rocky Mountain Nature Association, P.O. Box 147, Estes Park, Colorado 80517.

Ashton, Ruth E. *Plants of Rocky Mountain National Park*. Washington, D.C.: U.S. Government Printing Office, 1933.

Bird, Isabella L. *Lady's Life in the Rocky Mountains*. Norman, Oklahoma: Oklahoma University Press, 1960.

Clements, F. E. and E. S. *Rocky Mountain Flowers*. New York: Hafner Publishing Co.

Craighead, John J. and others. *Field Guide to Rocky Mountain Wildflowers*. Boston: Houghton Mifflin Co., 1963.

Mills, Enos A. *Rocky Mountain National Park*. New York: Doubleday & Co., 1931.

Packard, Fred Mallery. *Birds of Rocky Mountain National Park*. Estes Park, Colorado: Rocky Mountain Nature Association, 1950.

GLACIER

To secure pamphlets and books on local aspects of the park, write for catalog to Glacier Natural History Association, West Glacier, Montana 59936.

Campbell, Marius R. *Glacier National Park*. Washington, D.C.: U.S. Government Printing Office, 1921.

————. *Origin of the Scenic Features of Glacier National Park*. Washington, D.C.: U.S. Government Printing Office, 1921.

Edwards, Gordon J. *A Climber's Guide to Glacier National Park*. San Francisco, Calif.: Sierra Club Books, 1960.

Ruhle, George C. *Guide to Glacier National Park*. Minneapolis: John W. Forney, 1957.

Standley, Paul C. *Plants of Glacier National Park*. Washington, D.C.: U.S. Government Printing Office, 1926.

YELLOWSTONE

To secure pamphlets and books on local aspects of the park, write for catalog to Yellowstone Library and Museum Association, Box 117, Yellowstone National Park, Wyoming 83020.

Bauer, C. Max. *Yellowstone—its Underworld*. Albuquerque, New Mexico: University of New Mexico Press, 1962.

Beal, Merrill D. *The Story of Man in Yellowstone*. Yellowstone Library and Museum Association, 1960.

Bonney, Orrin H. and Lorraine. *Absaroka Range and Yellowstone Park Field Guide*. Denver, Colorado: A. Swallow, 1963.

Chittendon, Hiram M. *Yellowstone National Park*. (Richard A. Bartlett, ed.). Norman, Oklahoma: University of Oklahoma Press, 1964.

Fisher, Clay. *Yellowstone Kelly*. New York: Houghton Mifflin Co.

Fisher, William A. *Yellowstone's Living Geology*. Yellowstone Library and Museum Association, 1960.

Haynes, J. E. *Haynes Guide: Yellowstone National Park*. Bozeman, Montana: Haynes Studios Inc., 1964.

McDougall, W. B. and Herma A. Baggley. *Plants of Yellowstone National Park*. Yellowstone Library and Museum Association, 1956.

Mills, H. B. *Bugs, Birds, and Blizzards in the Yellowstone*. Ames, Iowa: Collegiate Press, 1937.

Randall, Leslie W. Gay. *Footprints along the Yellowstone*. San Antonio, Texas: Naylor Co.

Rush, William. *Yellowstone Scout*. New York: David McKay Co.

Thone, F. E. A. *Trees and Flowers of Yellowstone National Park*. St. Paul, Minnesota: J. E. Haynes, 1929.

GRAND TETON

To secure pamphlets and books on local aspects of the park, write for catalog to Grand Teton Natural History Association, Moose, Wyoming 83012.

Bonney, Orrin and Lorraine G. *Teton Range Field Guide*. Denver, Colorado: A. Swallow.
———. *Bonney's Guide to Jackson's Hole and Grand Teton National Park*. Houston, Texas: Bonney.

Carrighar, Sally. *One Day at Teton Marsh*. New York: Knopf, 1947.

Fryxell, Fritiof. *Tetons: Interpretations of a Mountain Landscape*. Berkeley, Calif.: University of California Press, 1953.

Harry, Bryan. *Teton Trails*. Moose, Wyoming: Grand Teton Natural History Association.

Leonard, Richard M. *Belaying the Leader*. San Francisco: Sierra Club Books, 1956.

Mattes, Merrill J. *Colter's Hell and Jackson's Hole*. Moose, Wyoming: Grand Teton Natural History Association.

Ortenburger, Leigh. *A Climber's Guide to the Teton Range*. San Francisco: Sierra Club Books, 1965.

OFFSHORE PARKS

HAWAII VOLCANOES AND HALEAKALA

To secure pamphlets and books on local aspects of both parks, write for catalog to Hawaii Natural History Association, Ltd., Hawaii Volcanoes National Park, Hawaii 96718.

Degener, Otto. *Ferns and Flowering Plants of Hawaii*. Honolulu: Honolulu Star-Bulletin, 1930.

Franck, Harry A. *Roaming in Hawaii*. New York: Frederick A. Stokes, 1937.

Hubbard, Douglass. *Ferns of Hawaii National Park*. Hawaii: Hawaii Natural History Association.

Kuck, Loraine E. and Richard C. Tongg. *Hawaiian Flowers and Flowering Trees*. Rutland, Vermont: Charles E. Tuttle Co.

Macdonald, Gordon and Douglass Hubbard. *Volcanoes of the National Parks in Hawaii*. Hawaii: Hawaii Natural History Association, 1961.

Munro, George C. *Birds of Hawaii*. Rutland, Vermont: Charles E. Tuttle Co. (rev. ed.)

Ruhle, George C. *Haleakala Guide*. Hawaii: Hawaii Natural History Association.

INDEX

COLOPHON

This book was printed and bound in San Francisco, California. Color and duotone pages were printed by A. Carlisle & Co., using lithograph film made by Balzer-Shopes; single-color signature printed by Jorgenson & Co. Jacket and cover lithographed by Charles R. Wood & Associates, binding by Cardoza Bookbinding Company. Body type is Monotype Bell 402 composed by Holmes Typography, Inc., San Jose, California. Type for headings is Dartmouth. Paper for body pages is Northwest Enamel furnished by Northwest Paper Co., Cloquet, Minnesota; paper for single-color signature is Antique Beckett Offset furnished by The Beckett Paper Company, Hamilton, Ohio.

Cover photographs: Front—Grand Tetons by David Muench; back—Vernal Fall, Yosemite, by Darwin Van Campen.